TURN-OF-THE-CENTURY DOLLS, TOYS AND GAMES

The Complete Illustrated Carl P. Stirn Catalog from 1893

by

CARL P. STIRN

New Introduction by
Mary Lynn Stevens Heininger

HENRY FORD MUSEUM & GREENFIELD VILLAGE

Published in association with
**HENRY FORD MUSEUM
& GREENFIELD VILLAGE**
Dearborn, Michigan
by
DOVER PUBLICATIONS, INC., New York

Copyright © 1990 by Henry Ford Museum & Greenfield Village.
All rights reserved under Pan American and International Copyright Conventions.

Published in Canada by General Publishing Company, Ltd., 30 Lesmill Road, Don Mills, Toronto, Ontario.
Published in the United Kingdom by Constable and Company, Ltd., 10 Orange Street, London WC2H 7EG.

This Dover edition, first published in 1990 in association with Henry Ford Museum & Greenfield Village, Dearborn, Michigan, is a republication of the *Illustrated Fall and Holiday Catalogue of Foreign and Domestic Dolls, Toys and Games,* published by Carl P. Stirn, New York, in 1893. The inside back cover of the original catalog has been moved to page 8 and the Index changed to reflect the new page number. A new Introduction has been written specially for this edition.

DOVER *Pictorial Archive* SERIES

Manufactured in the United States of America
Dover Publications, Inc., 31 East 2nd Street, Mineola, N.Y. 11501

Library of Congress Cataloging-in-Publication Data

Stirn, Carl P.
    [Illustrated fall and holiday catalogue of foreign and domestic dolls, toys, and games]
    Turn-of-the-century dolls, toys, and games : the complete illustrated Carl P. Stirn catalog from 1893 / by Carl P. Stirn ; new introduction by Mary Lynn Stevens Heininger.
        p.   cm.
    Reprint. Originally published: New York : C.P. Stirn, 1893 under title: Illustrated fall and holiday catalogue of foreign and domestic dolls, toys, and games.
    ISBN 0-486-26365-7
    1. Stirn, Carl P.—Catalogs. 2. Dolls—History—19th Century—Catalogs. 3. Toys—History—19th century—Catalogs. 4. Games—History—19th century—Catalogs. I. Title.
NK4893.S89   1990   90-33288
688.7'90'034—dc20   CIP

INTRODUCTION

Carl P. Stirn appeared to be riding high in 1893. A successful partner in the respected New York toy importing and wholesaling firm of Stirn and Lyon for nearly two decades, he had just struck out on his own. To inaugurate his venture, he issued an ambitious new catalog. It was a high-spirited enterprise, chock-full of the latest goods, generously illustrated and described in detail—a fancy, printed version of a confident peddler's pitch. We don't know how well Stirn's customers heard him. Apart from a City Directory citation marking the year he apparently went out of business, 1904, we know virtually nothing about the new firm. But if Stirn "the middleman" eludes our inquiry, perhaps instead we can learn something about the people who gave him his livelihood. This catalog, reprinted from the collections of the Henry Ford Museum & Greenfield Village, affords us a fitting occasion to peer into the nineteenth-century world of the young, and of those who would profit by their playthings.

In the 1990s, we assume that to be a child means to deserve a variety of toys and the leisure to enjoy them. However, this notion was a relatively new one in the 1890s, for American childhood, as we know it today, was a nineteenth-century creation. Until the 1820s, Puritan doctrine and sternness held great sway in Americans' attitudes toward the young. Children were characterized as by nature more bad than good, as embodiments of original sin in the world. Influential ministers of the 1820s and 1830s, however, shifted the blame for the world's evil from innate depravity to free will gone awry. Afire with reformist zeal, secular and religious leaders alike began to teach that virtue could be nurtured in the young, and that new generations of upright citizens would be the result. By mid-century, influenced first by European Romantics, and then by sentimental portrayals of children in popular art and literature, Americans' view of the young softened further. Children seemed not only capable of good, but actually predisposed toward it. Even naughty children—the kind who appeared in prints and posters with a broken vase in one hand and a baseball bat in the other—weren't really bad. Rather, they were seen as mischievous and comical; if anyone was at fault, it was the scowling adult in the doorway, for valuing possessions and rules over the high spirits of youth.

This increasing differentiation between the spheres of children and adults reflects shifts in behavior as well as attitude. In industrializing, nineteenth-century America, the site of earning a household's living began to move from homes and farms to urban factories and offices, thus diminishing many children's contributions to family economy. Among the burgeoning middle class, children's roles, like those of women, began to be measured more and more exclusively by what they contributed to home life. Women and children became responsible not only for care and maintenance of the domestic sphere, but also for sweetening it, serving as a foil to a competitive, stressful life of commerce and industry. But whereas women were called upon to impose the rules of cultivation and taste upon the chaos of the larger world, children in their innocence were to represent simplicity and lack of artifice. In a tacit cultural bargain, adults who afforded the young the means of their natural state—happy, carefree early years—would reap the benefits of a lightened, more joyful existence despite the cares of the world. Experts in the new field of child psychology concurred, predicting developmental benefits for the children themselves. By the end of the century, "having a childhood" had become an American right.

What all of this meant to the toy trade was growth and profit. If young people deserved a time set apart for development and play, what could be more appropriate than toys? Predictably, the same forces of industrialization that gave young Americans time on their hands also put toys in their hands. Before mid-century, toys had been relatively scarce, and were either home-made or were purchased as expensive specialty goods. But beginning around the 1860s, new techniques for formulating and manipulating materials ideal for toys were being perfected and mechanized. The advent of wood-pulp paper, aniline dyes, and chromolithography made possible not only a plethora of books for children, but also colorful and inexpensive card and board games, paper dolls, and all manner of doll houses and furnishings. Advances in metalworking technologies applied to toymaking brought about whole worlds of inexpensive tin-plated steel toys—locomotives and steamships, farm animals, carriages, and circus trains. Real steamships and railroads made for faster, more reliable, and cheaper transportation of great volumes of merchandise over land and sea. These developments allowed Stirn and his competitors to offer variety and price ranges sufficient to serve the street urchin with a penny in his pocket as well as the child of doting parents for whom money was no object.

It is hardly surprising, then, to discover that the major American concerns in the manufacture of toys and games date from the 1860s forward: Milton-Bradley was founded in 1860, Selchow & Righter in 1880, and Parker Brothers in 1888. Another way to chronicle expansion in the American toy industry is to note that it was in the early 1880s that the U.S. Bureau of Statistics' *Statistical Abstracts* first separated "Toys and Games" from the larger category of "Fancy Articles" in its reports of manufactures, imports, and exports. Making and selling toys had become an enterprise worth watching; from the 1880s forward, the Bureau recorded consistent and substantial growth well into the twentieth century.

Department stores for urban shoppers and mail-order outlets for rural customers provided new, convenient outlets for consumers and handsome profits for retailers. The example of Macy's, New York City, demonstrates the appeal of playthings to buyers and sellers alike during the second half of the nineteenth century. Macy's opened its doors in 1858, and included toys in its merchandise within two years. The store's "biographer," Ralph M. Hower, writes in his *History of Macy's of New York City* (1967) that by 1869, toys and dolls had earned themselves their own department. When the store calculated the profitability of each department late in 1877 and 1887—years during which Stirn and Lyon was a thriving concern—Toys and Dolls generated a higher percentage of profit to sales than any other department.

Paging through this catalog, we can understand the high demand that helped fuel the toy boom at Macy's and elsewhere. Like the toys that please our own children, Stirn's merchandise could delight and surprise, entertain and pacify, challenge and teach. Many of the forms they took are familiar— board games and puzzles, dolls of every description, colorful contraptions that whistle, pop, and rattle upon demand. Yet for all their similarities, toys such as those pictured here can also remind us of important differences between the 1890s and the 1990s. Toys featuring caricatures of African-Americans being thrown from animals or doing minstrel dances no longer find their way into mainstream consumer outlets, for the "joke" they tell is offensive today. In Stirn's turn-of-the-century America, however—when Reconstruction was dead and the civil-rights movement not yet born—such portrayals embodied racial stereotypes commonly accepted and openly enjoyed. Stirn's cast-iron banks in the shape of Gothic churches have given way to plastic ones modeled after Super Mario and Miss Piggy, giving contemporary meaning to the biblical adage that "where your treasure lies, there also your heart will be."

All toys, not just talking ones, have much to tell us about children and the world we offer them. As you *look* through this catalog, I urge you to *listen* as well.

Mary Lynn Stevens Heininger
Curator, Collections Division
Henry Ford Museum & Greenfield Village

ESTABLISHED SINCE 1875.

ILLUSTRATED FALL AND HOLIDAY CATALOGUE

OF

FOREIGN AND DOMESTIC

SPORTING GOODS,

FANCY GOODS

AND

NOVELTIES,

China and Bohemian

GLASSWARE

·· SPECIALTIES FOR ··

STATIONERY, DRY GOODS

AND

5 & 10-Cent Counter Trade.

DOLLS,

TOYS AND

GAMES.

CARL P. STIRN

Formerly of STIRN & LYON.

CARL P. STIRN,
597 BROADWAY.

European Offices:
COBURG, GERMANY,
PARIS, FRANCE.

Cable Address:
CARLSTIRN, NEWYORK.

597 BROADWAY,

NEW YORK, U. S. A.

Importer, Exporter and Commission Merchant.

≈ FALL CATALOGUE. ≈

SEASON 1893.

The most complete Catalogue ever published, containing full lines of goods, with Descriptions, Sizes and Prices.

❋ NEW STOCK, ❋ ❋ ❋ ❋ ❋ ❋ ❋ ❋
❋ ❋ ❋ ❋ NEW DESIGNS, ❋ ❋ ❋ ❋
❋ ❋ ❋ ❋ ❋ ❋ ❋ ❋ NEW PRICES, ❋

AND MOST SALABLE ARTICLES ONLY.

EVERY THING STAPLE and EVERY THING NEW made in the United States and Europe FOUND IN MY STORE.

BEING ONE OF THE LARGEST DIRECT IMPORTERS, I offer goods at prices which CAN NOT BE EQUALED, and a trial order only will convince you that I AM THE ONE FROM WHOM TO BUY.

HAVING HAD TWENTY-FIVE YEARS' EXPERIENCE in this line of goods, I know and continually study the wants of the trade, and try to please every one.

I HAVE MY OWN OFFICES IN EUROPE, and thus obtain all the latest foreign novelties as soon as out.

MY DOMESTIC DEPARTMENTS are stocked with full lines from all the leading factories in the country.

Do not fail to call when visiting New York, and you will see the MOST COMPLETE ASSORTMENT EVER SHOWN IN THE UNITED STATES.

All prices are NET, and SUBJECT TO CHANGE WITHOUT NOTICE. FOR CASH WITH ORDER a discount of 3 Per Cent. will be allowed. C. O. D. ORDERS must be accompanied with a remittance sufficient to cover freight or express charges both ways. If you want to buy on time, and your name is not already on my books, do not fail to send references, and if possible in New York City.

REGULAR TERMS:—All goods purchased for the Holidays—DUE NET JANUARY 1, 1894, or 1 PER CENT. DISCOUNT PER MONTH FOR PREPAYMENT, viz:

4 Per Cent. Discount if paid			September	1st to 10th.		
3	"	"	"	October	1st to 10th.	No Discount after December 10th.
2	"	"	"	November	1st to 10th.	
1	"	"	"	December	1st to 10th.	

☞ NO CHARGE FOR CASES OR CARTAGE. ☜

All goods are delivered free on board cars or steamer in New York City.

WHEN ORDERING do not neglect to mention Page of Catalogue, Numbers and Titles of the Articles.

CARL P. STIRN,

597 BROADWAY, NEW YORK.

☞ If you do not handle goods in this line, and have no use for this Catalogue, kindly hand it to some one who keeps such goods.

European Offices:
COBURG, GERMANY.
PARIS, FRANCE.

ESTABLISHED SINCE 1875.

Cable Address:
CARLSTIRN, NEWYORK.

Illustrated Fall and Holiday Catalogue

OF

FOREIGN AND DOMESTIC

DOLLS, TOYS and GAMES

❋

Toy Books,
Picture and
Spelling
Blocks,
Sporting
Goods.

Yours truly Carl P. Stirn

❋

School
Supplies,
Household
Goods,
Photographic
Outfits.

❋

❋

CHINA AND BOHEMIAN GLASSWARE, FANCY GOODS AND NOVELTIES.

Specialties for the Stationery, Dry Goods, and 5 and 10 Cent Counter Trade.

CARL P. STIRN,

Importer, Exporter and Commission Merchant,

597 BROADWAY, = = = **NEW YORK, U. S. A**

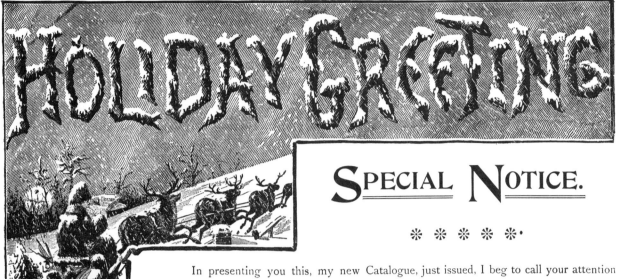

SPECIAL NOTICE.

❋ ❋ ❋ ❋ ❋·

In presenting you this, my new Catalogue, just issued, I beg to call your attention to the fact that during the 18 years that I was a member of the firm of Stirn & Lyon, the **ENTIRE** foreign business of the firm (which comprised the purchasing abroad of everything in the line of **DOLLS, TOYS, MUSICAL GOODS, CHINA AND BOHEMIAN GLASSWARE,** as well as **NOVELTIES, ETC.**), was attended to by me personally.

Since 1875 I have visited the European markets regularly and arranged for the manufacture of all the goods imported by the old firm.

I now beg to inform you that since opening my new establishment at **597 BROADWAY** (between Prince and Houston Streets), I have **LARGELY INCREASED** and **ADDED TO** my former foreign connections, and specially wish to say that I shall **CONTINUE** importing **DIRECT** and **ON A MUCH LARGER SCALE** than heretofore, all goods manufactured in foreign countries.

My Import Order Department

(Specialties being **DOLLS, TOYS, TEA SETS, MARBLES, HARMONICAS** and **NOVELTIES**), is under the supervision of an experienced buyer (for many years connected with the old house), who goes abroad regularly every Fall and procures everything new. On **JANUARY 15th** of each year my **IMPORT LINES** will be ready for inspection.

Regarding Domestic Toys, Fancy Goods, American Novelties, Etc.,

I desire to state that this Department is also largely increased, and is managed by an able buyer of many years' experience, and having made very large contracts with the leading and best American manufacturers in the various lines, places me in a position to offer the lowest possible prices.

Most respectfully,

CARL P. STIRN, (Formerly of the firm of STIRN & LYON,)

597 BROADWAY,

NEW YORK.

If you do not handle goods in this line and have no use for this Catalogue, kindly hand the same to a merchant in your place who buys such goods; by so doing greatly oblige.

INDEX.

Errata.

On page 45, Toy No. 435 should read $3.50 per dozen instead of $8.50.

❖ U. S. PLAYING CARDS. ❖

WHOLESALE DESCRIPTIVE PRICE LIST.

Number.		Per Dozen.	Per Gross.
343	CADETS, small size	$0.40	$4.80

For amusement, toy cards, Solitaire, etc. Perfectly rounded corners, indexed, and have all the qualities of full-sized playing cards. Two dozen packs in a carton.

343x.	EXTRA CADETS, small size	.80	9.60

These are Cadet cards with GOLD EDGES.

999.	STEAMBOAT, four color faces	.50	6.00

Rounded corners and indexed, six neat calico backs (blues, greens and browns). Each kind packed solid; twelve packs in a carton.

999x.	EXTRA STEAMBOAT	1.00	12.00

The Steamboat grade with GOLD EDGES.

101.	TIGERS, Extra Quality	.62½	7.50

Seven attractive plaid, star and calico backs, of different designs and colors. Each kind packed solid; twelve packs in a carton.

101x.	EXTRA TIGERS	1.12½	13.50

Grade No. 101, Tigers, with GOLD EDGES. One dozen packs in each carton.

155.	TOURISTS, finish and slip unequaled	1.00	12.00

Twelve beautiful and appropriate set pattern backs (reds, blues, greens and browns) in each dozen. Assorted colors in each dozen. Twelve packs in a carton.

155x.	EXTRA TOURISTS	1.50	18.00

This is the Tourist grade with GOLD EDGES.

155(A).	TOURISTS, enameled	1.00	12.00

Assorted designs and colors in each dozen.

155(A)x.	EXTRA TOURISTS, enameled, gold edges	1.50	18.00

29	FAUNTLEROY, small size	1.00	12.00

The "Fauntleroy" are small size, new and novel, with enameled ivory finish, and contain appropriate character backs—"Dick," "Mr. Hobbs," "Dearest," and "The Earl"—printed in red, blue and brown, making a complete assortment in each dozen.

29x.	EXTRA FAUNTLEROY, small size	1.50	18.00

This is grade No. 29 with GOLD EDGES.

21.	JUNIOR, known as "Bicycle Juniors"	1.50	18.00

A new brand, same grade as the Bicycle, and made the new Junior (three-quarter) size, which is a very peculiar shape, being nearer to the full regular size than the Cadet or Fauntleroy cards. The Junior embodies all the remarkable qualities of the Bicycle.

21x.	EXTRA JUNIOR	2.00	24.00

These are the Junior cards with GOLD EDGES.

808.	BICYCLE, ivory finish	1.50	18.00

Enameled. New bicycle designs—"Margin Star," "Angel," "Safety," "Emblem," "Rider," "Lotus," "Fan," "Acorn," and many others—assorted in all colors. Tested and tried everywhere. Used in card-playing countries all over the world.

808x.	EXTRA BICYCLE	2.00	24.00

These are the Bicycle cards with GOLD EDGES, in boxes printed in gold.

'45.	TEXAN, New Enameled Series	1.50	18.00

New designs—"Lone Star," "Palm Leaf," and "Saddle"—red, blue, green and brown, assorted.

'45x.	EXTRA TEXAN	2.00	24.00

These are the Texan cards—new enameled series, with GOLD EDGES.

'45.	TEXAN, triple strength	1.75	21.00

Plaid and calico backs, of different designs and colors. Made especially to meet the demands of players desiring cards with a higher finish than is obtained on cards of cheaper, unenameled grades.

93.	IVORY, Whist Series	2.00	24.00

Double enameled, size 2¼ x 3¾. A variety of designs and colors for Whist and other full-handed games.

93x.	EXTRA IVORY, Whist Series, gold edges	2.75	33.00

188.	CAPITOL, double enameled	2.00	24.00

Twelve beautiful, popular and fancy backs, in pink, blue and buff tinted and white enamel, assorted in each dozen.

188x.	EXTRA CAPITOL	2.75	33.00

These are the Capitol cards with GOLD EDGES.

Number.		Per Dozen.	Per Gross.
202.	SPORTSMAN'S	$3.00	$36.00

Linen stock. Highly finished enamel. Twelve handsome, appropriate sportsman's backs—red, blue, green and brown—assorted in each dozen.

202x.	EXTRA SPORTSMAN'S	3.75	45.00

These are the Sportsman's cards with GOLD EDGES.

707.	CABINET, new series; full packs	2.50	30.00

A revelation in playing cards. Made of fine linen stock; highly finished enamel; new and artistic landscape sketch backs without margins. The "Cabinet" are the most elegant line ever produced at a medium price.

707x.	EXTRA CABINET, new series	3.25	39.00

These are the NEW "Cabinet," No. 707, with GOLD EDGES.

303.	ARMY AND NAVY, all linen	4.00	48.00

Designed principally for Club use. Poker and Whist cards. Double enameled, high finish. Angel, London Club, etc. Each pack wrapped in a beautiful wrapper printed in five colors and inclosed in a handsome cloth (imported) telescope card case.

303.	ARMY AND NAVY, without cases	3.75	45.00

Wrapped and in cartons, but without the cloth telescope card cases.

303.	ARMY AND NAVY "SECONDS"	2.00	24.00

"Angel" or assorted backs, such as come from the regular editions of "firsts."

505.	EXTRA ARMY AND NAVY	5.50	66.00

These are the Army and Navy cards with GOLD EDGES, in blue cloth telescope card cases stamped in gold.

89.	Treasury, {FOR CLUBS AND EXACTING PLAYERS DESIRING PERFECT CARDS.}	6.00	72.00

Finest linen cards, highly finished. Each pack is gauged to standard thickness throughout, with cutting and margins accurate and true. This grade will be made to order with Monogram and special backs for Clubs.

404.	CONGRESS, gold backs	5.50	66.00

Finest linen. Extra double enameled. Each pack in a rich colored wrapper printed in gold and in a green silk card case stamped in silver. Handsome cards for holiday and fine trade.

606.	EXTRA CONGRESS	7.00	84.00

Great variety of artistic designs, printed in either green, copper, violet, aluminum or gold bronze, on backgrounds either red, blue, orange, maroon, black, green or white. Put up in elegant cases especially for card parties.

366.	SQUARED FARO	9.00	108.00

Fit any dealing box. Margin enough to trim many times. Three sizes in thickness—Eights, Nines and Tens. Perfect dealing cards. In ordering please specify thickness wanted.

1.	AMERICAN SKAT, German faces	4.00	48.00

Best quality. "Not enameled." 36 cards in a pack. German-American and fancy backs in red and blue. The only German cards having the POPULAR MODERN AMERICAN INDEXES on faces.

1.	AMERICAN SKAT, German faces	5.00	60.00

These are No. 1 with GOLD EDGES, and in ordering this grade please specify "No. 1 with gold edges."

2.	AMERICAN SKAT, German faces	6.00	72.00

For "SKAT" and other German games. 36 cards in a pack. Best quality of stock, double enameled.

2.	AMERICAN SKAT, German faces	7.00	84.00

These are No. 2 with GOLD EDGES, and in ordering this grade please specify "No. 2 with gold edges."

4.	AMERICAN SKAT, American faces	4.00	48.00

Full packs—53 cards. Double enameled. Twelve Whist backs—red, blue, green and brown; full assortment in each dozen.

4.	AMERICAN SKAT, gold edges	5.00	60.00

These are No. 4 with GOLD EDGES, and in ordering this grade please specify "No. 4 with gold edges."

Above "SKAT" cards, with German faces, have modern indexes, 36 cards in a pack. Size 2¼ x 3¾. For Skat and other German games.

Above "SKAT" cards, with American faces, have full packs—53 cards. Size 2¼ x 3¾. A variety of designs and colors for full-handed games.

ORDER BY THE ABOVE NUMBERS. ALL PREVIOUS LISTS ARE HEREBY CANCELED.

SPECIAL DISCOUNTS QUOTED ON QUANTITIES.

POSITIVELY NO CARDS RETURNED OR EXCHANGED.

FREIGHT PREPAID.—By sending your JOBBER a "TWO GROSS" assorted order or over, cards can be shipped direct from the manufactory, NO CHARGE for boxing and cartage, and FREIGHT FULLY PREPAID where the rate does not exceed $1.00 per 100 pounds. Where the rate is in excess of $1.00 per 100 pounds, $1.00 per cwt. will be allowed toward the freight on basis of the rate from Cincinnati or New York. This enables you to secure a complete assortment, from the cheapest to the finest, laid down at your depot for the SMALLEST OUTLAY OF MONEY, and at the same time receive a full supply of the "CARD-PLAYER'S COMPANION," NEW SHOW CARDS, HANGERS, ETC., for your store.

—≈THE TRADE SUPPLIED BY≈—

CARL P. STIRN, 597 BROADWAY, ✳ NEW YORK. ✳

Doll Department.

THIS is the largest Department in my establishment, and comprises everything new and novel in the line of Dolls and everything appertaining to Dolls.

My facilities for supplying Foreign Goods are unsurpassed, as I have a resident buyer permanently located in the Doll district in Germany; besides, I myself and also one of my buyers visit all the leading business centres in Europe every year in the Spring and Fall.

I control the output of several large Doll factories, and all foreign goods are imported by me direct, and are sold at prices which cannot be equaled by those not possessed of the advantages above mentioned.

Yours truly,

CARL P. STIRN.

CHINA LIMB DOLLS.

CHINA LIMB DOLLS, with glazed china heads, china arms and legs, plain cloth bodies.

No. 100.

7½	8	9	11½	12½	13	inches
30c	33c	38c	70c	75c	85c	per doz.
2	2	2	1	1	1	doz. in box

CHINA LIMB DOLLS, full bodies, with bisque china heads and bisque china arms and legs, assorted painted blond and black hair.

No. 105.

8½	9	11	inches
38c	45c	75c	per doz.
2	2	1	doz. in box

CHINA LIMB DOLLS, full·proportioned good quality bodies, full glazed limbs and heads.

No. 110.	7½	8½	10½	11	12½	inches
	33c	38c	70c	75c	$1.00	per doz.
	2	2	1	1	1	doz. in box

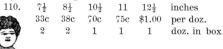

CHINA LIMB DOLLS, same style as before, with stitched cloth bodies.

No. 110.

13½	14½	15½	17	20	21	inches
$1.25	1.50	1.75	2.00	3.50	4.00	per doz.
½	½	½	½	⅓	⅓	doz. in box

CHINA LIMB DOLLS, with fancy bisque heads and assorted bisque fancy caps, fancy bisque shirt fronts trimmed with gold, bisque limbs.

No. 120.	7½	8	10½	11½	13	inches
	35c	38c	72c	80c	$1.25	per doz.
		2	1	1	1	doz. in box

Same as above, stitched body, full limbs.

No. 120.

15	16	inches
$1.75	2.00	per doz.
½	½	doz. in box

BISQUE LIMB DOLLS, fine quality bisque head and limbs, painted hair and eyes, full proportioned, stitched bodies.

No. 125.

7½	8	11	12	17	inches
70c	75c	$1.75	2.00	3.75	per doz.
1	1	½	½	½	doz. in box

CHINA PENNY BABIES.

PENNY BABIES, ALL BISQUE.

No. 250–1.   Plain babies, 2¾ inches
90c per gross
3 dozen in box

No. 250–2.   All bisque, assorted with and without bisque bonnets, painted shoes, length, 2½ inches
80c per gross.
6 dozen in box.

No. 250–3.   Glazed babies, painted hair, eyes and shoes, 2½ inches
90c per gross
12 dozen in box

No. 250–4.   Negro babies, glazed, same quality as 250–3.   2 inches, 90c per gross
12 dozen in box

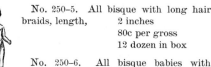

No. 250–5.   All bisque with long hair braids, length,   2 inches
80c per gross
12 dozen in box

No. 250–6.   All bisque babies with jointed arms, painted hair and colored assorted hats, painted shoes, length, 2¾ inches
90c per gross
12 dozen in box

No. 250–7.   All bisque babies with curly hair, painted shoes, length,   2 inches
90c per gross
12 dozen in box

No. 250–8.   All bisque with jointed arms, dressed in knit worsted dresses, length,   1½ inches
1 doz. on a card
1 gross in a box
90c per gross

CHINA GLAZED BABIES.

CHINA GLAZED BABIES, with open arms, good quality, glazed.

No. 260.

10/0	9/0	7/0	6/0	5/0	4/0	
1⅛	1¼	1⅜	1½	2	2½	inches
60c	70c	80c	$1.00	1.25	1.50	per gross
24	24	12	12	6	2	dz. in a box

No. 260.

3/0	0½	2	3	4	5	6	
2¾	3¼	3¾	4¼	4¾	5¼	5½	inches
$2.00	3.00	4.00	4.50	5.00	7.50	9.00	pr. gr.
2	1	1	1	1	1	1	dz. in box

CHINA GLAZED BABIES, with gilt shoes and open arms.

No. 261.

2	3	5	
3¾	4¼	5¼	inches
38c	40c	75c	per doz.
1	1	½	doz in box

CHINA GLAZED NEGRO BABIES, same quality as above 260 line.

No. 262.

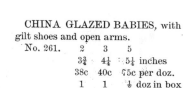

8/0	3	5	9	11	13	
1	1½	2¼	3½	4	4¾	inches
70c	90c pr gr.	20c	35c	40c	65c	per doz.
24	12	6	1	1	1	dz. in box

CHINA BISQUE BABIES.

BISQUE CHINA BABIES, jointed arms, painted china bonnets, crochet worsted dresses.

No. 263/1.

2	4		
3½	4	4¼	inches
33c	38c	75c	per dozen
1	1	½	dozen in box

BISQUE CHINA BABIES, jointed arms, with painted china bonnets, colored shoes.

No. 264/2.

Length, 4¼ inches.
35c per dozen
1 doz. in a box

BISQUE CHINA BABIES, jointed arms, painted blonde hair, gold shoes, length, 4½ inches

No. 265/3.
40c per dozen
1 doz. in a box

GLAZED CHINA BABIES, with long hair braids.

No. 266.
3½ inches
40c per dozen
1 doz. in a box

BISQUE CHINA BABIES, full jointed, with hair and painted eyes.

No. 270/.

0	1	
Length,		
2½	2¾	inches
33c	40c	per dozen
1	1	doz in a box

BISQUE CHINA BOYS, with all jointed bent limbs, painted eyes and hair.

No. 271.
2¾ inches
40c per dozen
1 dozen in a box

BISQUE CHINA BABIES, full jointed, painted eyes, Rembrandt style hair.

No. 272.
3¾ inches
75c per dozen
1 dozen in a box

BISQUE CHINA BABIES, swimmers, with painted hair and eyes and white painted tights.

No. 273.
3 inches
75c per dozen
1 dozen in a box

FINE BISQUE BABIES, GIRLS, jointed arms, natural hair, assorted styles, fancy painted slippers and stockings.

No. 275.

6/0	5/0	4/0	3/0	2/0	
3	3¾	4½	5	6	inches
75c	$1.00	1.35	1.75	2.00	per doz
1	½	½	½	½	doz in box

FINE BISQUE BABIES, same style as No. 275, with glass eyes.

No. 276.

7/0	6/0	5/0	4/0	3/0	2/0	
2½	3	3½	4½	5	6	inches
85c	$1.00	1.38	1.65	1.88	2.50	per dz.
1	1	½	½	½		doz. in box

FINE BISQUE BABIES, full jointed limbs, glass eyes, full hair wigs, assorted styles, fancy painted slippers and stockings.

No. 278.

6/0	5/0	4/0	3/0	
3½	4	5	5¾	inches
$1.00	1.50	1.75	2.00	per dozen
1	1	½	½	dozen in a box

FINE BISQUE BABIES, same as before, with painted eyes.

No. 277.   6/0.   Length,   3½ inches.
80c per dozen
1 dozen in a box

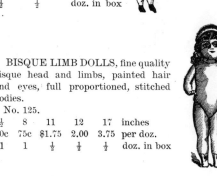

FINE BISQUE BABIES, full jointed, turning head, fine glass eyes, Rembrandt style hair wigs, fancy painted shoes.
No. 280/4.
5½ inches
$2.00 per dozen
1 dozen in a box

FINE BISQUE BABIES, jointed limbs, turning heads, painted eyes, natural hair in assorted styles, muslin shirts.
No. 281. 2   3
4¼   4½ inches
$1.75   2.00 per dozen

FINE BISQUE BABIES, same style as No. 281, with glass eyes and open mouth with teeth.
No. 282.
5   7   9
5½   6½   8 inches
$3.00   4.00   6.00 per doz.
one in a box

FINE BABIES, same style as No. 282, with moving eyes.
No. 283.   6   8   11
Length,   5¼   7   9 inches
$4.00   6.00   8.50 per dozen
in a box

FINEST BISQUE BABIES, jointed arms and legs, turning heads, moving glass eyes, open mouth showing teeth, Rembrandt style natural hair, painted shoes and stockings, dressed in fine muslin shirts. Put up one in a box.
No. 284.   2/0   0   1
5¾   6   6½ inches
$3.75   4.00   4.50 per dozen

FINEST BISQUE BABIES, "Zulus," full jointed, black curly hair, fine glass eyes, turning heads. Put up one in a box.
No. 285.   5/0   2/0
4   5½ inches
$2.00   3.75 per dozen

FINE BISQUE BABIES, jointed arms and legs, natural hair, assorted boys and girls, dressed in fine crochet dresses and hats to match. Half dozen in box.
No. 295.   7/0 $1.75 per doz.
3½   inches

FINEST BISQUE BABIES, jointed arms and legs, turning bisque heads, glass eyes, Rembrandt

style hair, painted colored stockings and slippers, assorted boys and girls, in silk crochet dresses with bonnets to match.
No. 296.   7/0   3/0   2/0   1
Length,   3¼   5   5½   6 inches
$2.00   3.50   4.00   7.00 per dozen
½   ¼   ¼   ⅙ doz. in a box

PATENT WASHABLE DOLLS.

WASHABLE DOLLS WITH HAIR, fixed glass eyes, plain shirts with colored fancy trimmings, papier mache limbs, cloth bodies.
No. 300.
9   10   14   15½   16 inches
38c   45c   75c $1.00   1.25 per doz.
3   2   1   1   1 doz. in box

18   20   22   24 inches
$1.50   1.75   1.88   2.00 per dozen
1   1   1   1   doz. in a box

WASHABLE DOLLS, BETTER QUALITY, with assorted hair wigs, fine fixed glass eyes, colored fancy trimmed shirts, papier mache limbs, cloth bodies.
No. 310.
16   18   20   22   24 inches
$1.50   1.75   2.00   2.50   3.00 per dozen
1   ½   ⅓   ⅓ doz. in a box

26   28   30   32   inches
$3.75   4.50   5.00   6.00   per dozen
⅓   ⅓   ⅙   ⅙ doz. in a box

WASHABLE DOLLS, BETTER QUALITY, with fine Matt heads, fine glass eyes, Rembrandt style hair, cream colored lace trimmed shirts, papier mache arms, cloth sitting body and cloth legs, with colored shoes and stockings.
No. 315.
18   20   26   28   30   34 inches
$2.00   2.50   4.00   5.00   7.50   8.50 per doz.
½   ½   ⅓   ⅓   ⅙   ⅙ doz. in box

WASHABLE DOLLS, same style as No. 315, with moving eyes.
No. 315½.

18   26   32   inches.
½   ⅓   ⅙   doz. in box
$2.00   4.00   8.00   per dozen

WASHABLE DOLLS, FINE QUALITY, same style as No. 315, with shoes and stockings to take off.
No. 317.
15   22   23   30   33 inches
$2.00   4.00   4.50   8.00   9.00 per doz.
1   ⅓   ⅓   ⅙   ⅙ dz. in pk.

WASHABLE BABY DOLL, fine washable patent head, with fine glass eyes, with baby cap and in fancy colored cream shirt.
No. 318.   16   22 inches
$2.00   4.00 per doz.
1   ½ doz in box

WASHABLE INFANT DOLLS, fine quality, fine washable heads, with Rembrandt style hair, fine glass eyes, fine muslin shirts trimmed with lace, cloth stockings and leather shoes.
No. 319.   14   19
$2.00   4.00 per dozen
1   ½ dozen in box

PAPA AND MAMMA DOLLS.

PAPA AND MAMMA DOLLS, WITH CLOTH BODIES, WASHABLE HEADS, hair wigs, fine glass eyes, cream colored shirts with colored fancy trimmings, papier mache limbs, fancy colored caps; speaking "Papa" and "Mamma."
No. 316.   15   22 inches
$2.00   4.00 per doz.
1   ⅓ dz. in box

SPEAKING DOLLS, with half kid bodies, fine Bisque heads with hair, fine glass eyes, open mouth showing teeth, bisque hands, cream-colored shirts trimmed with colored lace; saying "Mamma."
No. 450.   12 inches
$2.50 per dozen
1 doz. in a box

PAPA AND MAMMA DOLLS, same style as No. 450, with fancy trimmed colored caps; saying "Papa" and "Mamma."
No. 452.   15½   inches
$4.25   per dozen
½   dozen in box

Other styles of Papa and Mamma Dolls, in great variety, ranging in prices from, $8.00 to $36.00 per dozen.

SHOW DOLLS.

These dolls are suitable for dressing up for window attractions; they are very large and well finished.

SHOW DOLLS, WITH FINE WASHABLE HEADS, fine quality, fine glass eyes, assorted styles of fine hair-dress, muslin shirts, with fancy lace trimmings, cloth bodies, papier mache limbs, painted shoes and stockings. Each doll in wooden box.
No. 320.   36   38   44 inches
$2.50   3.00   4.00 each

SHOW DOLLS, FINEST QUALITY, washable heads, fine hair wigs, fine glass eyes, painted eye lashes, teeth, earrings, pearl bead necklaces; fine muslin shirts trimmed with colored braid and white lace, fine washable arms and legs, colored stockings to take off. Each doll in a wooden box.

No. 982.   34   42   inches
$6.00   10.00   each

For Fine Large Dolls Suitable for Show,

SEE FINE BISQUE JOINTED DOLLS.

WASHABLE DOLLS, with hair stuffed, cloth sitting bodies, patent heads, with painted hair and painted eyes, leather arms, cloth legs with colored shoes and stockings.

No. 350.
11	14	15½		17½	19	inches
45c.	75c.	$1.50		1.75	2.00	per doz.
1	1	½	½	½	½	doz. in box

WASHABLE DOLLS, fine Matt heads, assorted hair wigs, fine glass eyes, stitched hair stuffed sitting bodies, leather arms, cloth legs with colored shoes and stockings.

No. 355.
16	17	18	21	23	inches
$1.75	2.00	2.50	3.75	4.00	per dozen
1	1	1	½	½	doz. in box

HAIR STUFFED BODY DOLLS with bisque heads, hair dress and painted eyes.

No. 360.   11½ inches   85c per dozen

BISQUE HEAD, HAIR STUFFED DOLLS, with fine glass eyes, open mouth showing teeth, leather arms, fine stitched muslin bodies, with colored shoes and stockings.

No. 361.
13	16	17	18	inches.
$1.50	1.75	2.00	3.00	per doz.
1	1	1	½	doz. in box

BISQUE HEAD, HAIR STUFFED DOLLS, same as above, with full sitting muslin bodies, papier mache arms.

No. 362.
21	inches
$4.00	per dozen
½	dozen in box

BISQUE HEAD, HAIR STUFFED BODY DOLLS, with bisque arms and full proportioned pink colored sitting bodies, with colored stockings and shoes to take off, fine bisque head with fine glass eyes, Rembrandt style of hair.

No. 365.
14	19	inches
$2.00	4.00	per dozen
1	½	doz. in a box

COLORED FELT BODY DOLLS, with fine bisque heads, human eyes, Rembrandt style of hair, bisque hands, jointed in seat and knees; black, white, red and blue assorted in a box.

No. 370. 11-inch style Doll comes with painted eyes.
11	13	16	21	inches
80c	$2.00	4.00	9.00	per dozen
1	1	½	⅓	doz. in a box

FINE QUALITY CLOTH BODY DOLLS, hair stuffed with fine bisque head, human eyes, fine long or curly hair, with painted shoes and stockings or bare feet; with fine muslin shirts; 3 kinds assorted.

No. 375.
	11 inches
	$2.00 per dozen
	1 doz. in a box

CLOTH BODY DOLLS, with bisque head, painted eyes, hair wig; shoes and stockings.

No. 244.
	10 inches
	$1.00 per dozen
	1 doz. in a box

CLOTH BODY DOLLS, imitation kid body style, with bisque head, painted eyes, hair wig; 1 dozen in a box.

No. 258.
10	11 inches
80c	$1.00 per dozen

KID BODY DOLLS.

KID BODY DOLLS, with good quality kid body, jointed at the knees, with bisque head, fine eyes, hair wig.

No. 400.
12	14	15	inches
$1.75	2.00	3.00	per dozen
1	½	½	doz. in a box

No. 400½. Same style as before with moving eyes.
12	14	15	inches
$2.00	3.00	3.50	per dozen
1	½	½	doz. in a box

KID BODY DOLLS, good quality kid body with bisque arms, bisque head, showing teeth, with fine glass eyes, hair wig; jointed knees; shoes and stockings.

No. 405.
14	14½	inches
$2.25	3.00	per dozen
1	1	doz. in a box

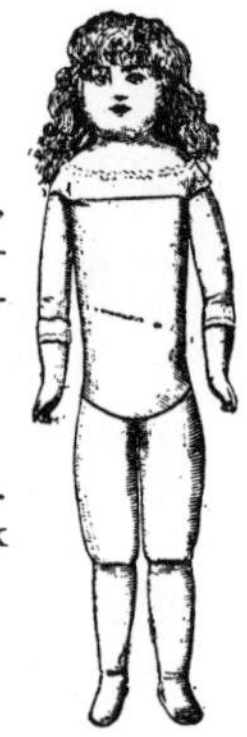

KID BODY DOLLS, good quality, same style as before with leather covered breast and shoulders; body jointed in seat and knees.

No. 406.
12	14	16½	17	21	inches
$2.00	2.25	3.75	4.00	8.00	per doz.
1	1	½	½	1/12	dz. in box

KID BODY DOLLS, similar to No. 406; fuller proportioned bodies, with all-black shoes and stockings.

No. 408.
15	17	18	21	23	inches
$3.75	4.00	5.00	9.00	10.50	per doz.
½	½	½	1/6	1/12	doz. in box

KID BODY DOLLS, same style as No. 408, with moving eyes.

No. 408½.
16	21	23	inches
$4.00	9.50	12.00	per doz.
½	1/6	1/12	dozen in a box

KID BODY DOLLS, good quality kid, with bisque arms, bisque heads, fine eyes, hair wigs, leather covered breast and shoulders. ½ dozen in a box.

No. 409.
16	18	inches
$3.75	4.50	per doz.

KID BODY DOLLS, finest quality kid with bisque arms, bodies jointed in seat and knees, fine bisque head with fine eyes and full Rembrandt hair wigs. 1/12 dozen in a box.

No. 410.
18	20	22	24	inches
$7.50	8.00	9.00	10.50	per dozen

KID BODY DOLLS (BOYS), fine kid body, fine bisque head with curly lambs wool wig, fine glass eyes.

No. 412.
12	16	inches
$2.00	4.00	per dozen
1	½	doz. in a box

No. 412. 20-inch. Same style as before, with shoes and stockings. One piece in a box. $9.00 per dozen.

KID BODY DOLLS, full proportioned body with bisque arms, shoes and stockings, fine bisque head with sewed long curly hair wig, fine glass eyes, teeth, leather covered breast and shoulders.

No. 415.
13	15	16	19	20	inches
$2.00	4.00	5.00	9.00	12.00	per doz.
1	½	½	1/12	1/12	doz. in box

KID BODY DOLLS, finest quality kid leather, with fine bisque arms, jointed limbs, fine black stockings and light colored leather shoes with rubber straps, fine bisque head with sewed wig, fine moving eyes, teeth, leather-covered breast and shoulders. One in a box.

No. 420.
17½	19	20	inches
$9.00	12.00	15.00	per doz.

22	23	25	inches
$16.50	21.00	24.00	per doz.

KID BODY DOLLS, finest quality kid leather, full proportioned body with fine bisque arms, all jointed limbs, fine assorted colored stockings and light leather shoes with straps and buckles, finest quality bisque head with fine moving eyes, sewed curly hair wig, open mouth, showing teeth. One in a box.

No. 425.

15·	16	19	20	22	24 inches
$9.00	10.50	16.50	18.00	24.00	30.00 per dozen

KID BODY DOLLS, finest quality stitched kid leather bodies (French style of body), jointed bisque arms, leather upper arms, assorted colored shoes and stockings, finest quality turning bisque head, with fine moving eyes, fine long hair wig, open mouth, showing teeth. One in a box.

No. 428.

14	15	20 inches
$9.00	10.50	18.00 per dozen

KID BODY DOLLS WITH REAL HUMAN HAIR (NEW). This doll is one of the latest productions of the European markets. The bodies are made of fine quality kid leather with bisque arms, jointed limbs, colored shoes and stockings, fine bisque heads with long real human hair wig, which can be combed, braided and made up; fine moving eyes, open mouth showing teeth, leather covered breast. One in a box.

No. 431.

12	16	19	21 inches
$4.00	9.00	18.00	24.00 per doz.

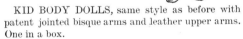

KID BODY DOLLS, same style as before with patent jointed bisque arms and leather upper arms. One in a box.

No. 435.	21	22	23	24 inches
	$27.00	36.00	42.00	48.00 per dozen.

QUARTER KID BODY DOLLS, with fine cream colored mull shirts, trimmed with satin ribbons and lace; full proportioned body; bisque head with long Rembrandt style of hair, fine fixed human eyes, open mouth showing teeth.

No. 440.	14	17 inches
	$2.00	4.00 per dozen
	1	½ doz. in a box

QUARTER KID BODY DOLL, with cream colored mull shirt, trimmed with ribbons and lace; patent jointed leather and bisque arms; shoes and stockings to take off; fine bisque head with stationary eyes, Rembrandt style hair wig, open mouth showing teeth. One in a box.

No. 445.

22 inches
$9.00 per dozen

QUARTER KID BODY DOLLS, same style as before with moving eyes. One in a box.

No. 445½.	20	21 inches
	$8.50	9.00 per dozen

QUARTER KID BODY DOLLS, with shoes and stockings, white mull shirt, with bib; bisque head with lace cap. One dozen in a box.

No. 442.

13 inches
$2.00 per dozen

QUARTER KID BODY DOLLS, same style as before with cream colored shirt and lace baby cap to match. One dozen in a box.

No. 443.

13 inches
$2.00 per dozen

QUARTER KID BODY DOLLS, plain body, not full jointed with bisque arms; colored stockings, and leather shoes with buckles; colored Mother Hubbard chemise trimmed with lace; fine bisque head, full wig of hair, fine moving eyes, open mouth showing teeth; lace cap to match chemise. One in a box.

No. 446½.

14	18 inches
$4.00	6.50 per dozen

HALF KID BODY DOLLS, with bisque head, Rembrandt style of hair, fine fixed glass eyes, open mouth with teeth; muslin shirt trimmed with lace; half kid leather body with bisque arms; colored stockings and leather shoes to take off. One dozen in a box.

No. 454.

13 inches
$2.00 per dozen

HALF KID BODY DOLLS, same style as before; fancy lace trimmed cream colored chemise.

No. 455.

13	16	17	21	24 inches
$2.00	3.75	4.00	6.50	9.00 p.doz.
1	½	½	¹⁄₁₂	¹⁄₁₂ dz. in box

HALF KID BODY DOLLS, same style as before with moving eyes.
No. 455½.

13	16	23 inches
$2.25	4.00	9.00 per dozen
1	½	¹⁄₁₂ doz. in a box

HALF KID BODY DOLLS with sewed long curly wig, fine bisque head with stationary fine eyes; open mouth showing teeth; half kid body with bisque arms; lace trimmed white mull shirt, black stockings, leather shoes to match.

No. 460.	15	17	20 inches
	$4.00	5.00	9.00 per dozen
	½	½	½ dozen in a box

HALF KID BODY DOLLS with fine quality bisque head; fine curly hair wigs, fine human eyes, open mouth showing teeth; half kid, full proportioned body, with fine lace trimmed muslin shirt, pleated at the bottom and puffed sleeves; black stockings and leather shoes with buckles. One in a box.

No. 462.

17	19	20 inches
$8.00	9.00	10.50 per dozen

HALF KID BODY DOLLS, finest quality, with fine bisque head; sewed curly hair wig; moving human eyes; open mouth showing teeth: half kid body, with fancy lace trimmed chemise, with pleats at the bottom and puffed sleeves; fine black stockings and fine leather shoes with buckles. One in a box.

No. 465.	17½	19	20 inches
	$9.00	12.00	15.00 per dozen

HALF KID BODY DOLLS, same style as before, with turning head; fine chemise with a lace yoke and wide silk ribbons; ribbed black stockings; light colored leather shoes with buckles and straps. One in a box.

No. 470.

20	22	24 inches
$21.00	27.00	30.00 per dz.

BISQUE HEAD JOINTED DOLLS.

BISQUE HEAD JOINTED DOLLS, with turning head; curly hair wig; painted eyes; muslin shirt; wood jointed body and papier mache limbs.

No. 500.

7 inches
38c per dozen
3 dozen in a box

BISQUE HEAD JOINTED DOLLS. Same style as before, with glass eyes; white shirt.

No. 501.

8½ inches
75c per dozen
1 dozen in a box

BISQUE HEAD JOINTED DOLLS, better quality; turning head with fine glass eyes; jointed limbs; assorted colored muslin shirts. One dozen in a box.
No. 502.

8½	9	10	inches
85c	$1.00	1.25	per dozen.

BISQUE HEAD JOINTED DOLLS, fine quality, with fine bisque head; full wig of hair; fine glass eyes; open mouth showing teeth; jointed limbs, with painted shoes and stockings; fine muslin shirt. One in a box.
No. 503.   7½ inches
80c per dozen

BISQUE HEAD JOINTED DOLLS; fine bisque turning head with full wig of hair; fine glass eyes; open mouth showing teeth; fine muslin shirt; larger sizes with silk ribbons; limbs double jointed. Our leading line.
No. 505.

11½	13	14	inches
$1.75	1.88	2.00	per dozen
1	½	½	doz. in a box

15½	20	22	inches
$3.75	8.00	8.50	per dozen
½	1/12	1/12	doz. in a box

BISQUE HEAD JOINTED DOLLS, fine quality; large turning bisque head with fine full hair wig; fine glass eyes; open mouth showing teeth; full proportioned papier mache body; double jointed limbs; fine muslin shirt trimmed with lace.
No. 506.

16 inches
$4.00 per dozen.
½ dozen in a box

BISQUE HEAD JOINTED DOLLS, same style as before, with double jointed limbs and jointed hands; fine lace trimmed pleated muslin shirts.
No. 506.   17½ inches
$4.50 per dozen
½ dozen in a box

BISQUE HEAD JOINTED DOLLS, fine quality turning bisque head, with full long hair wig, large fine glass eyes, open mouth showing teeth; papier mache body with jointed limbs and turning wrists; fancy puffed sleeve chemise with colored yoke and satin ribbons to match. One in a box.
No. 507.

21   22 inches
$8.50 9.00 per dozen

BISQUE HEAD JOINTED DOLLS, same quality and style as No. 505, with moving eyes.
No. 510.   11½   13 inches
$2.00   2.50 per dozen
1   ½   dozen in a box

BISQUE HEAD JOINTED DOLLS, same style as before, with jointed wrists and fine hair wig; moving eyes.
No. 511.

15	16	21	inches
$4.00	5.00	9.00	per dozen
½	½	1/12	doz. in a box

BISQUE HEAD JOINTED DOLLS, full proportioned infant body, fine bisque head with long curly hair wig, moving eyes, open mouth showing teeth; full jointed, with fine muslin lace chemise.
No. 513.   12 inches
$3.00 per dozen

BISQUE HEAD JOINTED BABIES, with lace cap; fine bisque heads with full hair wig, fixed eyes, baby shape body, full jointed with turning wrists.
No. 515.

11	13	inches
$3.00	4.50	per dozen
1	½	doz. in a box

BISQUE HEAD JOINTED DOLLS, (NEW), with papa and mamma voice, with new style of eyes, with real hair lashes, eyes move to right and left; fine bisque turning head, with full hair wig, open mouth showing teeth, bead necklace; full proportioned body with double jointed fine limbs; lace trimmed fine quality shirt. One in a box.
No. 520.

12½   18 inches
$9.00   18.00 per dozen

BISQUE HEAD JOINTED DOLLS, (NEW), with fine bisque head with 3 faces, crying, laughing, and sleeping; full jointed body. One in a box.
No. 521.   14 inches
$9.00 per dozen

BISQUE HEAD JOINTED DOLLS, finest quality bisque turning head, sewed long curly hair wig, fine human eyes, papier mache body, double jointed limbs with turning wrists; fancy white mull chemise with puffed sleeves and satin and lace "V" shape front, trimmed with satin ribbons. One in a box.
No. 525.

18   19 inches
$9.00   12.00 per dozen

BISQUE HEAD JOINTED DOLLS, same style as before, with moving eyes. One in a box.
No. 525½.   18 inches
$12.00 per dozen

BISQUE HEAD JOINTED DOLLS, very fine quality bisque turning head, sewed long curly wig, fine human eyes (fixed), papier mache body, full jointed limbs, turning wrists; fine white muslin shirt with lace yoke. One in a box.
No. 530.   11 inches
$4.50 per dozen

BISQUE HEAD JOINTED DOLLS, same style as before, with moving eyes; shoes and stockings. One in a box.

No. 535.

14	18	20	22	inches
$9.00	13.50	18.00	24.00	per doz.

23	25	28	30	inches
$33.00	42.00	51.00	66.00	per doz.

BISQUE HEAD JOINTED DOLLS, finest quality; of best material throughout —perfect in every way. Full size finest bisque china turning head with fine full-sewed Rembrandt style hair wig, fine moving human eyes, open mouth showing teeth; full proportioned all jointed body with turning wrists; fine muslin shirt, pleated and trimmed with lace around the neck, and puffed sleeves with lace around the wrists, satin bows and ribbons; ribbed stockings and fine leather shoes to match. Finest quality doll in the market. One doll in a box.

No. 540.

21	23	24	inches
$3.25	4.00	4.75	each

27	29	32	inches
$5.50	6.50	7.50	each

BISQUE JOINTED NEGRO DOLLS, style and quality like No. 540 dolls, with fine curly black woolly hair; fancy colored satin shirts trimmed with colored satin ribbons; colored beaded necklace. One in a box.

No. 545.

13	16	18	19	21	inches
$1.38	1.65	2.00	2.50	3.00	each

NEGRO DOLLS.

NEGRO DOLLS, muslin bodies, waxed papier mache head with curly, wooly hair, glass eyes; colored striped shirt; wood arms, papier mache legs.

No. 560.	8	12	19	inches
	38c	75c	$2.00	per dozen
	3	1	1	dozen in a box

NEGRO JOINTED DOLLS, with voice; papier mache turning head with curly and long hair; papier mache jointed limbs; colored striped shirt. One dozen in a box.

No. 562. 7½ inches
75c per dozen

NEGRO JOINTED DOLLS, turning bisque china head, long black hair, glass eyes, open mouth showing teeth; wood body, papier mache jointed limbs; colored shirt. One dozen in a box.

No. 563. 8½ inches
75c per dozen

NEGRO JOINTED DOLLS, washable head, curly black woolly hair, glass eyes; jointed papier mache limbs; colored shirt. ½ dozen in a box.

No. 565. 11 inches
$2.00 per dozen

NEGRO JOINTED DOLLS, BOYS AND GIRLS ASSORTED, bisque turning head with glass eyes, open mouth showing teeth; papier mache limbs; fancy negro costumes. ½ dozen in a box.

No. 566. 10 inches
$2.00 per dozen

NEGRO REVERSIBLE DOLLS (NEW). A new style of doll, which can be turned from a negro baby into a white baby; dressed in a colored costume for the negro, and blue dress for the white baby.

No. 567.	25	30	inches
	$1.75	2.00	per dozen
	1	½	dozen in a box

ZULU DOLLS (NEW), papier mache jointed figure, with black curly hair; painted eyes, with fur breach-cloth. 1 dozen in a box.

No. 580.

5	10	
3¾	5¾	inches
38c	80c	per dozen

ESQUIMAUX JOINTED DOLLS (NEW). These dolls are dressed in white fur, representing the costume of Esquimaux; wood body; papier mache jointed arms and legs; fine bisque china head with glass eyes.

No. 570.

1	3	5	
7	9	13½	inches
$2.00	3.75	9.00	per doz.
1	½	1/12	doz. in box

DRESSED DOLLS.

DRESSED DOLLS WITH WASHABLE HEADS, painted hair, painted eyes, cloth body, papier mache arms; cloth feet with colored stockings and shoes; dressed in a plain muslin colored shirt. One dozen in a box.

No. 600.	14	18	inches
	75c	$2.00	per doz.

DRESSED DOLLS, with washable head, fine glass eyes, hair wig, papier mache limbs; dressed in assorted colored dresses with fancy trimmings and with bonnet to match. One in a box.

No. 601. 15 inches
$1.75 per doz.

DRESSED DOLLS, BETTER QUALITY WASHABLE HEADS, hair wigs, fine glass eyes, cloth body, papier mache limbs; Assorted lace and muslin dresses trimmed with lace and satin fronts, bonnets to match.

No. 605.

14	15	18	20	22	inches
$1.75	2.00	3.25	3.75	4.00	per dozen
⅓	1/12	1/12	1/12	1/12	doz. in box

DRESSED DOLLS, WITH GOOD QUALITY WASHABLE HEADS, same style as before; cloth feet, shoes and stockings to take off. One in a box.

No. 606. 26 inches
$8.00 per dozen

DRESSED DOLLS, WITH FINE WASHABLE HEADS, with full hair wig, fine glass eyes; full proportioned body, fine papier mache limbs; colored muslin dresses with lace, satin and velvet trimmings, bonnets to match.

No. 608.	13	18	inches
	$2.00	3.75	per dozen
	½	1/12	dozen in a box

DRESSED DOLLS, WITH BISQUE CHINA HEADS, hair wig, fine glass eyes, open mouth showing teeth; excelsior stuffed cloth body, papier mache limbs; assorted dresses with satin and lace fronts and lace trimmings, bonnets to match. ½ dozen in a box.

No. 610. 12 inches
$1.75 per dozen

DRESSED DOLLS, same style as before with cloth feet, shoes and stockings. ½ dozen in a box.

No. 611½.	No. 611.	
11	13	inches
$2.00	2.25	per dozen

DRESSED DOLLS, same style as before, with shoes and stockings to take off. One in a box.

No. 612. 22 inches
$8.50 per dozen

DRESSED DOLLS, WITH FINE BISQUE CHINA HEADS, hair wig, fine glass eyes, open mouth showing teeth; short stout hair-stuffed baby shape body; shoes and stockings to take off. Dolls dressed in white, pink and blue fancy cashmere dresses, baby caps to match.

No. 625.	12	14	inches
	$2.25	4.50	per dozen
	⅓	1/12	dozen in a box

DRESSED DOLLS, WITH FINE BISQUE HEADS, hair wig, glass eyes, open mouth showing teeth; hair-stuffed body; colored shoes and stockings to take off; dressed in 3 different styles of fancy dresses, trimmed with satin fronts and lace, bonnets to match. One in a box.

No. 626.

14	15	16	inches
$4.00	4.50	6.50	per dozen

DRESSED DOLL WITH FINE BISQUE HEAD, same quality as before; fine satin and cashmere dresses assorted, bonnets and hats to match. One in a box.

No. 627.

18	20	inches
$9.00	12.00	per dozen

KID BODY DRESSED DOLLS.

KID BODY DRESSED DOLL, with fine bisque head, full wig of hair, fine eyes, open mouth showing teeth; half kid body with shoes and stockings to take off. Latest style of satin dresses with lace and velvet trimmings, assorted bonnets to match the dresses. One in a box.

No. 650.

15	17	inches
$4.00	9.00	per dozen

KID BODY DRESSED DOLL, same quality as before. Fine assorted wool and satin dresses, made in the latest styles, with silk ribbons, lace trimmings and satin fronts, handsome bonnets to match. One in a box.

No. 651. 16 inches
$8.50 per dozen

KID BODY DRESSED DOLL, same style as before, with moving eyes. One in a box. No. 652.

16 inches
$9.00 per dozen

KID BODY DRESSED DOLL, same style as before; larger, with fixed eyes. One in a box.

No. 653. 18 inches
$12.00 per dozen

KID BODY DRESSED DOLL, fine bisque head; fine eyes; open mouth showing teeth; full curly hair wig; half kid body, jointed arms; black stockings and black leather shoes to take off. These dolls come dressed in different styles—child's cashmere dress, cape and hood and sash; cashmere blouse and satin skirt, and lace hat with flowers; cashmere puffed blouse, satin skirt and Eaton jacket, straw hat with feathers; handsome satin child's dress profusely trimmed with ribbons and handsome lace, and lace hat to match dress. One in a box.

No. 654. 21 inches
$18.00 per dozen

KID BODY DRESS-ED DOLL, same style as before, with moving eyes. One in a box.

No. 655.

21 23 inches
$21.00 36.00 per dozen

JOINTED DRESSED DOLLS.

JOINTED DRESSED DOLL, bisque turning head; hair wig; glass eyes; jointed limbs; cream colored long baby dress. One in a box; 12 boxes in a package.

No. 15/1. 80c per dozen

JOINTED DRESSED DOLL, same quality as before. Assorted colored sailor costumes. One in a box; 12 boxes in a package.

No. 15/2. 80c per dozen

JOINTED DRESSED DOLL, with bisque china turning head, papier mache jointed limbs, painted shoes and stockings; fancy colored dress trimmed with lace. One dozen in a box.

No. 700. 6½ inches
75c per dozen

JOINTED DRESSED DOLL with bisque turning head, hair wig, fine glass eyes, open mouth showing teeth, jointed papier mache limbs; cloth stockings and shoes to take off. Different styles cambric and lace colored dresses trimmed with ribbons and lace, with lace poke bonnets to match. One in a box.

No. 705. 9 inches
$1.88 per doz.

JOINTED DRESSED DOLL, similar to No. 705; colored stockings and leather shoes to take off. All lace dresses with satin fronts. One in a box.

No. 706. 9 inches
$2.00 per dozen

JOINTED DRESSED DOLL, with fine bisque turning head, hair wig, fine glass eyes, open mouth showing teeth, jointed limbs, shoes and stockings to take off; colored Mother Hubbard dresses with lace trimmed hoods; 6 in a box.

No. 707. 8½ inches
$2.00 per dozen

JOINTED DRESSED DOLL, same style as before; painted shoes and stockings, assorted colored wool dresses with colored cloth or lace skirts, trimmed with lace and ribbons, lace trimmed poke bonnets; 6 in a box.

No. 708. 8½ inches
$1.87 per dozen

JOINTED DRESSED DOLL, same style as No. 708, with shoes and stockings to take of; 6 in a box.

No. 709. 8½ inches
$2.00 per dozen

DRESSED JOINTED DOLL, same quality doll as before; painted shoes and stockings; dressed boys and girls assorted, in child's velvet costume with cap to match; 2 pieces in a box.

No. 710. 9 inches
$2.00 per dozen

DRESSED JOINTED DOLL, turning bisque head, full hair wig, fine eyes, open mouth showing teeth; jointed limbs; leather shoes to take off; children's cloth sailor costumes with striped fronts, stockings and caps to match; assorted boys and girls; 6 in a box.

No. 712. 9 inches
$2.00 per dozen

DRESSED JOINTED DOLLS, same style as No. 708; 6 in a box.

No. 713. 9½ inches
$2.00 per dozen

DRESSED JOINTED DOLL, same style as No. 709; 6 in a box.
No. 714.   9½ inches
                          $2.25 per dozen

DRESSED JOINTED DOLL, bisque turning head, hair wig, glass eyes, papier mache limbs, painted shoes and stockings, knit worsted assorted dresses. One dozen in a box.
No. 715.   8 inches
                          $1.00 per dozen

DRESSED JOINTED DOLL, with bisque head, good hair wig, fine eyes, open mouth showing teeth, papier mache limbs, painted shoes and stockings; assorted good quality knit worsted dresses, with caps or bonnets to match; six in a box.
No. 715.   9   10 inches
                    $2.00   2.25 per dozen

DRESSED JOINTED DOLL with fine bisque turning head, good hair wig, fine glass eyes, open mouth showing teeth, papier mache limbs, shoes and stockings to take off. Assorted fancy colored cloth and lace dresses, trimmed with velvet, satin or lace, and with lace bonnets to match. One in a box.
No. 725.
                    12   14 inches
                  $3.75   4.00 per dozen

DRESSED JOINTED DOLL, same style as before, with moving eyes.
No. 725¼.   12 inches
                          $4.00 per dozen

DRESSED JOINTED DOLL, same style as before.
No. 726.   16 inches
          $9.00 per dozen

DRESSED JOINTED DOLL, fine bisque turning head, full hair wig, fine glass eyes, open mouth showing teeth, double jointed limbs, black shoes and stockings to take off; children's long dresses of the latest design, assorted, figured and plain fine material, fancy cloth or lace caps or bonnets to match. One in a box.
No. 730.
          12   16 inches
        $4.50   9.00 per dozen

DRESSED JOINTED DOLL, same style and quality as before, with moving eyes; Cashmere baby dresses, cloth hood to match.
No. 731.   16 inches
                    $9.00 per dozen

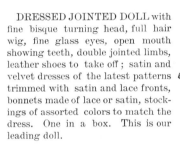

DRESSED JOINTED DOLL with fine bisque turning head, full hair wig, fine glass eyes, open mouth showing teeth, double jointed limbs, leather shoes to take off; satin and velvet dresses of the latest patterns trimmed with satin and lace fronts, bonnets made of lace or satin, stockings of assorted colors to match the dress. One in a box. This is our leading doll.

No. 735.
   11   14   14½ 16   17   19   20 inches
$4.00 5.00 6.00 9.00 12.00 18.00 21.00 per dozen

DRESSED JOINTED DOLL, same style as before, with moving eyes and long fine curly wig. One in a box.
No. 736.
   19   21 inches
$24.00 36.00 per dozen

DRESSED JOINTED DOLL, finest quality bisque turning head, fine full hair wig, open mouth showing teeth, fine eyes; double jointed limbs; black stockings and black shoes to take off. Latest style dress made of lace over satin skirt, fancy satin jacket over puffed lace waist, lace trimmed underclothing, lace hat with ribbons, satin trimmings and feathers. One in a box.
No. 740.
        12 inches
      $10.00 per dozen

DRESSED JOINTED DOLL, same style as before with moving eyes. One in a box.
No. 741.
        15 inches
      $18.00 per dozen

DRESSED JOINTED DOLL, fine turning bisque head, long curly hair wig, fine moving glass eyes, open mouth showing teeth; short ribbed stockings and shoes with straps and buckles; latest style dresses made of best plain and ribbed silk, satin and velvet, in plain and mode colors trimmed with lace, ribbons, large hats and bonnets to match. One in a box.
No. 745.

   19   20   22   24   26   28   30   32 inches
$3.75 4.50 5.50 6.00 7.00 8.00 10.00 12.00 each

DRESSED SAILOR DOLLS.

WASHABLE HEAD DRESSED SAILOR DOLL, fine glass eyes; papier mache limbs; excelsior stuffed body, cambric sailor costumes, assorted colors.
No. 750.   11   16 inches
              80c   2.00 per dozen
               1   ½ doz. in a box

DRESSED JOINTED SAILOR DOLL, (boys only), bisque turning head, fine glass eyes, open mouth showing teeth; papier mache double jointed limbs; painted shoes and stockings; assorted sailor cloth costumes. 6 in a box.
No. 755.   11 inches
                  $2.00 per dozen

DRESSED JOINTED SAILOR DOLL, same style as before with shoes and stockings to take off. One in a box.
No. 756.   14 inches
                  $4.00 per dozen

DRESSED JOINTED SAILOR DOLL, (boys and girls), bisque turning head, hair wig, fine glass eyes, open mouth showing teeth; papier mache jointed limbs. Satin sailor costumes.

No. 284.   9   inches
$2.50   per dozen

DRESSED JOINTED SAILOR DOLL, (boys and girls), fine bisque turning head, full curly hair wig, fine eyes, open mouth showing teeth; double jointed limbs; black shoes and stockings to take off. Fine merino two colored sailor costumes. 2 in a box.

No. 757.   14   inches
$9.00   per dozen

DRESSED JOINTED SAILOR DOLL, (boys and girls assorted), fine quality bisque turning head, fine glass eyes, open mouth showing teeth; double jointed limbs. Cashmere and velvet sailor costume. One in box.

No. 758.   16   inches
$9.00   per dozen.

DRESSED JOINTED DOLL. Baby Doll, bisque turning head, fine moving eyes, open mouth showing teeth; papier mache limbs; long white muslin baby dress trimmed with lace and silk ribbons with baby cap to match.

No. 760.

9	12	16	inches
$2.00	4.00	9.00	per dozen
¼	1/12	1/12	doz. in a box

DRESSED JOINTED BABY DOLL, fine washable head; cloth body, papier mache limbs; pink and blue long cloth dress, trimmed with lace, baby rattle attached. One in a box.

No. 765.   12   14   inches
$4.00   4.50 per dozen

DOLLS DRESSED IN FANCY COSTUMES.

RED RIDING HOOD, wood jointed, bisque turning head, fine glass eyes, hair wig, open mouth showing teeth; jointed limbs; plain child's Red Riding Hood dress with red hood and red cape. One in a box.

No. 775.

    9   12   inches
$2.00   4.00 per dozen

SCOTCH DRESSED BOYS AND GIRLS, fine bisque turning head, full hair wig, fine glass eyes, open mouth showing teeth; double jointed limbs. Scotch Highlander costume. Two in a box.

No. 782.

   9   12   16   inches
$2.25 4.50 9.00 per dz.

LORD FAUNTLEROY DOLL. Bisque jointed doll. Velvet Lord Fauntleroy costumes of different colors.

No. 783.   16   inches
$9.00 per dozen

DRESSED NURSE WITH BABY, jointed bisque doll. Gray cloth nurse costume with white apron and cap with baby in her arms. One in a box.

No. 777.   12   inches
$4.00   per dozen

DRESSED COLORED NURSE WITH BABY, Southern nurse costume with baby in her arms. One in a box.

No. 778.

     16   inches
$9.00 per doz.

DRESSED BRIDE, bisque jointed doll, white muslin dress with lace trimmings, and long white veil; wreath in her hair and boquet in her hand, white shoes and stockings. One in a box.

No. 780.   14   inches
$9.00 per dozen

MARGUERITE DRESSED DOLL, bisque jointed doll. Costume of blue cashmere with white yoke and sleeves, blue cap, black velvet side pocket. One in a box.

No. 781.   14   inches
$9.00 per dozen

MOURNING DOLL, mourning costume of black cloth with black velvet trimmings, crepe hat and veil. One in a box.

No. 779.   11   inches
$4.00 per dozen

QUAKER DRESSED DOLL, bisque jointed doll. Quaker costume, gray dress with bonnet to match and white linen cloth worn over shoulder, coming to the waist.

No. 784.   9   11   inches
$2.00   4.00
    1   ½   dozen in a box

RAG BABY DOLL, long baby dress with colored hood and colored cape with lace trimmings. One dozen in a box.

No. 825/15.   No. 825/25.
80c $1.75 per dozen.

RAG DOLLS IN RED RIDING HOOD COSTUME. 6 in a box.

No. 827/50 $3.75 per dozen

DRESSED JOINTED FRENCH WALKING DOLL. (New).

This is a new doll brought out by us this season. By taking the doll by the hands, you can make it walk on the floor just like a baby. This doll is dressed in fine silk chemise with lace trimmings. The larger one in silk dress with a bonnet to match. Each with fine ribbed baby socks and leather shoes with buckles and bows. Fine bisque French China head which turns as the doll walks.

No. 1582.	No. 1583.
20	24 inches
$5.00	10.00 each

GERMAN WICKELPUPPEN.

BABY DOLL ON PILLOW, WITH VOICE, bisque head, curly hair, papier mache limbs. White mull dress trimmed with satin ribbons and lace cap. Moving arms.

No. 830.

10	25	50	
80c.	$2.00	4.00	per dozen
1	1	½	dozen in a box

KNIT WORSTED DOLLS.

These dolls are intended for small children, they are made entirely of cloth, covered with knit worsted in bright colors. They are very durable and very attractive to the eye.

No. 800.

6/0	4/0	3/0	1	
7	9½	10	13	inches
75c.	$1.75	2.00	3.75	per doz.
1	1	1	½	doz. in box

KNIT WORSTED DOLL CLOWNS, same style of doll as described before. Bright colored clown costume with bells.

No. 802.

4/0	
10	inches
$1.75	per dozen
1	dozen in a box

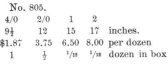

KNIT WORSTED DOLL CLOWNS, same style as before with voice.

No. 805.

4/0	2/0	1	2	
9½	12	15	17	inches.
$1.87	3.75	6.50	8.00	per dozen
1	½	1/12	1/12	dozen in box

KNIT WORSTED SAILOR BOYS AND GIRLS, same style as described before. Knit blue and white sailor costumes.

No. 808.

3/0	2/0	
10	12	inches
$2.00	3.75	per dozen
1	½	dozen in a box

KNIT WORSTED BOYS AND GIRLS. Fine knit fancy dresses. One in a box.

No. 809. No. 4/0
9 inches
$2.00 per dozen

KNIT WORSTED DOLLS, covered with fine Jersey cloth. Fine knit worsted dresses.

No. 810.

No. 2/0	No. 2	
$4.00	8.00	per dozen
11	15	inches
½	1/12	dozen in box

KNIT WORSTED RATTLES.

Made of very bright colored worsted. Very attractive for babies.

No. 816/1. Square shape, with long handles. 75c per dozen

No. 816/4. Same as before, large size. $1.75 per dozen

No. 812. Baby head, with wood handle and bells. $2.00 per dozen

WASHABLE, CHINA AND BISQUE DOLL HEADS.

PATENT GLAZED DOLL HEADS, painted hair and eyes; ⅔ light and ⅓ black painted hair.

No. 2015.

0	1	2	
2½	2¾	3	inches across the shoulders
33c	37c	50c	per dozen
1	1	1	dozen in a box

3	4	5	
3½	3¾	4	inches across the shoulders
67c	75c	87c	per dozen
1	1	½	dozen in a box

6	7	8	
4½	4¾	5	inches across the shoulders
$1.00	1.25	1.50	per dozen
½	⅓	⅓	dozen in a box.

WASHABLE DOLL HEADS, Fine Matt quality, with hair wigs and fine glass eyes.

No. 2020.

0	1	2	
3½	3¾	4	inches across the shoulders
75c	$1.00	1.25	per dozen
1	1	1	dozen in a box

3	4	
4½	4¾	inches across the shoulders
$1.75	2.00	per dozen
½	½	dozen in a box

CHINA GLAZED DOLL HEADS, with painted hair and eyes.

No. 200.

2/0	0	1	
2¼	2½	2¾	inches across the shoulders
37c	45c	60c	per dozen
1	1	1	dozen in a box

1½	2	3	
3	3¼	3½	inches across the shoulders
70	75c	87c	per dozen
1	1	1	dozen in a box

4	5	6	
3¾	4	4¼	inches across the shoulders
$1.00	1.25	1.50	per dozen
½	½	½	dozen in a box

CHINA GLAZED DOLL HEADS, better quality, with painted hair and eyes.

No. 205.

0	2	3	
3	3¼	3½	inches across the shoulders
67c	75c	$1.00	per dozen
½	½	⅓	dozen in a package

4	5	6	
3¾	4	4¼	inches across the shoulders
$1.25	1.50	1.75	per dozen
⅓	⅓	⅓	dozen in a package

7	9	11	
4½	4¾	5¼	inches across the shoulders
$2.00	3.00	4.00	per dozen
¼	¼	1/6	dozen in a package

BISQUE CHINA DOLL HEADS, with assorted styles of painted hair, and with painted eyes.

No. 210.

4	5	6	
3¼	3½	3¾	inches across the shoulders
$1.65	1.75	2.00	per dozen
½	⅓	⅓	dozen in a box

7	8	9	
4	4¼	4½	inches across the shoulders
$2.50	3.00	3.50	per dozen
⅓	¼	¼	dozen in a box.

BISQUE CHINA DOLL HEADS, same style as before, with fine glass eyes.

No. 220.

3	4	5	
3	3¼	3½	inches across the shoulders
$2.00	2.50	3.00	per dozen
½	½	⅓	dozen in a box

6	7	8	
3¾	4	4¼	inches across the shoulders
$3.50	3.75	4.00	per dozen
⅓	⅓	¼	dozen in a box

BISQUE CHINA BOY DOLL HEADS, with painted hair and eyes.

No. 215.

5	6	7	8	
3½	3¾	4	4½	inches across the shoulders
$1.65	1.75	2.00	3.00	per dozen
⅓	⅓	⅓	⅓	dozen in a box

BISQUE CHINA DOLL HEADS, with assorted hair wigs, fine glass eyes, open mouth showing teeth.

No. 225.

4/0	2	3	5	6	
2¼	3¼	3½	4	4¼	ins. across shoulders
75c	$1.75	2.00	3.50	4.00	per dozen
1	½	½	⅓	¼	doz. in a box

BISQUE CHINA DOLL HEADS, with assorted sewed, long curly hair wigs, fine glass eyes, open mouth showing teeth. One in a box.

No. 230.

0	1	2	3	4	
3	3½	3¾	3¼	4	ins. across shoulders
$1.88	2.00	3.00	3.50	3.75	per dozen

5	6	7	8	
4⅛	4¼	4½	5	ins. across shoulders
$4.00	5.00	6.00	7.50	per dozen

BISQUE CHINA HEADS, same style as before, with moving eyes. One in a box.

No. 235.

2/0	0	2	4	5	7	
$2.00	2.50	3.50	4.00	4.50	6.50	per dozen

BISQUE CHINA HEADS, fine quality, with sewed curly hair wigs, fine glass eyes, open mouth showing teeth. (New model head.) One in a box.

No. 240.

4	6	8	10	
3½	4	5	5¾	ins. across shoulders
$4.00	6.50	9.00	12.00	per dozen

BISQUE CHINA HEADS, fine quality, same style as before, with moving eyes.

No. 241.

5	7	9	11	
3¾	4½	5	6	ins. across shoulders
$6.00	9.00	12.00	15.00	per dozen

BISQUE CHINA HEADS, finest quality, with fine long curly hair wigs, fine glass eyes, open mouth showing teeth. One in a box.
No. 1166.

4				
3¼ ins. across shoulders				
$5.00 per dozen				
5	6	8	10	12
3½	4	4¾	5½	6½ ins. across shoulders
$6.00	7.00	9.00	12.00	15.00 per dozen

BISQUE CHINA HEADS, finest quality, same style as before, with moving eyes. One in a box.
No. 1167.

4	5	7
3¼	3½	4½ ins. across shoulders
$5.50	6.50	8.00 per dozen
9	11	13
5	6	7 ins. across shoulders
$12.00	15.00	18.00 per dozen

BISQUE CHINA BOYS' HEADS, finest quality, with fine short curly hair wigs; fine eyes. One in a box.
No. 242.

4	6	8	10
3	4	4¾	5½ ins. across shoulders
$4.00	6.00	7.50	9.00 per dozen

BISQUE CHINA BOYS' HEADS, fine quality, with lamb's wool short wigs. One in a box.
No. 245.

5/0	2/0	3
2½	3	4 ins. across shoulders
$1.50	2.00	4.00 per dozen

BISQUE CHINA GIRLS' HEADS, with lamb's-wool wigs, curly bangs and back comb, fine glass eyes, open mouth showing teeth. One in a box.
No. 246.

4	6	7	9	11
3½	4	4½	5	6 ins. across shoulders
$4.00	6.50	7.50	9.00	12.00 per dozen

MUSLIN AND KID DOLL BODIES.

DOLL BODIES, WHITE MUSLIN with leather arms, colored corsets, colored stockings and black cloth shoes with tassels.

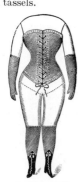

No.	Length of Body.	Length across Shoulders.	Price per Dozen.
0	10½ inches	3½ inches	$1.00
1	11 "	4 "	1.13
2	12 "	4¼ "	1.25
3	13½ "	4½ "	1.50
4	15 "	4¾ "	1.75
5	16½ "	5 "	2.25
6	18 "	5¼ "	2.75
7	19½ "	5½ "	3.25
8	21 "	5¾ "	3.75
9	22½ "	6 "	4.00
10	24½ "	7 "	5.00
11	26½ "	8 "	6.00

DOLL ARMS, WHITE KID LEATHER, MUSLIN UPPER ARM, WITH OPEN FINGERS.

No. 2/0,	3¼ inches long,	$ .60 per dozen pairs.
" 0	3¾ "	.70 " "
" 1	4½ "	.85 " "
" 2	5 "	1.00 " "
" 3	5½ "	1.20 " "
" 4	6 "	1.35 " "
" 5	6½ "	1.50 " "
" 6	7 "	1.65 " "
" 7	7½ "	1.85 " "
" 8	8½ "	2.00 " "
" 9	9 "	2.25 " "
" 10	10 "	2.50 " "
" 11	11 "	2.75 " "

FINE WHITE KID LEATHER BODIES with bisque arms, jointed limbs, full shaped body.
No. 1040.

	Length of Body.	Length across Shoulders.	Price per Dozen.
2	10 inches	2¾ inches	$2.50
3	12 "	3 "	3.25
4	13 "	3½ "	4.00
5	14 "	3¾ "	4.50
6	16 "	4½ "	5.50
7	17 "	4¾ "	6 50
8	18 "	5½ "	8.00
9	19½ "	6 "	9.00
10	21½ "	6½ "	12.00

KID DOLL BODIES, fine white leather, same style and sizes as 1040, with assorted colored stockings and leather buckled slippers to take off.

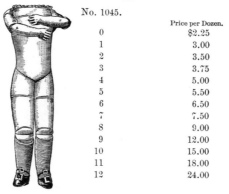

No. 1045.

	Price per Dozen.
0	$2.25
1	3.00
2	3.50
3	3.75
4	5.00
5	5.50
6	6.50
7	7.50
8	9.00
9	12.00
10	15.00
11	18.00
12	24.00

DOLLS' SLIPPERS, SHOES, STOCKINGS, ETC.

All doll slippers and shoes are put up 1 dozen in a box, 6 sizes, assorted.

DOLLS' SLIPPERS, black and bronze leather with rosettes, strings to tie and heels, assorted sizes, from 1 to 6.
Assortment No. 1...........$1.50 per dozen pairs.

SLIPPERS, same style as before, assorted sizes, from 6 to 9.
Assortment No. 2...........$2.00 per dozen pairs

DOLLS' SHOES, 6 assorted sizes, from 1 to 6, black leather with buckles.
No. S/5.....................$ .38 per dozen pairs.

DOLLS' SHOES, black and russet leather, assorted, with buckles and single buttoned strap, assorted as before.
No. S/10....................$ .75 per dozen pairs.

DOLLS' SHOES, same style as before, all solid tan colored leather.
No. S/15....................$ .75 per dozen pairs.

DOLLS' BUTTON GAITERS, russet and black leather assorted, with buttons, buckles and heels, assorted sizes, 1 to 6.
Assortment No. 3...........$2.00 per dozen pairs.

DOLLS' BUTTON GAITERS. Fine black and bronze leather, with bronze buttons and heels and silver buckles; sizes from 1 to 12.
Assortment No 4, $3.00 per dozen pairs.

DOLLS' STOCKINGS, put up 1 dozen pairs, 6 assorted sizes.
No. R/1, assorted solid colors, 38c per doz. pairs
No. R/2, assorted solid colors,
    short feet, for jointed dolls, 35c " "

DOLLS' HATS AND BABY CAPS.

One dozen in a box, assorted sizes and styles.

DOLLS' HATS, made of lace, with assorted feathers and ribbons to match.
No. H/10.......................75c per dozen

STRAW HATS, with feathers, ribbons and other ornaments.
No. H/25 ....$2.00 per dozen

FELT HATS, assorted shapes of the latest styles, with ribbons, feathers and pon-pons.
No. H/30 ....$2.00 per dozen

DOLLS' BABY CAPS, with ruchings and white muslin strings.
No. 501 (plain).................$ .37 per dozen
No. 502 (embroidered).......... .75 " "
No. 503 (with lace ruchings).... 1.25 " "
No. 504 (embroidered and with
    lace ruchings)....... 1.75 " "

PLUSH BABY CAPS, with ruchings and silk ribbons.
No. 704.......................$ .85 per dozen
No. 705. Same style as before
    (lined) .... 1.00 " "

KNIT WORSTED DOLL GOODS.

DOLLS' KNIT WORSTED BABY SHOES.

No. 25 (4 sizes) ....$1.65 per dozen

DOLLS' KNIT HOODS, four assorted colors and four assorted sizes.

No. 30........................$2.00 per dozen

DOLLS' KNIT TAM O'SHANTER CAPS.

No. 50........................$1.75 per dozen

DOLLS' KNIT WORSTED BABY JACKETS, four assorted styles and colors.

No. 100.......................$2.00 per dozen

MISCELLANEOUS.

DOLLS' GOSSAMERS OR RUBBER CLOAKS, with hoods, assorted sizes and assorted colors.

$1.75 per dozen

DOLLS' FANS, colored, with plain white sticks and tassels.

No. 134.........................38c per dozen

DOLLS' PARASOLS, colored cambric, natural wood stick.

No. P/25 ....$2.00 per dozen

Same style as before, colored satin, trimmed with white lace, natural wood stick.

No. P/50......................$4.00 per dozen

DOLLS' RUBBER COMB SETS, put up on cards, consisting of round comb, back comb, fine comb, and toilet comb.

No. 30....$1.25 per dozen

DOLLS' JEWELRY SETS.

DOLLS' JEWELRY, put up on cards, consisting of beaded necklace with metal cross, bead earrings and gilt metal back comb.

No. J/5...37c per dozen

DOLLS' JEWELRY, consisting of colored bead necklace, with locket, earrings, bracelets, breast pin, watch, or with button hook, back comb and fine comb. Each set put up in a box.

No. FJ/25 ....$1.75 per dozen
No. FJ/50 .... 4.00 " · "
No. FJ/100 ....12.00 " "

DOLLS' TOILET SETS.

DOLLS' TOILET SETS, consisting of hand mirror, sponge, soap, baby, box of powder, or nursing bottle, sachet, hair brush, comb, etc.

No. J/10......................$ .75 per dozen
No. J/30...................... 2.00 " "
No. J/50...................... 4.00 " "

DOLLS' NURSING BOTTLES, with rubber tube. One dozen in a box.

No. N/5.......................35c per dozen

DOLLS' HAMMOCKS, assorted colors and sizes.

No. 15.........................75c per dozen

NICKEL DOLL STANDS.

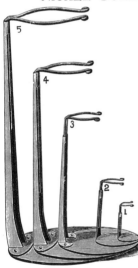

NICKEL-PLATED METAL DOLL STANDS, a new patent device for supporting dolls in a standing position; a very useful article for show windows.

No. 1   No. 2
$1.00   2.00 per doz.

No. 3   No. 4
$4.50   13.50 per doz.

EXTENSION WIRE DOLL STANDS, with cast-iron base. A new patent device for supporting dolls in a standing position.

Very convenient for show windows.

1	2	3
$1.75	2.50	3.75 per dozen

PATENT WIRE DOLL HANGERS. An ingenious device to hang dolls on, suitable for stores. (See back of doll on accompanying picture.)

02   03

50c   75c per dozen

FLANNEL, PLUSH AND KNIT WORSTED TOYS.

FLANNEL RABBITS.   One dozen in a box.

1	2	3	5
35c	63c	75c	$1.75 per dozen

FLANNEL DOGS.

		Per Dozen
No. 1.	Assorted colors...................	$ 0 35
No. 2.	Black and white on wood casters, with bell........................	75
No. 3.	Black and white, larger, on wood casters, with bell	1 25
No. 4.	Black and white, extra, size on wood casters, with bell	1 75
No. 50.	Velvet covered, with colored ribbons and basket	4 00

CLOTH OR FLANNEL ANIMALS.

No. 6.	Dog and monkey rider............	75
No. 7.	Monkey rider on Donkey with wood casters and bell.................	1 38
No. 10.	Elephant with bells on wooden casters	75
No. 20.	Plush monkeys with fur trimmings	75
No. 30.	Plush monkeys, same as before, with bells ; larger size..........	1 75
No. 2/10.	Creton cats, stuffed with excelsior, with ribbon and bell	70
No. 4/25.	Same as before, very large size..	2 00

FINE IMPORTED FLANNEL POODLE DOGS, assorted colors and sizes.   One dozen in a box.

No. 818. $2.00 per dozen

FINE KNIT WORSTED ASSORTED ANIMALS with bells, viz:—sheep, dogs, horses, etc. One dozen in a box.

No. 817. $2.00 per dozen

KNIT WORSTED BALLS WITH RATTLE INSIDE.   One dozen in a box.

$ .75 per dozen

FOR KNIT WORSTED DOLLS AND RATTLES, See Index.

FINE KNIT WORSTED DOMESTIC ANIMALS FOR SMALL CHILDREN.

No. 1, cat standing. No. 1, dog lying. No. 1, dog sitt'g. No. 1, dog stand'g.

Very fine crochet worsted animals stuffed with cotton batting.   Suitable for first-class trade.

Small cats, dogs and rabbits assorted lying,
$2.50 per dozen

Small birds assorted................ 2.50	"
No. 1, cats lying................... 4.50	"
" 3, cats lying...................12.00	"
" 1, cats sitting................. 4.50	"
" 2, cats sitting................. 8.50	"
" 1, cats standing................ 7.25	"
" 3, cats standing...............16.50	"
" 1, dogs lying.................. 4.50	"
" 2, dogs lying.................12.00	"
" 1, dogs sitting................ 4.50	"
" 2, dogs sitting................ 8.50	"
" 1, dogs standing.............. 7.25	"
" 2, dogs standing.............. 8.50	"
" 3, dogs standing..............18.00	"

Also Monkeys, Rattles, Dolls and Bean Balls.

HARMONICAS.

(Richter's Harmonicas, Nickel Covers.

No.
33½–10 Zinc Plate 10 holes, metal cover on one side only.................................$0 35

Richter's Harmonicas, Nickel Covers.
Brass Plates, with screws.

No. 33	8	10	12	20	24 notes
	33c.	37c.	48c	75c.	96c Per Doz

Excelsior Harmonicas, New Design.
Nickel Covers, Zinc Plates, Fancy Colored Wood.

No.
45–10 ½ Dozen in Package $0 70

Imitation Hohner Style Harmonicas.
Nickel covers, zinc plates, screws, broad silver reeds.

No.
50–10 ½ Dozen in a Package..$0 75

Gilt Cover Imitation Hohner Harmonicas,
Zinc plates, screws, broad silver reeds, gilt covers

No.
60–10 ½ Dozen in a package...$0 80

Vienna Shape Fancy Harmonicas,
Imitation Vienna Concert.   Red and yellow polished wood, nickel cover.

No.
51–10 6 Notes, 1 Dozen in a Package....................................$0 35

Solo Concert Harmonicas.
Red stained wood, nickel covers.

No.
52–16 ½ Dozen in a Package...$0 75

Vienna Concert Harmonicas.
White polished wooden ends, fine nickel covers, German silver reeds.

No.
53–16 ½ Dozen in a package..$1 00

Tremolo Concert Harmonicas.
Polished wood ends, best nickel covers, fine German silver reeds.

No.   Per Doz
62–16 ½ Dozen in a Package...$1 75

Fancy Gilt Cover Tremolo Concert Harmonicas.
Handsome gilt covers with trumpet holes.

No.   Per Doz
63–16 ½ Dozen in a Package...$2 00

Gebrueder Ludwig's Harmonicas. Pine Tree Brand.
Brass plates, single reeds, nickel covers, assorted keys.   ½ Dozen in a package.

No. 133	10	12	20	24
	90	1 10	1 80	2 20 Per Doz

Richard Wagner Concert Harmonicas.
Oval Mouthpiece, nickel plated, sliding covers, silver reeds.   Each one in a neat box.

No.   Per Doz
70 10 Notes. ½ Dozen in a Package....................................1 88

Original Emmet Harmonicas.
Finest quality, Richter shape, best nickel covers, silver plates, real silver reeds.
Each Harmonica bears a facsimile of J. K. Emmet's signature.

No   Per Doz.
69–10 ½ Dozen in a Package..$1 50

Genuine M. Hohner Harmonicas.
Best nickel covers, brass plates, double reeds, assorted letters.

No.   Per Doz
50B–10 ½ Dozen in a Package..$1 70

34B–10 Same as before, single reeds, ½ Dozen in a Package...........1 70

Professional Hohner Concert Harmonicas.
German silver covers, silver reeds, finest quality.

No.   Per Doz
3–C. N. D.–20 ½ Dozen in a Package..................................$4 00

✤HARMONICAS ✦ AND ✦ IRISH ✦ HARPS✤

Novelties in Celluloid Harmonicas.

F. A. Böhm's Genuine Richter.

No.   Per Doz

534-10. 10 Note, fine nickel covers with celluloid panels, gold letters, silver reeds.

½ dozen in package...$1 50

F. A. Böhm's Orchestra Harmonicas.

No.   Per Doz

600-10. 10 Note, celluloid covers, silver letters, silvered plates, silver reeds.......... ..... 1 75

75-10. Celluloid Concert, **Our Special**; the best 25c Harmonica in the market. Celluloid

covers with gilt letters, white polished wood, nickel buttons. 10 double notes. 2 00

F. A. Böhm's Celluloid Emmet's Delight Harmonicas.

No.   Per Doz

626-10. Fine quality, celluloid covers, with bone front, gilt letters $2 50

Brentano's Delight Harmonicas.

No.   Per Doz

752-10 The Finest Harmonica made, in a sliding celluloid case; best brass plates, finest

German silver tongues...3 50

Crystal Palace Harmonicas, (new).

Per Doz

One of the novelties of the season. A brass plate harmonica in a solid glass cover, which keeps it always clean, is not affected by saliva or moisture. Each one in a substantial sliding cover box..$ 3 25

Irish Harps.

Irish Harps, plain iron frames, steel tongues.

No.	Per Doz
013	$0 20
015	25
017	30
019	35
021	40

Genuine J. B. Smith Harps.

These Harps are especially made for us by one of the leading Belfast makers; they are warranted to be made of the very best material, and are perfect club harps, with finest steel tongues.

J. B. Smith's Plain Harps.

No.	Per Doz
50	$0 75
75	1 00
78	1 25

J. B. Smith's Fancy Shape Harps.

No.	Per Doz
30	$0 75
45	1 25

J. B. Smith's Tinned Harps.

With blue steel tongues.

No.	Per Doz
01	$0 75
02	1 25
03	1 50

Accordeons and other Musical Instruments.

☩ACCORDEONS☩

Large Accordeons.

No.		Per Doz
120–10.	10 keys, polished wooden sides, nickel trimmings, 2 basses and 1 stop, paper bellows with leather corners.	$8 50
125-200.	Accordeons, imitation rosewood with colored metal and nickel trimmings, 10 keys, 2 basses, 2 stops, 5 trumpets, leather corners, cloth bellows	18 00
125-300.	Fine oak case with nickel trimmings, 10 keys, 2 basses, 2 stops, leather edges, cloth bellows, a fine instrument	24 00

Fine Quality Accordeons.

Large size Accordeons, plain black top, heavy nickel ornaments, corners and clasps, double bellows, with 2 sets of reeds, 2 stops.

No.		Each
855.	10 keys	$2 50

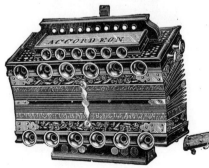

Regular Size Accordeons, black and gold moulding, colored top, silver stamped depressed keyboard, open action, nickel keys, corners and clasps, double bellows, 2 sets of reeds

No.		Each
405.	10 keys	$3 00

Regular Size Accordeons, with white enameled frame, polished, open nickel keys, corners and clasps, heavy metal corners, double bellows, 2 sets of reeds, 2 stops.

No.		Each
610.	10 keys	$3 50

Kalbe's Imperial Accordeon, with ebonized mouldings, nickel corners and clasps, open key action, double bellows, leather strap, 2 sets of reeds, 2 stops.

No.		Each
1190.	10 keys	$4 00

Occarinas.

A new instrument which can be learned without any teacher, and on which the finest concert pieces can be performed.

GERMAN SILVER.

No.		Per Doz
01.	Small	$2 50
03.	Medium	3 75
05.	Large	6 00

Toy Violins.

No.		Per Doz
115–30.	Varnished with bow, one in a box.	$2.00.
115–50.	Same style, larger with a better bow, one in a box	$4.00

Large Violins.

No.		Per. Dozen.
116–1.	Fine polished with a screw bow, full size, one in a paper bag.	$9.00.
116–2.	Fine full polished instrument with a good screw bow	$12.00.
116–3.	Extra good quality, fine polished violin, with polished fine screw bow.	$18.00.

Banjos.

No.		Per Doz.
7 ½ inch vellum head		$1.85.
P. 7 ½ inch, same as before with picture		$2.00.
6 ½ inch, sheep-skin head, 4 screws, wood rim.		$4.00.

No.		
9 inch, sheep-skin head, 4 screws wood rim		$8.00.
10 " " " " "		$9.00.
8 inch calf-skin head, nickel rim, 6 screws.		$8.50.
356.	9 inch calf-skin head, all nickel rim, 6 screws	$13.50.
358.	10 inch, same as before,	$18.00.
608.	10 " 12 screws	$24.00.

Musical Cup and Ball.

		Per Doz
5 Notes		$0 75
6 "		80

The Calliope.

It is a wooden instrument of ten whistles, each of a different note, and the average small boy can be depended on to make life miserable for everybody within half a mile of him. Packed 1 dozen in a package.
Per dozen $0 70

Kazoo.

No.		Per Doz
310.	It is a musical instrument that any one can play at a moments notice without any instruction. There is nothing about the Kazoo to get out of order, and it can be carried in the pocket without injury. The variety of tunes produced on the Kazoo, unlike any other instrument, is almost limitless. Packed 1 dozen in a package.	$0 60

Toy Castanets.

We hereby show you cut of our new 5c novelty, size 6x1. Made of hard wood with steel spring and double weighted strikers, stained red and black. Put up 1 dozen in a box. This is a good thing, and a seller.
Per dozen $0 35

Harmonica Flutes.

These instruments are made of bright metal, nickel and wood. Are very showy and any one can learn to play them without a teacher in a short time.

No. 110.		Per Doz.
25.	6 keys	$1.85.
35.	6 keys, all nickel	$2.00.
50.	8 keys and 2 basses, case all nickel	$4.50.
100.	10 bone keys, 2 basses, case all nickel.	$9.00.

No. 112		Per Doz.
50.	6 keys, nickel with wood ends	$4.00.
100.	10 keys, 2 basses, polished wood,	$8.50.
150.	10 keys, 2 basses, fine polished wood with gilt trimmings	$12.00.

TOY DRUMS.

TOY DRUMS, plain metal, with belt and cord.
No. A.

6	7	8	9 ins.
$1.75	2.00	3.25	3.87 PER DOZ.

10	11	12	13 ins.
$5.25	6.00	7.50	8.00 PER DOZ.

TOY DRUMS, embossed metal, Morning Glory pattern, with hook and belt, and red, white and blue cord.
No. B.

8	9	10	11	12	13	inches
$3.75	5.00	6.00	7.00	8.00	9.00	per dozen

TOY DRUMS, metal with assorted colored pictures, Children's scenes, Landing of Columbus, etc.
No. C.

8	9	10	11	12	13	inches
$4.00	5.50	6.50	8.00	8.50	9.00	per dozen

TOY DRUMS, wood with calfskin heads, with strap and belt, and red, white and blue cord, a good Boys' Military Drum.
No. D.

8	9	10	11	12	13	14	inches
$6.00	7.00	8.00	9.00	12.00	13.50	15.00	per dozen

TOY DRUMS, fine nickel metal, with calfskin heads, belt, and red, white and blue cord, a very fine article.
No. E.

10	11	12	13	14	inches
$15.00	16.50	18.00	24.00	30.00	per dozen

DRUM MAJOR STICKS.

No. X. $2.00 per dozen

TAMBOURINES.

TAMBOURINES VARNISHED.
No. 0.   7 inch parchment,   75c per dozen

TAMBOURINES, VARNISHED SHEEPSKIN HEAD, WITH THREE JINGLES.

No. 1.	7	8	10 inches
	$1.85	3.00	3.50 per dozen

TAMBOURINES RED PAINTED AND VARNISHED, sheepskin head with three jingles.

No. 2.	7	8	10 inches
	$3.00	3.50	3.75 per dozen

FINE RED PAINTED AND VARNISHED TAMBOURINES, calfskin head.

No. 3.	8	10 inches
	9 jingles	9 jingles
	$4.00	6.00 per dozen

FANCY TAMBOURINES.
No. 857   10 inches $2.00 per dozen

METALLOPHONES.

METALLOPHONES, plain with bronzed keys.

No. 350/5.	8 keys	$ .38 per dozen
No. 350/10.	15 "	.75 " "
No. 122/15.	15 " larger	1.85 " "
No. 124/22.	22 " "	3.75 " "

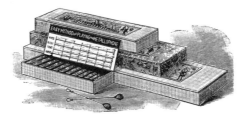

METALLOPHONES, in fancy paper boxes.

No. 128.	12 keys	$2.00 per dozen
No. 128.	22 "	3.75 " "

FINE METALLOPHONES, harp shape, put up in paper boxes.

No. 135.	8 keys	$2.00 per dozen
	15 "	3.75 " "
	22 "	7.50 " "

XYLOPHONES OR WOOD INSTRUMENTS.

No. 161.	8 keys	$4.25 per dozen
	18 "	8.50 " "

ZITHERS.

8 strings	$2.00 per dozen
10 "	4.00 " "
15 "	7.50 " "
20 "	8.50 " "

THE AMERICAN HARP.

THE AMERICAN HARP, a fine quality zither; the best instrument for the price in the market.
No. 1. 18 strings .... $8.50 per dozen

IDEAL HARP.

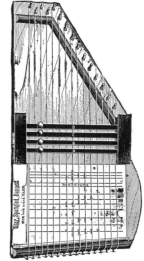

This is not a toy, but a musical instrument on which various tunes can be played by picking the strings as on a regular zither.

$16.50 per dozen

PHONOHARPS.

A beautiful musical instrument on which almost any tune can be played.
No. 1.
15 strings, $12.00 per doz.

No. 2.
Finer finished instrument.
17 strings, $24.00 per doz.

TOY PIANOS.

TOY SQUARE PIANOS.

No. 354. 10 keys, cover to open....$2.00 per dozen
No. 100.   8 " on carved legs,
           single cover to open.... 4.00 " "
No. 104. 15 keys, single cover to
           open, carved legs...... 8.00 " "
No. 103. 22 keys, with full hinged
           cover to close.........18.00 " "

UPRIGHT PIANOS.

No. 114.   8 keys ....$4.50 per dozen
"   " 15 "   .... 8.50 " "

FINE UPRIGHT PIANOS, fancy front, candle
brackets, metal or wood carved legs.

No. 113. 15 keys ....$18.00 per dozen
No. 112. 18 " .... 30.00 " "
No. 112. 22 " .... 51.00 " "

EXTRA FINE UPRIGHT PIANOS, with half
notes

No. 118. 30 keys.....................$8.00 each
No. 111. 37 " ....12.00 "

TOY PIANO STOOLS.

No. 1.
Plain........$6.00 per dozen

No. 2.
Upholstered..$8.00 per dozen

TIN TRUMPETS.

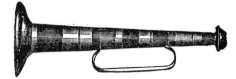

PLAIN TRUMPETS, painted in fancy colors,
with metal mouth pieces.   One dozen in a box.
No. 70.

1	2	3	3½
3½	7½	9	12 inches long
8c	20c	30c	35c per dozen

PLAIN TIN TRUMPETS, painted in fancy colors, with china mouth pieces.   One dozen in a box.
No. 70.

4	5	6	7
9½	12	13½	18 inches long
35c	38c	67c	$1.00 per dozen

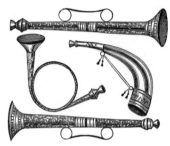

FANCY TIN TRUMPETS, assorted, double call
with china mouth pieces.   One dozen in a box.
No. 72.

5	8	10	15	25
9½	15	16	18	18 ins. long
38c	70c	75c	$1.25	$1.75 per dozen

NICKEL TRUMPETS, double call with china or
metal mouth pieces.   One dozen in a box.
No. 75.

5	10	15	18
9½ in.	15 in.	12 in., full shape	13 in., full shape
38c	75c	75c	$1.00

20	25	30
14 in., full shape	19 in., extra long	13 in., fine quality
$1.50	$1.75	$2.00

50	55
19 in.,	19 in.,
extra large, colored tassel,	full shape, extra fine,
$3.75	$3.75 per doz.

NICKEL TRUMPETS, round French horn shape,
china mouth pieces, double call.   One dozen in a box.
No. 76.

5	10	25
38c	75c	$2.00 per dozen

MUSICAL SONG TRUMPETS, nickel round
and straight shapes.   They play a tune by moving
a lever.

No. 77.	straight	round
	1	2
	$2.00	$2.00 per dozen

COW HORNS.

COW HORNS, metal and china mouth pieces.
One dozen in a package.
No. 12.

5	10	15	25
38c	67c	75c	$1.75 per dozen

COW HORNS, same as before, with brass trimmings and brass mouth pieces and colored tassels.
One dozen in a box.

No. 12.	30
	$2.00 per dozen

TOY TROMBONES.

TOY TROMBONES, metal mouth pieces; all
nickel.
No. 100.

4 keys...........$2.00 per dozen
8 " .... 3.75 " "

TOY CORNETS.

TOY CORNETS, all nickel, china mouth pieces,
large shape.
No. 102.

4 keys...........$2.00 per dozen
8 " .... 3.75 " "

FANCY COLORED METAL TOPS.

COLORED METAL HUMMING TOPS.

15/1   3/46
$ .08   .35 per doz.

METAL MUSICAL TOPS, will make a singing noise when spun. They are made of metal stained in bright colors. One dozen in a box.

No. 15.

5	10	15
$ .37	.75	1.25
20	25	
1.50	2.00	per dozen

NICKEL METAL TOPS.
No. 16/35. $2.00 per dozen
½ dozen in a box

METAL CHORAL TOPS. The top when spun, will change the tune by simply touching the handle. One dozen in a box.

No. 18.

10	15	25
$ .75	1.50	2.00 per dozen

FANCY METAL TOPS, with two clown figures on top.

No. 269/25.
$2.00 per dozen
½ dozen in a box

FRENCH METAL SPRING TOPS, made of brass. One dozen in a box.
No. 19/25
$1.75 per dozen

PLAIN AND FANCY COLORED TIN RATTLES.

A-B-C, PLAIN TIN RATTLES, round shape with whistle. 1 dozen in a package.
$1.50 per gross

STAR PLAIN TIN RATTLES, with whistle.
$1.75 per gross

COLORED METAL RATTLES, with tin handles.
No. 60/1. $ .08 per dozen
3 dozen in a box

COLORED METAL RATTLES, assorted shapes with red or white wood handles. One dozen in a box.
No 60.

3	5	6	8	10
$ .30	.35	.38	.38	.67 per doz.

15	25
$ .75	1.75 per dozen

FANCY SHAPE NICKEL RATTLES, with white wood or bone handles. One dozen in a box.

No. 760/10   60/12   60/20
$ .80   .75   1.75 per dozen

FRENCH CELLULOID RATTLES, VARIEGATED COLORS.

One dozen in a box.
No. 600/10, All Celluloid with celluloid handles,
$ .75 per dozen
No. 600/15, Celluloid Rattles with red wood handles,
$ .75 per dozen
No. 600/25 Celluloid Rattles with gilt and colored stripes and colored striped polished wood handles,
$1.75 per dozen

VEGETABLE IVORY RATTLES.
No. 100,   15/16 assorted
75c. $1.75 per dozen. 1 dozen in a box

FOR KNIT WORSTED, CHIME AND RUBBER RATTLES, See Index.

TOY GUNS AND AIR RIFLES.

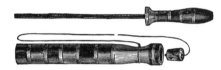

WOODEN POP PISTOLS. No. B, bright striped colors, varnished.......................$ .35 per dz.

POLISHED SPRING GUNS, with tin barrels; to shoot paper caps.

Per Doz.

No. 846/10.	21 in. long	........$ .75
" 846/25.	26 "	.... 1.75
" 846/35.	30 "	with bayonet............ 2.00
" 846/50.	36 in. long, fine polished, with shoulder strap............. 3.75

POP PISTOLS and POP GUNS.

Per Doz.

No. 840/5.	13½ in. long (pistol) ..$ .38
" 840/10.	18 " (gun).... .75
" 840/25.	31 " (gun).... 1.75

BREECH LOADING POP GUN (New).

Per Doz.
No. 844.   25 in. long (polished gun)..............$2.00

TOY REVOLVERS (new), nickel barrel, polished handle; shoots a cork.
No. 845...........$2.00 per dozen

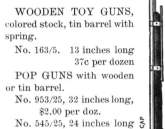

WOODEN TOY GUNS, colored stock, tin barrel with spring.
No. 163/5.   13 inches long
37c per dozen
POP GUNS with wooden or tin barrel.
No. 953/25, 32 inches long,
$2.00 per doz.
No. 545/25, 24 inches long
fine quality...$1.75 per doz.
No. 166, 26 inches long,
$1.88 per dozen
No. 172, 31 inches long,
$4.00 per dozen
PERCUSSION GUNS, for shooting paper caps.
No. 171/1, 26 inches long,
$1.88 per dozen
No. 171/2 B, 36 inches long, with bayonet, $4.00 per doz.

SCHOOL DRILL GUNS. Hardwood, well finished percussion lock, for boys 12 to 16 years old, with bayonet.

No. 175/42B, 42 inches long,.....$8.75 per dozen

Pawtucket. Buffalo Bill. Globe. Matchless. Expert.

WOODEN GUNS WITH ELASTIC. King Philip, nicely finished, single barrel, $1.50 per dozen

Pawtucket, double barrel,........$1.85 per dozen

Indian Chief, single barrel, a neat fine shooter,
$3.00 per dozen

Buffalo Bill, best made, 36 inches long,
$3.50 per dozen

Harmless gun, finely finished gun, shoots small hollow rubber ball,.................$4.00 per dozen

Globe Air Rifle, nickel steel barrel, most improved movement, a strong and very accurate gun of handsome design...................$8.00 per dozen

Matchless Air Rifle, steel barrel, black walnut stock shoots 60 BB shots without reloading..$18.00

Expert, a new Air Rifle similar to the Matchless, shoots 200 BB shots without reloading.......$24.00

TOY SWORDS WITH BELTS.

TIN SWORDS, tin blade, metal colored tin scabbard, tin pocket and belt.

No. 20/5.   18 inches long..........38c per dozen

TIN SWORDS, iron blade, brass colored tin scabbard, colored tin pocket and belt.

No. 20/8.   22 inches long...........75c per dozen

TIN SWORDS, iron blade, striped and brass colored tin scabbard, large colored tin pocket and belt.

No. 20/10.   24 inches long.......$1.00 per dozen

METAL SWORDS, large brass handle, iron blade, heavy metal scabbard, large colored fine tin pocket, leather belt with buckles.

No. 20/25.   25 inches long.......$1.75 per dozen

IRON SWORDS, fine brass open work handle with tassel, steel blade, iron scabbard with brass trimmings, leather belt with brass buckles.

No. 20/50.   25 inches long........$3.75 per dozen

BOYS' SOLDIER SUITS AND OUTFITS ON CARDS.

No. 4000/1.

OUTFIT consisting of fatigue cap, sword and trumpet on card.

  No. 62/50..................$4.00 per dozen

OUTFIT consisting of cloth cap, sword, gun and knapsack on card.

  No. 4000/4.................$4.50 per dozen

OUTFIT consisting of soldier's cap or helmet, cloth breastpiece, gun, sword and epaulettes on large card.

  No. 62/100................$8.50 per dozen

OUTFIT (7th Regiment), consisting of gray helmet, gray breastpiece shoulder straps, white belt, officers' epaulettes, gun, short sword and cartridge box.

  No. 655/2.................$16.50 per dozen

FINE OUTFIT (French Hussar), consisting of officers' red fatigue cap with silver lace, cloth breastpiece laced, with metal buttons, colored shoulder straps, polished gun, long sword with colored metal pocket and leather cartridge box.

  No. 487.....................$18.00 per dozen

FINE OUTFIT (French Uhlan), consisting of red fatigue cap with silvered lace, cloth breastpiece with metal buttons and white cord with tassels, epaulettes, cloth officer's cuffs, polished gun, long sword, leather belt and leather cartridge box.

  No. 488...................$27.00 per dozen

No 2000/1.

FINE OUTFIT (American Cavalry), consisting of officers' regulation helmet with gilt eagle, red cloth breastpiece with metal buttons, knapsack, cartridge box, cloth and gilt epaulettes, polished gun, long sword with colored metal pocket.

  No. 489/1.................$36.00 per dozen

FINE OUTFIT (7th Regiment) consisting of white helmet with hair plume, gray breastpiece with white leather belts, leather knapsack and cartridge box, shoulder straps, polished gun, short sword with leather belt.

  No. 655/4.................$36.00 per dozen

BOYS' OUTFITS, POLICEMEN, FIRE= MEN, ETC.

No. 980.

POLICE OUTFIT, consisting of regulation blue cloth police helmet, blue cloth breastpiece with metal buttons and shield, wood polished club, handcuffs and leather belt with metal buckle.

  No. 980......... ....$8.50 per dozen

No. 999.

FIREMAN'S OUTFIT, consisting of red or white fireman's helmet, fire ax, 16 inch fireman's trumpet and leather belt with metal buckle.

  No. 999....................$8.50 per dozen

FIREMAN'S OUTFIT, consisting of large fine red or white helmet, cloth breastpiece with black letters "F. D." Large fireman's ax, 21 inches long, extra long fireman's trumpet and leather belt. Mounted on a heavy card.

  No. 1000/1................$18.00 per dozen

MARINE OUTFIT, consisting of blue sailor's cap with a hat band marked "U. S. Navy," blue cloth breastpiece and blue cloth cuffs with gilt buttons.

  No. 650/100...............$9.00 per dozen

DRUM MAJOR'S OUTFIT, consisting of cloth cap, epaulettes, drum major's stick, sword with leather belt and metal pocket.

  3000/5....................$9.00 per dozen

No. 2000.

DRUM MAJOR'S OUTFIT, consisting of fine cloth cap, drum major's stick, long sword, colored metal pocket, epaulettes, blue cloth belt. On a large card.

  No, 2000.................$18.000 per dozen

BOY'S SOLDIER CAPS AND HELMETS.

No. 60/1, Cloth Military Caps, plain colors,
  75c. per dozen

No. 60/1½, Gray Military Caps with Gilt Eagle,
  $1.50 per dozen

No. 60/7, American Helmets, black or white,
  $2.00 per dozen

No. 60/8, American Helmets, black or white, with Plume,
  $2.50 per dozen

No. 60/4 Metropolitan Policemens' Hats, $2.00 per dz.

No. 60/9, Fireman's Helmets, assorted colors,
  $4.00 per dozen

TOY WATCHES WITH CHAINS.

No. 90/1. Nickel Watch, with colored paper face, short steel chain. One gross in a box. 96c per gross

No. 90/3. Nickel Watch, same quality, with white face, moving hands, silvered chain. One dozen in a box.....................30c per dozen

No. 90/5. Large Nickel Watch, stem winder, with silvered chain. One dozen in a box. 38c per doz.

No. 90/8. Hunting Case Silvered Watch, large shape, stem winder, with assorted silvered chains. One dozen in a box..................40c per dozen

No. 89. McGinty Surprise Watch, nickel, with chains. One dozen in a box..........38c per dozen

No. 96. Hunting Case Watch, stem winder, gilt and silver assorted, with heavy long gilt and silvered chains. One dozen in a box..70c per dozen

No. 90/10. Open face, extra large Nickel Watch, stem winder, with assorted silvered chains. One dozen in a box.......................70c per dozen

No. 85. Hunting Case Watch, large shape, silvered chased covers, with plain silvered chains. One dozen in a box...................75c per dozen

No. 90/12. Hunting Case Watch, stem winder, silvered chased covers, with spring movement to run when wound up. One dozen in a box...75c per doz.

No. 90/15. Large Nickel Open Face Watch, stem winder, with spring movement, silvered chain. One dozen in a box...................75c per dozen

No. 90/20. Open face gilt watch, stem winder, with spring movement to run, gilt chain. Each watch in a separate little box. One dozen in a package..........................$1.50 per dozen

No. 90/22. Open face gilt watch, stem winder, with spring movement to run, striking a bell when running, assorted gilt chains with charm. Each one in a fancy box ; 12 boxes in a package
$1.75 per dozen

No. 90/25. Open face, large shape gilt watch, stem winder, with spring movement ; fine watch hands and minute hand moving. Each one in a little box ; 12 boxes in a package ...$2.00 per dozen

No. 90/30. Large shape open face gilt watch, spring movement, with hands to move separate, running several minutes, and with minute hand moving ; assorted heavy gilt chains. Each one in a fancy box ; 12 boxes in a package, $2.25 per dozen

TOY CLOCKS.

No. 95/5. Fancy shape toy clock, with imitation spring movement. One dozen in a box, 40c per doz.

No. 95/25. Larger nickel clock on a black japanned base, with pendulum ; moving when wound up ; brass figure strikes a bell on top. One in a box ; one dozen in a package...$1.75 per dozen

TOY SCALES.

Put up each one in a box. One dozen in a package.

No. 55/5. Brass stand scales......38c per dozen

No. 55/10. Brass balancing apothecaries' scales, with black japanned platform........75c per dozen

No. 55/25. Same as before. Extra large sizes.
$2.00 per dozen

METAL KALEIDOSCOPES.

Fancy colored metal case. One dozen in a box.

No. 8/5.   No. 8/10.
38c   75c   per dozen

Same as before, all nickel. Half dozen in a box
No. 8/25.................$1.75 per dozen

Nickel Kaleidoscopes on stands. Each one in a box. Half a dozen in a package.
No. 8/35...................$2.00 per dozen

ZŒOTROPE OR WHEEL OF LIFE.

Wheel of Life, a very amusing toy for children. Made of metal on a wood stand ; when set in motion it will show figures or animals in comical or natural moving positions.

No. 20.	25	50
	$2.00	4.00 per dozen

MAGNETIC TOYS.

Put up in glass covered boxes. Assorted animals and a magnet in each box, viz., gold and silver fishes, turtles boats, ducks, swans, lobsters, frogs, etc., to be drawn by the magnet.

		Per Dozen
No. 10/5.	Box contains 3 pieces......	$ .37
No. 10/10.	Box contains 5 pieces......	.75
No. 10/25.	Box contains 9 pieces......	2.00
No. 10/50.	Box contains 12 pieces......	4.00
No. 10/100.	Box contains 18 pieces......	8.50

HORSE-SHOE MAGNETS made of best quality steel, painted bright red.

		Per Dozen
No. 625/1.	2 inches long ..	$ .08
No. 625/5.	3 inches long ..	.38
No. 625/10.	4 inches long ..	.75

JUGGLERS' TRICK BOXES.

JUGGLERS' TRICKS put up in fancy paper boxes.

No. 65/1.	Box contains 7 pieces........	$2.00
No. 65/2.	Box contains 9 pieces........	4.00
No. 65/5.	Box contains 14 pieces........	9.00
No. 65/8.	Box contains 24 pieces........	18.00

FINER BOXES containing finer and more complicated tricks ranging in price from $3.00 to $6.00 each box.

MAGIC LANTERNS.

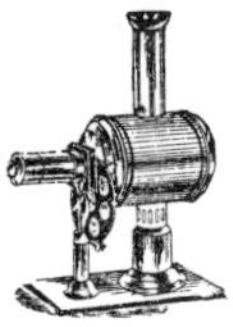

MAGIC LANTERNS, new upright shape, nickel and black japanned chimney, with nickel rim and black japanned base, with glass slides. Each one in a box.

No. 25.

50	65	75	
$4.00	4.50	8.00	per dozen

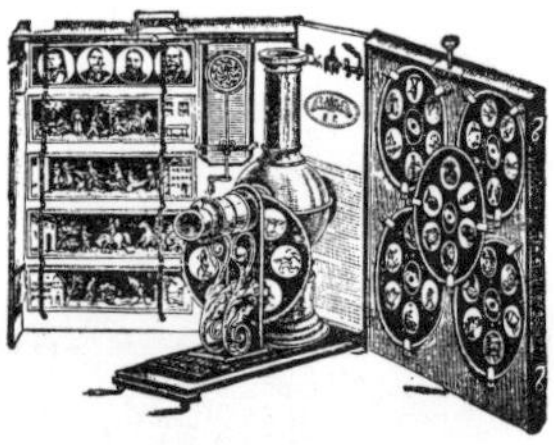

MAGIC LANTERNS, same style as before in wood folding boxes with square and round painted glass slides. Each lantern in a box.

No. 25.

100	150	200	300	500	
$9.00	16.50	21.00	36.00	45.00	per dozen

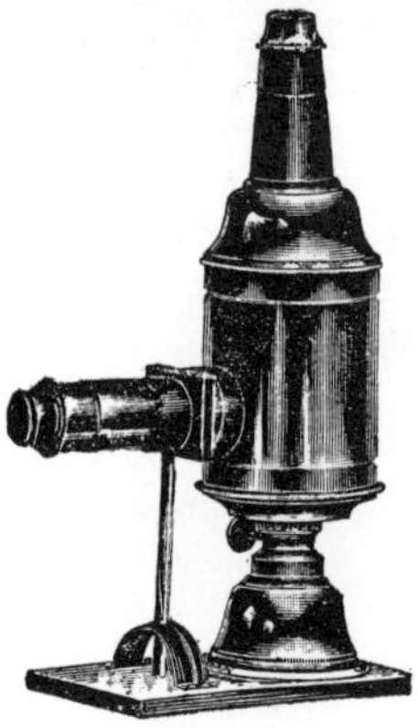

MAGIC LANTERNS, new upright shape, Russia iron with brass trimmings and nickel lens tube, with painted glass slides. Each Lantern in a box.

No. 30.

50	100	200	
$4.50	9.00	18.00	per doz.

MAGIC LANTERNS, Columbus egg shape, (new). This lantern is made in shape of a large egg, with gilt lettering and gilt eagle. On a nickel and polished wood base with nickel lens tube and assorted glass slides.

No. 35. 100
$9.00 per dozen

MAGIC LANTERNS, extra fine quality, black polished Russia iron, with large Russia iron chimney, Duplex burners, solid brass lens tube with arrangement to lengthen and shorten the lens. Each one in a box.

No. 40.

1	2	3	4	5	
$6.50	8.50	10.50	13.50	15.00	each

MAGIC LANTERN GLASS SLIDES.

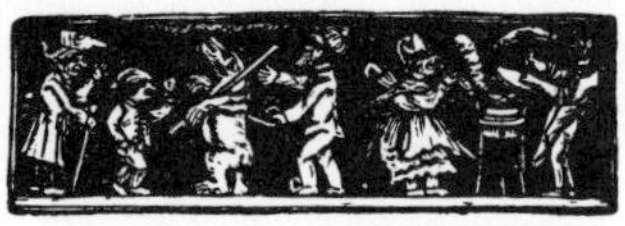

These slides are all specially selected for our lanterns, handsome assortments of comics, landscapes, children's scenes and historical views. Twelve slides in a box.

No. 42.

3½	4	4½	5	6	
1¼x5	1½x6	1¾x6½	2x7	2¼x8	inches
$3.50	4.50	5.00	8.00	9.00	per doz. boxes

7	8	9	10	
2½x8½	3x10	3½x11	4x12	inches
$13.50	18.00	24.00	30.00	per doz. boxes

PEWTER SOLDIERS.

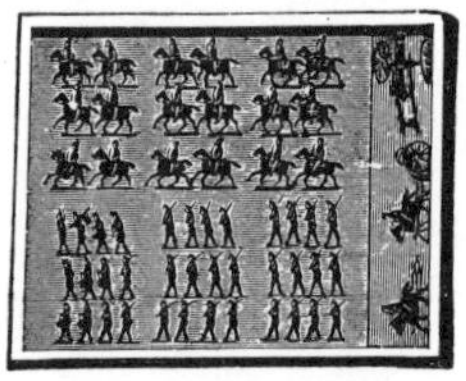

	Per doz. boxes.
No. 160, containing 12 flat American soldiers	$ .70
No. 161, containing 10 sailors and 2 White Squadron ships	.70
No. 164, containing 12 Zouaves	.70
No. 171, containing 12 American cavalry.	.70
No. 700/25, containing 18 infantry or 9 cavalry, fine painted	1.75
No. 700/35, containing 4 cavalry and 16 infantry	2.00
No. 700/50, containing 10 cavalry and 20 infantry	4.00

PEWTER ARTILLERY.

	Per doz. boxes
No. 150/25 containing 4 riders, one cannon with carriage, 2 horses and driver...	$2.00
No. 150/50, containing 12 cavalry and 24 infantry, one cannon with carriage, 4 horses and 2 drivers	4.00
No. 150/100, containing 8 riders, 12 artillery on foot, 4 cannons with carriage and two horses and driver each	8.50

FINE LEAD SOLDIERS, HEAVY FIGURES.

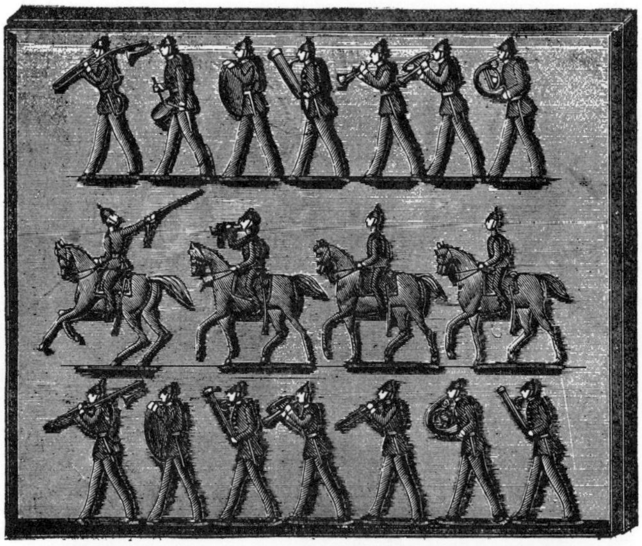

	Per doz. boxes
No. 702/50, containing 3 kinds assorted Buffalo Bill Show, sea battle or fighting cavalry	$4.00
No. 705/50, containing American soldiers (7th regiment, etc.), 9 infantry with commander on horseback...	4.00
No. 705/100, containing American infantry, marines, Indians on foot, or indians on horseback, from 10 to 20 figures	9.00
No. 705/200, containing 28 infantry and cavalry assorted, handsomely painted	18.00
No. 706/50, containing 12 American infantry (regulars) in white coats and blue pants, or 6 cavalry, assorted....	4.50
No. 706/100, containing 28 infantry with one officer on horseback or 18 English red hussars and American cavalry...	9.00
No. 707/200, containing 30 pieces fine painted Indians, in various positions on foot and on horseback	18.00
No. 708/200, containing 20 infantry and 20 marines, assorted, fine painted, in fighting positions	18.00
No. 706/300, containing infantry and cavalry, assorted American, German and English soldiers, extra fine painted..	30.00
No. 705/400, containing American infantry (7th regiment) and American cavalry, large and very fine	36.00

I always carry in stock, in addition to the above, a large assortment of fine boxes of Lead Toys, viz:—Buffalo Bill Shows, Military Reviews, Camps, Battle Scenes, Ostrich Hunts, Artillery Parks, Marine Scenes, etc., ranging in price, from $9.00 to $60.00 per dozen.

NOAH'S ARKS.

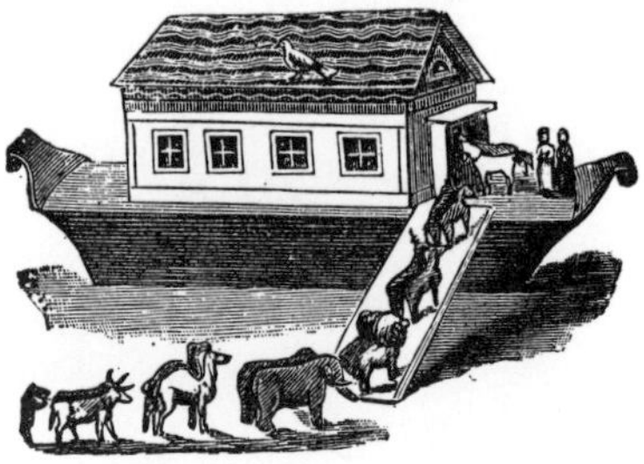

NOAH'S ARKS painted in bright colors, with colored animals.

No. 340.

	Per Dozen
0 Containing about 10 animals and figures	$0 35
1 Containing about 12 animals and figures	40
3 Containing about 20 animals and figures	75
4 Containing about 24 animals and figures	1 00
5 Containing about 27 animals and figures	1 25
6 Containing about 36 animals and figures	1 75
7 Containing about 40 animals and figures	2 50
8 Containing about 45 animals and figures	3 00
9 Containing about 50 animals and figures	4 00
12 Containing about 75 animals and figures	8 00

WOODEN BOX TOYS.

BOX TOYS in oval boxes containing villages, farms and sheep-folds assorted.

No. 325.

5	10
38c	75c per dozen

BOX TOYS, same style as before, in square boxes; better finished.

No. 325.

25	35	50	60	
$1.75	2.00	3.75	4.00	per dozen
100	125	250		
$9.00	12.00	24.00		per dozen

BOX TOYS, assorted fine white Swiss villages with white animals and figures.

No. 328.

10	25	50	100	
75c	$2.00	4.00	9.00	per dozen

BOX TOYS, white wood animals on platforms with metal wheels, in paper covered wood boxes.
No. 330.

25	50	100	
$2.00	4.00	8.00	per dozen

BOX TOYS, wood kitchen sets and tea sets.

No. 335	No. 336
10	25
75c	$2.00 per dozen

PENNY BOX TOYS, containing 144 pieces assorted wood penny toys from 12 to 20 different kinds.

No. 346.   96c per box

TOY FURNITURE SETS.

Complete Parlor, Bedroom and Dining Room Sets in nice paper covered square wood boxes.

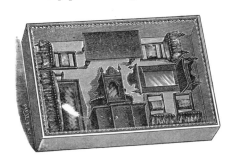

PARLOR SETS.

No. 360/ 10.	Light wood, 6 piece set........$0 75
" 20.	Oak set, upholstered, 8 pieces. 1 75
" 25.	Polished imitation mahogany, upholsterd, 9 pieces.......... 1 88
" 30.	Light wood, ornamented and upholstered, 7 pieces........ 2 00
" 33.	Oak set, upholstered, 8 pieces... 2 00
" 35.	Light wood, with lithographed picture, upholstered, with plush, 8 pieces.............. 2 00
" 50.	Ebony wood, upholstered, 8 pieces, larger............... 3 75
" 55.	Ebony or polished wood, upholstered with plush, 7 pieces.... 4 00
" 60.	Old oak with imitation carvings, upholstered, 10 pieces........ 4 00
" 110.	Imitation Ebony with gilt decorations, embossed plush upholstery, 11 pieces 9 00
" 120.	Fine polished set, upholstered in assorted colored material, 12 pieces 9 00
No. 366/100.	Embossed plush, new style parlor set, 7 pieces............. 9 00
No. 370/1.	White wood, ornamented in colors, dining room set, 8 pieces 8 50
No. 370/2.	Same as before, larger, 8 pieces, 18 00
No. 373.	Ebony, white engraved parlor set, 11 pieces............... 24 00
No. 373/2.	Fine old oak upholstered parlor set, with piano, 8 pieces......18 00
No. 373/5.	Fine old oak dining room set, upholstered with embossed plush, 9 pieces...............27 00

BEDROOM SETS.

No. 365/30.	Polished wood set, 6 pieces $2 00
" /33.	White wood, ornamented, 6 pieces 2 00
" /55.	Polished imitation mahogany, upholstered with plush, 8 pieces, 4 00
" /100.	Same style as before, larger..... 8 50

RATTAN FURNITURE SETS.

Consisting of sofa, two chairs, table and mirror, upholstered in green cloth with fringe,

No. 250/25.................$2.00 per dozen

Fine large furniture sets in different styles of wood, upholstered in silk or plush, in large variety, ranging in price from $2.00 to 10.00 per set.

WOODEN HORSE STABLES.

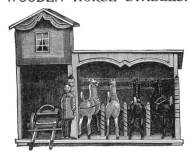

Stables painted in bright colors, with horses wagons, drivers, etc.

		Per Doz.
No. 890/10.	Containing 3 horses............$ .75	
" 890/25.	Containing 2 larger horses and wagon........................ 2.00	
" 890/50.	Contents same as before, larger . 4.00	
" 890/100.	Containing 4 horses, four-wheel wagon........................ 9.00	
" 890/200.	Finer style, containing 4 horses on platforms with wheels, and four-wheel wagon..............18.00	
No. 892/25.	Fine style, containing 4 horses, two-wheel cart and driver...... 2.00	
" 892/50.	Same as before, larger.......... 3.75	
" 892/100.	" " " extra large size. 9.00	
" 892/200.	Fine new style, with double roof, 4 horses on platforms with metal wheels, and four-wheel wagon..18.00	
" 892/300.	Same as before, with 6 horses, larger stable 30.00	

Finer stables, ranging in price from $3.00 to $10.00 each. A full line always in stock.

WAREHOUSES.

Fine new style, highly decorated, painted in bright colors, with glass windows, boxes, barrels, truck and horses.

No. 312.	100	200	300
	$9.00	18.00	36.00 per dozen

BUTCHER SHOPS.

Exact imitation of butcher shops, handsomely decorated with imitation tiles inside, with a butcher, counter and imitation of articles such as are found in a butcher shop.

No. 300.			
25	50	100	2 00
$2.00	4.00	9.00	18.00 per dozen

WOODEN KITCHENS.

New style this season, with bright colored range, tin dishes, larger sizes with wooden furniture, with cook; the kitchen is decorated with imitation tiles.

No. 305.					
25	50	100	200	500	600
$2.00	4.00	9.00	18.00	45.00	72.00 per doz.

DOLL HOUSES.

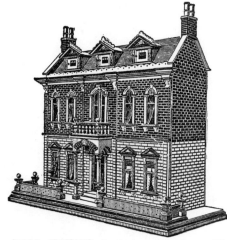

DOLL HOUSES, 2 stories, with fancy lithographed front; two larger sizes with glass windows, with gable roof and 2 chimneys.

No. 308.	25	50	100
	$2.00	4.00	9.00 per doz.

DOLL HOUSES, fancy design, with bay window, porch, balcony, glass windows, gable roof and chimney and furniture.

No. 308.	125	200	500
	$12.00	18.00	48.00 per doz.

GROCERY STORES.

GROCERY STORES, painted in bright colors and fitted up with counters, scales, drawers, etc.

No. 315.	100	200
	$9.00	18.00 per dozen

THEATRES.

Fancy fronts, with cloth curtain, assorted sceneries, figures on wires, and text book, ranging in price from $15.00 per dozen to $10.00 each.

BELLOWS TOYS.

BELLOWS TOYS, put up in flat boxes, from 6 to 12 different kinds, assorted. The largest and best for the money in the market. All kinds of domestic and wild animals and birds. One dozen in a box.

B/5	B/8	B/10	B/15
35c	40c	70c	$1.00 per doz.

B/25, 6 kinds of birds, assorted.....$2.00 per dozen
B/30, 6 " " animals, assorted.. 1.75 "

TOY ASSORTMENTS IN BOXES.

These assortments are put up specially for the small trade, and consist of 12 different salable toys, viz.: Jumping jacks, clapping figures, wood horses, surprise boxes, donkeys, sheep, birds in cages, stables, etc. One dozen in a box.

No. 2/5	2/10	2/25
38c	75c	$1.75 per doz.

SURPRISE BOXES.

SURPRISE BOXES, plain styles, colored paper covered boxes, with fur trimmed comic figures with voices. One dozen in a package.

No. 800/5.	10
	38c 70c per doz.

No. 802/10.

SURPRISE BOXES, with assorted comic figures, 75c per dozen.

No. 803/25.

Large size, with 6 different comic figures, box covered with fancy paper and colored picture in front, $1.75 per dozen.

WOODEN CANNONS.

WOODEN CANNONS, colored lithographed sides; to shoot peas.

No. 352.	$ .38 per dozen

WOODEN CLOWNS KICKING BALL.

A new wooden toy, representing a clown kicking a little ball; figure 10 inches high. One dozen in a package.

No. 353.	$ .40 per dozen

COMIC BELLOWS FACES WITH VOICES.

No. 50/5	10
	$ .38 .75 per doz.

DEVIL'S FIDDLES.

A toy made of a tambourine shaped box on a string with a wooden handle, which, when swung around, makes a loud noise.

No. 850/5. $ .38 per dozen

MUSICAL PIG.

A new toy just out, made of colored card board and wood; a negro pulling a pig's tail; it has a trumpet attachment. A very comical toy. One dozen in a package.

No. C/10. $ .75 per dozen

CLAPPING FIGURES.

Comic figures and clowns with clappers, assorted; dressed in bright colored muslin, cloth or silk costumes with voices. One dozen in a box.

No. 810/5	10	25	
	9	12	18 inches long
$ .38	.75	1.75	per dozen

Assorted clowns with clappers and with moving eyes. One dozen in a box.

No. 812/25. $2.00 per dozen

WHISTLING FIGURES.

Boys, comic figures and clowns, dressed in fancy costumes on long sticks with whistle. One dozen in a box.

		Per Dozen
No. 815/5.	Clowns in assorted dresses, 10 inches long	$ .38
No. 816/10.	Birds assorted on stick, 12 inches long	.75
No. 817/10.	Boys with china heads, in colored dresses, 12 inches long	.75
No. 818/10.	Assorted whistling and cricket figures in fancy costumes, 12 inches long	.75
No. 820.	Assorted clowns and figures in fancy costumes, 14 inches long.	2.00

DRESSED COMIC FIGURES.
WHISTLING, CLAPPING, STRETCHING, ETC.

Per Dozen

No. 821. Assorted comic stretching figures with clappers, voice and moving tongue, etc. $2.00

No. 825. Stretching figures with 2 revolving side figures, dressed in fancy colored costume. One dozen in a box.. $1.75

No. 826. Standing monkey with voice, throwing baby over his head from one arm to the other. One dozen in a box................. 1.75

No. 827. Large double clapping figure in bright colored dress with gold trimmings. One dozen in a box. 2.00

No. 828. Double revolving cricket figures. One dozen in a box 2.00

No, 829. New style of fancy jumping clown with stretching tongue; figure 16 inches high. One dozen in a box.......................... 1.75

No. 830. Comic fighting men and women; 2 figures moving. One dozen in a box........................... 1.75

MUSICAL RATTLING DOLLS, OR TURNING FIGURES.

Musical turning figures with bisque China heads, dressed in fine colored satin costumes with caps to match. These toys are made to revolve, and have a music box attachment, which will play while the toy revolves. Each one in a box.

No. 885/50   100

$4.00   8.50 per dozen

No. 886/100 $9.00 per dozen

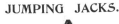

No. 1750/5 $9.00 per dozen

JUMPING JACKS.

WOOD JUMPING JACKS, painted in bright colors, with large hats, double faces. One dozen in a package.

No. 850/5	10	
	11	15 inches long
38c	75c	per dozen

No. 852/10. 15 inches long, assorted figures and clowns.   75c per dozen

MEN AND MONKEYS ON STICKS.

One dozen in a package.

		Per Doz.
No. 858/ 5.	Colored monkey with baby on back, 20 inches long	.38
No. 858/10.	Same as before, in white wood, 25 inches long	.70
No. 860/ 5.	Clowns on sticks, 18 inches long	.40
	Clowns on trapeze, No. A, single figure	.38
	Clowns on trapeze, No. B, double figures	.65

DRESSED COMIC FIGURES AND CLOWNS.

ON PLATFORMS WITH WHEELS.

Half dozen in a box, assorted.

No. 835. $2.00 per dozen

Comic figures and clowns on box with voices. Shoemaker working, clown playing fiddle, woman washing, etc. Six kinds assorted. Half dozen in a box.

No. 838 $2.00 per dozen

BUTTERFLIES ON WIRES.

A nice toy, which by reversing makes the butterflies ascend and descend the wires. One dozen in a box.

No. 862/5 38c per dozen.

BABIES IN CARRIAGES.

Willow or rattan carriages, with a bisque head baby in bright colored muslin or silk dress with lace trimmings. The babies move arms and legs when the carriage is wheeled.

		Per Doz.
No. 875/25.	Carriage and baby, with voice	$2.00
" 876/50.	" " " with papa and mamma voice	4.00
" 876/100.	Carriage and baby, with papa and mamma voice (larger)	9.00

FANCY DRESSED BOYS IN WHEEL CHAIR.

The chairs are made of gilt rattan. A bisque head boy, dressed in fine colored costume with lace trimmings, when wheeled, will move his head and arms. ⅙ doz. in a box.

No. 878.	50	100	
	$4.00	9.00	per dozen

BABIES IN CRADLES,

WITH PAPA AND MAMMA VOICE.

RATTAN CRADLE, with a cloth canopy and with a baby dressed in long baby dresses, trimmed with lace, with papa and mamma voice. ⅙ doz. in a box.

No. 879. $9.00 per dozen.

BIRDS, with colored feathers, on platform and wheels, with voice. 1 doz. in a box.

No. 1716. 75c per dozen

BIRDS IN WIRE CAGES, with bird whistle. ½ doz. in a box.

No. 856. $1.75 per dozen

PAPIER MACHE DONKEYS.

PAPIER MACHE DONKEYS on platform, with moving heads.

No. 805/5	805/10	805/25	
5	6½	9	inches high
38c	75c	$1.75	per dozen
1	1	½	doz. in a box

WOODEN HORSES ON PLATFORMS.

WOODEN HORSES, painted, with hair mane and tail. On platform with wheels.

No. 806/5	806/10	806/15	806/20	806/25	
6½	7½	8	9½	10	ins. high
38c	70c	75c	$1.75	2.00	per doz.
1	1	1	½	½	doz. in box

WOODEN AND PLUSH STICK HORSES.

No. 1018/10. Wood horses, with long colored sticks; 1 dozen in a package ....75c per dozen

No. 280/25. Imitation skin horse head, with varnished stick and iron wheels; 1 dozen in a box. $2.00 per dozen

PAPIER MACHE ELEPHANTS.

PAPIER MACHE ELEPHANTS with moving heads, on platform. Half dozen in a box.

No. 808/25. $2.00 per dozen

WOODEN HORSES AND WAGONS

One dozen in a box.

		Per Dozen
No. 894/ 5.	White wood horse and cart	$ .38
No. 894/25.	White wood horse and 4-wheeled truck, with baggage	2.00
No. 895/10.	Painted horse and 2-wheeled hay cart	.75
No. 895/25.	Painted horse and 2-wheeled hay and sand carts, larger size	2.00
No. 896/25.	Painted horse with hair mane and tail, and fine painted sand cart and baggage wagon assorted; ½ dozen in a package.	2.00
No. 897/50.	Sand and hay carts assorted, with painted horse with hair mane, on platform with iron wheels	4.00

For finer wagons with imitation and real skin covered horses, see Index.

FUR COVERED ANIMALS.

WOOLY LAMBS with voice, on polished platform with wheels; ½ doz. in a box.

No. 905/25	50	
6½	8½	inches high
$2.00	4.00	per dozen

No. 906/100

10 inches high
$9.00 per dozen
⅙ dozen in a box

FINE FRENCH WOOLY LAMBS with voice and gilt horns, covered with fine long white lamb's skin, and decorated with silk ribbons.

No. 908/100   200
    13½   15 inches high
    $9.00 $18.00 per dozen.

Finer lambs, ranging in price from $3.00 to $10.00 each, in great variety.

FUR COVERED RABBITS in sitting position with voice, moving ears and tail.

No. 910/25 50
    $1.75 4.00 per dz.
    ½   ⅓ dz. in box

FUR COVERED RABBITS, same style as before, in an upright sitting position, with cabbage leaves and basket on back.

No. 911/100   11 inches high
    $8.50 per dozen
    1/6 dozen in a box

FUR COVERED RABBITS on rockers with moving ears and tail, or with moving ears and fore feet.

No. 913/25   50   100
    7 x 8   8 x 12   12 x 18 inches
    $2.00   4.00   8.50 per dozen
    ½   1/6   1/6 dozen in a box

BLACK FUR DOGS ON PLATFORMS WITH WHEELS.

No. 940/10   15   25   50
    4½ x 6   7 x 8   8 x 10 10 x 14 inches
    70c   75c   1.75   3.75 per dozen

Black Fur Dogs, same style as before, on iron casters.

No. 941/50   100   150
    8 x 9   12 x 13 13 x 15 inches
    $4.00   8.00   9.00 per dozen

FRENCH FUR POODLE DOGS.

FINE FRENCH WHITE FUR POODLE DOGS, with voice and moving mouth.

No. 916/65   100   200
    8   12   14 inches high
    $4.00   9.00   18.00 per dozen

FUR COVERED GOATS with voice, on polished platform with wheels.

No. 920/25   50   100
    7 x 7½   8½ x 10 12 x 13 inches
    $2.00   4.00   9.00 per dozen
    1   ½   1/6 dozen in a box

         150   200
      12 x 14 14 x 16 inches
      $12.00   18.00 per dozen
      1/12   1/12 dozen in a box

FUR COVERED GOATS AND DOGS WITH CLOWN RIDERS on polished platform.

No. 935. Assorted. $9.00 per dozen
                         ⅓ dozen in a box

FUR COVERED CATS, with voice.

No. 922/25. $2.00 per dozen

FUR COVERED MONKEY, with young on his back, on velocipede.

No. 925/25.

$2.00 per dozen
1 dozen in a box

FUR COVERED DONKEYS on platform with wheels.

No. 930/50.   100
    10x8¼   13x10 inches
    $4.00 $9.00 per dozen

I carry in stock besides the above mentioned fur animals, a large variety of finer sheep, goats, donkeys and dogs, ranging in price from $2.50 to $10.00 each.

LEATHER COVERED COWS.

LEATHER COVERED COWS, with voice and moving head on polished platform with wheels.

No. 940/1   2   3   4
    7½x9   9x11   10x13   11x14 inches
    $8.00 $12.00 $15.00 $18.00 per dozen

          6   7   8
      12x18 14x20 15x24 inches
      $36.00 45.00   60.00 per dozen

LEATHER COVERED COWS, same style as before, milking. These cows are made with a tin reservoir inside, arranged so that children can milk them.

No. 945/2.   5
    10x13   11½x16 inches
    $18.00 $36.00 per dozen

IMITATION AND SKIN COVERED HORSES.

IMITATION SKIN COVERED OR PLUSH HORSES on platform with iron wheels. These horses are covered with plush in exact imitation of the real skin, are very durable and large for the money.

No. 950/2/0.   2   5
    6x7   8½x9   13x13 inches
    $2.00 $4.00 $8.50 per dozen

          7   9
      13x15   21x20 inches
      $16.50 $24.00 per dozen

REAL SKIN COVERED HORSES, finest quality, on platforms with iron wheels, made of best quality hide with leather saddle and leather harness.

No. 960/5   7   9   11   13
    $3.00 $5.00 6.75 9.00 12.00 each

REAL SKIN COVERED HORSES on rockers. Same style of horse as No. 960, on large strong varnished rockers.

No. 965/9	10	12	14	
$7.00	8.00	10.00	13.50	each

PLUSH COVERED HORSES, with jockey and monkey riders, mounted on platform with iron wheels.

No. 636/37, assorted.
10x12 inches
$7.50 per dozen

IMITATION SKIN COVERED HORSES with wagons.

Per Dozen

No. 970.	Assorted hay, sand and dump carts	$4.00
No. 975/1.	One horse dump cart	8.50
No. 975/2.	" " butcher cart	9.00
No. 975/3.	" " cart with 2 barrels	9.00
No. 975/4.	" " 2 wheel baggage cart	9.00
No. 975/5.	" " 4 wheel express wagon	9.00
No. 975/6.	" " 4 wheel milk cart	9.00
No. 975/7.	" " American truck	9.00
No. 975/8.	" " 4 wheel sand wagon	9.00
No. 975/9.	" " 2 wheel open hay wagon	9.00
No. 975/10.	One horse 2 wheel large sand cart	9.00
No. 976/11.	2 horses, 4 wheel express wagon with baggage	18.00
No. 976/13.	2 horses, 4 wheel sand wagon	18.00
No. 977/14.	One horse (large size), with 2 wheel open hay cart	16.50
No. 977/15.	One horse (large size) 4 wheel baggage wagon, with boxes and barrels	18.00
No. 977/16.	One horse (large size) 2 wheel sand cart	18 00

FINE SKIN COVERED HORSES WITH WAGONS.

One horse baggage wagon.

No. 980/3	4	5	6	
$5.00	6.00	7.00	9.00	each

Two horse baggage wagon.

No. 982/4	5	6	
$7.00	9.00	12.00	each

Upholstered two wheel carriage with one horse.

No. 990/1	3	5	7	
$2.50	5.00	7.50	10.00	each

American trucks with one horse.

No. 985/2	4	5	
$3.00	5.00	7.50	each

A large variety of fine horses and wagons different styles from the above mentioned, such as freight wagons, express wagons, etc., with one or two horses always on hand.

SANTA CLAUS FIGURES.

SANTA CLAUS FIGURES with Christmas trees; figures covered with snow flakes.

No. 870/5	10	25	
6	8½	12 ins. high	
$ .38	.75	2.00 per doz.	
	50	100	
	14	18 ins. high	
	4.00	8.50 per doz.	

SANTA CLAUS FIGURES, similar to No. 870 with transparent faces to be illuminated. Large figures suitable for show windows.

No. 872/200	300	500	
$18.00	27.00	42.00 per doz.	

FINE LITHOGRAPHED AND EMBOSSED SANTA CLAUS FIGURES on strong cardboard stand; a beautiful and attractive show window ornament.

36 inches high, $9.00 per dozen.

WAX ANGELS FOR CHRISTMAS TREES.

Wax angels with spun glass wings, suspended on rubbers.

No. 230/5	10	25	50	100	150	
$ .38	.75	2.00	3.75	8.00	13.50 per doz.	

GLASS CHRISTMAS TREE ORNAMENTS.

Glass Balls on strings, assorted colors.

No. 200/0	800 in a box	$ .75 per box
" 1	100 "	1.75 per 1000
" 2	100 "	2.50 "
" 3	100 "	4.00 "
" 4	100 "	6.00 "

Glass Balls on strings, bright silver with colored spots. 100 in a box.

No. 202/1	$ .40 per 100
" 2	.50 "
" 3	.60 "

Glass Balls on strings, fine matt silver with colored spots.

No. 204/1	50c per 100
2	60c "
3	75c "

Glass Balls on strings, fine matt copper bronze color, with silver spots; 100 in a box.

No. 205/3 .... 75c per 100

Glass balls put up one dozen in a box, assorted fine colors, with brass rings to hang on.

No. 206/1	20c per doz. balls
2	25c "
3	35c "

Glass Ornaments, round, oblong, cone, acorn, star, balloon and numerous other shapes in very bright colors, which will make them attractive ornaments for the Christmas tree. One dozen in a box.

No. 210/1 to 18. 18 different assortments.
35c per box of 12 pieces.

No. 212/1 to 9. 9 assortments, finer and larger sizes.   40c per dozen pieces.

No. 214/1 to 2. Put up half dozen in a box assorted.   63c per dozen pieces.

Glass Balls, round ball shape, in assorted colors, with variegated colored spots, stripes and other ornaments.

No. 215/1	2	3	
38c	75c	$1.00	per dozen
1	½	½	dozen in a box

Glass Balls, round shape, transparent colors, covered with spun silver tinsel, and with a tinsel tree inside. One dozen in a box.

No. 216/1.   67c per dozen

No. 218/1. Same as before, larger.
80c per dozen

No. 218/2. New style, silver band covering, with tree inside.   80c per dozen

No. 218/3. Same as before, oval shape.
80c per dozen

Glass Balls, fine red satin color, round ball shape; ½ dozen in a box.

No.   880/10   12
        75c $1.00   per dozen

Solid Glass Balls, assorted colors, with brass rings.

No.   885/4   7   10
        35c   70c $2.00   per dozen
        1   1   ½   dozen in a box

Glass Christmas Tree Points for top of tree, made of brilliant colored glass; very ornamental.

No.   226/5   10   15   20
        8   9   10   12   inches long
        38c   70c $1.00 1.50 per dozen
        1   1   1   ½   dozen in a box

Cornucopias with glass balls on the end (new). One dozen in a box.

No.   227.   38c per dozen

GLASS THERMOMETERS.

Matrimonial Thermometers.   A very amusing glass toy. One dozen in a box.

No. 220.   38c per dozen

Glass Thermometer with comic negro and old woman's head with glass eyes, which are illuminated by holding the thermometer in your hand. One dozen in a box.

No. 222.   75c per dozen

DECEPTION GLASSES.

Imitation of liquor glasses. One dozen in a box

No.   225/5.   10
        38c   70c   per dozen

TINSEL ORNAMENTS FOR CHRIST-MAS TREES.

Tinsel Lametta, put up in paper bags.

No. 1200/10.   Pearled..........35c per dozen bags
        12.   Silver.............35c   "   "
        13.   Gold..............35c   "   "
        14.   Assorted colors...35c   "   "

COLORED TINSEL GARLANDS.

COLORED TINSEL GARLANDS, (small) silver, gold and copper color assorted, 36 yards in a box,
                        $ .85 per box

COLORED TINSEL GARLANDS, (medium,) silver, gold and copper color, 6 yards in a box,
                        $ .50 per box

COLORED TINSEL GARLANDS, (extra heavy), silver, gold and copper color, 6 yards in a box,
                        $ .75 per box

TINSEL ORNAMENTS.

Per gross

No. 635. SILVER AND GOLD STARS with tinsel, ½ gross in a box.................. $ .85

No. 779. GELATINE AND TINSEL ORNA-MENTS, ½ gross in a box.............. .85

No. 868. GELATINE AND TINSEL STARS, ½ gross in a box....................... .85

Per doz.

No. 841. TINSEL AND GELATINE COMETS, 2 dozen in a box............. $ .35

No. 840. LARGE TINSEL STARS, 2 dozen in a box.............. .... .35

No. 833. TINSEL AND GELATINE ORNA-MENTS with angel, 2 dozen in a box.... .35

No. 835. TINSEL AND GELATINE ORNA-MENTS with children's figures, 2 dozen in a box....................... .35

No. 829. TINSEL AND GELATINE ORNA-MENTS with angels, 2 dozen in a box... .35

No. 862. TINSEL AND COLORED PAPER ANGELS, 2 dozen in a box............. .35

No. 853. TINSEL AND COLORED PAPER CHERUBS, 2 dozen in a box........... .35

No. 805. PAPER ANGELS with gold wings and tinsel and colored paper ornaments, 2 dozen in a box...................... .35

No. 814. FANCY PAPER, TINSEL AND GOLD STARS, one dozen in a box...... .70

No. 811. LARGE TINSEL AND GELA-TINE STARS, one dozen in a box...... .70

No. 822. LARGE COLORED PAPER AND TINSEL STARS with children's pictures, one dozen in a box..................... $ .70

No. 821. LARGE TINSEL STARS, with gelatine back and colored Cupid, one dozen in a box......................... .70

GREEN MOSS FOR CHRISTMAS TREES, in bundles...................$ .75 per dozen bundles

GOLD AND SILVER PAPER FISHES.
No. 509. 2 dozen in a box..........$ .35 per dozen

GOLD AND SILVER PAPER STARS.
No. 515. one dozen in a box........$ .35 per dozen

COLORED CHRISTMAS TREE GLASS LANTERNS, made of different colored glass and metal, very handsome ornaments for Christmas trees.

No. 622/5   10
        $ .35   .75   per dozen
        2   1   dozen in a box

FANCY CORNUCOPIAS.

No. 769. SMALL GELATINE CORNUCOPIA with crépe fringe, 2 dozen in a box..$ .35 per doz.

No. 866. GOLD AND SILVER PAPER CORNU-COPIA with tissue paper fringe, 2 dozen in a box.......................:.$ .35 per dozen

No. 810. GOLD AND SILVER PAPER CORNU-COPIA, filled with colored tinsel, 2 dozen in a box.........................$ .70 per dozen

48   36   24   18
        Cable.   Diamond.

Christmas Tree Candles.

CHRISTMAS TREE CANDLES.

CABLE CHRISTMAS TREE CANDLES, assorted colors, in boxes of 72, 48, 36, 24 and 16 candles.....................$1.20 per dozen boxes

DIAMOND CHRISTMAS TREE CANDLES, finest quality, brilliant colors; new pattern, put up in boxes of 48, 36, 24 and 16 candles...............
                        $1.50 per dozen boxes

CANDLE HOLDERS FOR CHRIST-MAS TREES.

No. 4. PLAIN TIN CANDLE TACK BRACK-ETS, one gross in a box........$ .25 per gross

No. 2. Safety tin candle holders with spring, as-sorted colors, one gross in a box.$ .75 per gross

Per Gross

No. 1. Gold and silver ball candle holders, ½ gross in a box...... $ .75

No. 22. Assorted colored ball candle holders, ½ gross in a box....... .85

No. 7. Tin star balanc-ing candle holders, ½ gross in a box....... .90

No. 3. Brilliant reflector balancing candle holders, ½ gross in a box............... 2.50

CHRISTMAS TREE HOOKS.

CHRISTMAS TREE HOOKS, a simple device for hanging ornaments and presents on the Christmas tree; put up 100 hooks in a box, 70c per dozen boxes.

CORNUCOPIAS.

Plain colored glazed paper cornucopias.

				Per Gross
No. 1.	1 oz.,	plain		$ .18
" 2.	1 "	better paper		.30
" 10.	2 "	glazed		1.20
" 19½.	4 "	"		2.25
" 41.	6 "	"		3.00
" 24½.	8 "	"		3.50
" 39½.	16 "	"		5.50

Plain gold and silver paper cornucopias.

			Per Gross
No. 4.	1 oz		$ .60
" 9.	2 "		1.35
" 15.	4 "		2.50
" 20.	6 "		4.25
" 26½.	8 "		5.00
" 29½.	16 "		7.00

Decorated colored paper cornucopias.

			Per Gross
No. 11.	2 oz., with flowers or pictures		$1.75
" 18.	4 " " " "		3.25
" 42.	6 " " " "		3.50
" 34½.	8 " " " "		5.50
" 39.	16 " " " "		8.00

COTTON, WIRE AND PAPER MASKS.

COTTON DOMINOES, with curtains in white, black, pink, dark red, blue and orange......
per gross, $3.00

SATIN DOMINOES, with curtains, same colors as above......
per dozen, 2.00

LULU MASKS, satin, half masks, same colors as above.. ....per dozen, 1.25

MASK FASTENERS...............per 100, 1.00

433. GAUZE MASKS, gents and ladies, fine quality............per dozen, .75

8G11. GAUZE MASKS, clowns, negroes, Indians, etc............per dozen, 1.00

3050. WIRE MASKS, gents and ladies....
per dozen, 1.75

3051. WIRE MASKS, comics and characters...................per dozen 3.00

3053. WIRE MASKS, gents, with hair beards.................per dozen, 3.00

PAPER MASKS.

A. Common Paper Masks, children's size, assorted....per gross, $ .90

Ax. Glazed Paper Masks, children's size, assorted...............per gross, 1.00

A, Special. Glazed with hair moustaches, children's size, assorted, per gross, 1.25

B. Glazed Paper Masks, assorted caricatures, 12 kinds, full size........
per gross, 3.00

C/I. Glazed Paper Masks, assorted caricatures, better quality, 12 kinds....
per gross, 4.00

C/II. Paper Glazed Masks, assorted, 12 kinds, nationalities.....per gross, 4.80

E/10. Waxed Paper Masks, better quality, assorted............ ...per gross, 9.00

D. Paper Masks, nationalities, fine quality, assorted, 12 kinds .. ..
per gross, 9.00

F. Glazed Paper Masks, ladies and gents, assorted in box.........per gross, 4.00

G. Fine Waxed Paper Masks, ladies and gents, assorted.........per gross, 9.00

H. Glazed Paper Masks (fine), old men, women, school boys and girls, Indians, squaws, Yankees..per gross 9.00

K/5. Glazed Paper Masks, assorted, clowns, Chinese, Indians, etc....per gross, 4.80

K/10. Fine Paper Masks, assorted clowns, etc....................per gross 9 00

M/5. Glazed Paper Masks, men's, with hair moustaches........per gross, 4.80

M/10. Waxed Paper Masks, men's, with hair moustaches ......per gross, 9.00

N/5. Varnished Paper Masks, assorted negroes ....per gross, 4.00

N/10. Fine Varnished Paper Masks, assorted negroes, full face........per gross, 9.00

N/25. Fine Waxed Paper Masks, assorted negroes, with wool hair, extra quality.................per dozen, 1.75

55/2. Fine Matt Paper Masks, Santa Claus and Ermits, with flax beards......
per dozen, 1.25

ANIMAL MASKS.

250²/o. Varnished Paper Animal Face Masks, assorted kinds..........per gross, $4.00

250/1. Full Size Animal Masks, assorted 12 kinds, flocked and varnished, consisting of monkey, frog, dog, cat, pig, bear, wolf, fox, sheep, goat, tiger, duck, parrot, eagle, etc .....
per dozen, 1.75

179-182. Fine large Animal Heads, viz., horse, monkey, sheep, tiger, frog, dog, crow, eagle, etc...per dozen, 5.00

206-210. Extra large Animal Heads, viz., cat, dog, fox, wolf, bear, etc......
per dozen, 24.00

SANTA CLAUS HEADS.

265/2. Large Santa Claus Heads, with long flax beads ....per dozen, $10.00

265/3. Same as above, with long wool beards................. per dozen, 12.00

266/8. Fine large Santa Claus Heads with flax beards......... ...per dozen, 16.00

LARGE COMIC HEADS.

365/A to P. Fine large Comic Heads, viz.: Englishman, dwarf, soldier, professor, hermit, school-boy, negro, dude, colored lady, tramp, etc..
per dozen, 12.00

266/A to M. Extra large fine Painted Comic Heads, viz.: Chinaman, Punch, monk, policeman and Scotchman. '...............per dozen, 24.00

PAPER NOSES.

7/5. Comic Paper Noses, assorted........ .35

7/10. Large Comic Paper Noses, assorted, with hair moustaches...per dozen, .75

HAIR GOATEES, assorted colors.......... .25

HAIR MOUSTACHES, per gross ....
No. 1, 75c; No. 2, $1.50; No. 3, 3.00

HAIR BEARDS, assorted colors, small sizes ....per dozen, 2.00

HAIR BEARDS, assorted colors, large sizes..................per dozen, 3.00

HAIR BEARDS, assorted colors, extra large sizes.............per dozen, 4.00

HAIR BEARDS, fine long white or grey hair.............per dozen, 6.00

HAIR WIGS, negroes..........per dozen, 4.50

HAIR WIGS, assorted...per dozen, $6.00 to 12 00

COSTUME BELLS.

ALL BRASS.

Nos.	1	2	3	4	5
Per gross.	25c	30c	35c	40c	45c

FOOLS' CAPS.

Nos. 33-41. Paper Muslin Carnival Caps, assorted colors and shapes, one, two and three bells..per dozen, 1.00

No. 18. Same style as above, better quality, with gold braid, 4 bells..........
per dozen, 2.00

VOCOPHONES OR BIGOTOPHONES.

These new instruments are made of pasteboard, covered with bronzed or colored paper, and are imitations of leading instruments. Any person can play them by simply singing into the instrument. To be used for masquerades, serenades, surprise parties, picnics, excursions, etc. They create quite a sensation wherever seen and heard. See illustration.

No. 92. Vocophones all straight, per dozen, $ .75
" 93. " " " " 1.75
" 94. " " " " 4.00
" 100. Vocophones in sets of 8 instruments, per set.... 4.50

DECORATED CHINA TOY TEA SETS.

Per Dozen

CHINA TOY TEA SETS, decorated in bright colored designs and spread in large square paper box; assorted flower decorations; size of box, 3x4, D/5, 7 pieces in box...... $ .37

D/10.   Blue and red decorated; size of box, 5x6½, 15 pieces in box............   .70

D/11.   Flower decorations; size of box, 5x7, 12 larger pieces in box...........   .75

D/12.   Flower decorations; size of box, 5½x8, 16 pieces in box.................   .87

D/15.   Flower decorations; size of box, 6x8½; 11 pieces and spoons in box.......   1.00

D/20.   Assorted decorations; size of box, 6½x10; 16 pieces in box............   1.65

D/25.   Raised decorations; size of box, 7¼x11; 15 pieces and spoons in box........   1.75

D/26.   Fine assorted decorations; size of box, 6½x10; 15 pieces and spoons in box.   1.88

D/27.   Blue underglazed; size of box, 8x10; 16 pieces and spoons in box........   2.00

D/28.   Flower decorations; size of box, 7x9½; 16 pieces and spoons in box........   2.00

D/29.   Flower and colored stripe decorations; size of box, 8x11; 15 pieces in box,   2.00

D/30.   Assorted flower decorations; size of box, 9½x11; 22 pieces in box.......   2.25

D/35.   Extra heavy decorations; size of box, 9x12; 22 pieces and spoons in box..   3.25

D/40.   Blue underglazed; size of box 10x13; 23 pieces and spoons in box.......   3.50

D/50.   Flower decorations; size of box 10x13; 23 pieces and spoons in box.......   3.75

D/51.   Flower decorations; size of box 10x13; 16 large pieces and spoons in box..   3.75

D/52.   Flower decorations; size of box 10x13½; 23 pieces with plates in box.......   4.00

D/53.   Blue underglazed decorations; size of box 10x13; 23 pieces and spoons in box............................   4.00

D/54.   Flower decorations; size of box 10x14; 23 pieces in box..................   4.00

D/60.   Assorted heavy flower decorations; size of box 10x14; 19 large pieces in box   4.50

D/61.   Bright flower decorations; size of box 11x15; 23 pieces and spoons in box   5.00

D/62.   Blue underglazed decorations; size of box 11x15; 23 pieces and spoons in box............................   6.00

D/65.   Assorted flower decorations; size of box 12x16; 23 pieces and spoons in box 6.50

D/66.   Colored stripe decorations; size of box 12x16; 23 pieces and spoons in box   6.50

D/75.   Assorted flower decorations; ribbed pattern; size of box, 13½x18; 23 large pieces in box................   7.50

D/76.   Assorted flower decorations; size of box 13½x17½; 23 large size pieces in box   8.00

D/77.   Blue underglazed; size of box, 12x17, 17 pieces (extra large size) and spoons in box 8.50

D/78.   Fine flower decorations; size of box 13x16; 16 pieces and 2 large cake baskets in box...................   9.00

D/79.   Fine flower decorations; ribbed pattern; size of box 13x19; 23 pieces (large size) in box 9.00

D/80.   Fine flower decorations; size of box 13½x19; 23 pieces in box..........   10.50

D/90.   Very fine flower and colored stripe decorations; size of box 16x21½; 23 pieces (extra large size) in box 18.00

DECORATED FANCY CHINA TEA SETS

Per Dozen

D/100.   All gold decorations; size of box 8x10; 17 pieces in box.... ....   4.00

D/102.   All gold decorations; round box 9½ inches in diameter; contents same as before........................   4.50

D/103.   Fine flower decorated with gold leaves, spread in fancy style, in box; size of box 12x16, 23 pieces in box............................   9.00

D/105.   Fine gold decorations, with colored shading, laid out in fancy style in box; size of box 14½x20; 23 large pieces in box......................   24.00

D/110.   Highly decorated design with flowers and gold handles; size of box 20x27; 23 large pieces in box..............   30.00

Besides the above decorated tea sets, a full line of finer sets, ranging in price from $3.00 to $8.00 each, and some of them large enough for use, will be always found in my stock.

DECORATED CHINA TOY DINNER SETS.

Per Dozen

D/130.   Assorted flower decorations; size of box 7x10; 11 pieces in box........   2.00

D/132.   Assorted flower decorations; size of box 9x12; 11 pieces (larger) in box,   4.00

D/134.   Fine flower decorations; size of box 13x18; 16 pieces (extra large size) in box............. ....   9.00

Toy dinner sets, ranging in price from $12.00 to $48.00 per dozen, in various designs.

DECORATED CHINA WASH SETS.

Per Dozen

D/120.   Assorted flower and colored stripe decorations; size of box 5x8; 6 pieces in box..................   2.00

D/121.   Finer flower decorations; size of box 5½x8; 5 pieces in box 2.25

D/125.   Assorted flower and colored stripe decorations; size of box 7x9½; 7 pieces in box..................   3.75

D/126.   Fine flower decorations; size of box 9x10½; 7 pieces in box...........   4.50

D/128.   Finest gold and colored fancy decorations; size of box 9x12; 7 pieces (extra large) in box..............   8.50

Better and larger sets up to $30.00 per dozen always on hand.

DECORATED CHINA CUPS AND SAUCERS.

All cups and saucers come assorted in packages, from three to six different decorations, and are packed up one half dozen in a package, except 5c and 10c sizes, which are put up one dozen in a package.

SAXON SHAPE CUPS AND SAUCERS.

Per Dozen

No. C/205. Toy cup and saucer, with gold band and red colored handle; cup, $1\frac{3}{4}$ inches high, saucer, $3\frac{1}{2}$ inches in diameter.............................$ .37

No. C/210. Toy cup and saucer, handsomely decorated with colored flowers and gilt vines; cup, 2 inches high, saucer, $4\frac{3}{4}$ inches in diameter............................ .80

No. C/211. Cup and saucer, decorated with colored flowers and garlands; cup, 3 inches high, saucer, 6 inches in diameter.............. 1.50

No. C/212. Cup and saucer, with similar decoration and same size as 211; cup and saucer ribbed..................... 1.65

No. C/213. Cup and saucer, ribbed pattern, with large colored flowers and scroll decorations; cup, $3\frac{1}{2}$ ins. high, saucer, $6\frac{1}{2}$ ins. in diameter.............. 1.75

No. C/112. Cup and saucer, large size, with assorted colored fancy broad bands and gilt stripes; cup, $3\frac{1}{4}$ inches high, saucer, 6 inches in diameter.................. 1.65

No. C/119. Cup and saucer, large size, decorated with flowers and mottoes, assorted; cup, $3\frac{1}{2}$ inches high, saucer, $6\frac{1}{2}$ inches in diameter.................... 1.75

No. C/131. Cup and saucer, with fine fancy flower and scroll ornaments and mottoes, assorted; cup, 3 ins. high, saucer, 6 ins. in diam. 1.75

No. C/132. Cup and saucer, large size, with fancy flower, bird, gilt decorations and mottoes, assorted; cup, $3\frac{1}{2}$ inches high, saucer, $6\frac{1}{2}$ inches in diameter........... 1.88

No. C/135. Cup and saucer, with colored flower decoration and raised gilt motto; cup, 3 inches high, saucer, $5\frac{1}{2}$ inches in diameter.............................. 1.75

Per Dozen

No. C/140. Cup and saucer, large size, with moss roses and other flower decorations; cup, $3\frac{1}{2}$ inches high, saucer, $6\frac{1}{2}$ inches in diameter............................ 1.87

No. C/1020. Cup and saucer, large shape with fine flower decorations and motto in colors; cup, $3\frac{1}{2}$ ins. high, saucer, 6 ins. in diameter.. 2.00

No. C/214. Cup and saucer, extra large shape, with vine, flower and bird decoration; cup, $3\frac{1}{2}$ inches high, saucer, $6\frac{1}{2}$ inches in diameter.................... 2.00

No. C/215. Cup and saucer, extra large shape, decorated with bright large colored flowers and assorted colored shadings; cup, $3\frac{1}{2}$ inches high, saucer, $6\frac{1}{2}$ inches in diameter.................... 1.88

No. C/216. Cup and saucer, similar to 215; cup, $3\frac{1}{2}$ inches high, saucer, $6\frac{1}{2}$ inches in diameter.............................. 2.00

No. C/225. Cup and saucer, with large colored flower decoration and colored band decoration; cup, $3\frac{1}{2}$ inches high, saucer, $6\frac{1}{2}$ inches in diameter 2.00

No. C/226. Cup and saucer, extra large size, with scalloped rim, bright colored flower and gilt decorations; cup, $3\frac{1}{2}$ inches high, saucer, $6\frac{1}{2}$ inches in diameter..... 2.00

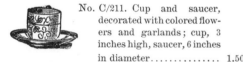

No. C/227. Cup and saucer, extra large size, all colored in pink, blue and buff, with bright flower decorations, fluted Saxon pattern; cup, $3\frac{1}{2}$ inches high, saucer, $6\frac{1}{2}$ inches in diam... 2.00

No. C/1047. Cup and saucer, with raised colored flower and gilt ornaments (new decorations this season); cup, 3 inches high, saucer, 6 inches in diameter...... 1.75

No. C/232. Cup and saucer, similar to 1047, and same size, with raised colored flower and raised gilt motto decorations....... 2.00

No. C/233. Cup and saucer, same size as before, with raised large flowers (new decorations this season).................. 2.00

No. C/425. Cup and saucer, same size and style as before, with colored shadings and raised butterfly and flower decorations.................................. 2.25

No. C/250. Cup and saucer, with new style of beaded raised colored flower and gilt decorations with colored shadings; cup, $3\frac{1}{2}$ inches high, saucer, $6\frac{1}{2}$ inches in diameter 4.00

No. C/251. Cup and saucer, same size and decoration as before, without colored shading..... .... 3.75

No. C/252. Cup and saucer, same size and style as before, marble decorations with beaded center and raised gold ornaments.................................. 4.00

DECORATED CHINA CUPS AND SAUCERS.

Fancy Shapes.

No. 257.

Per Dozen

No. C/217. Cup and saucer, tapering shape, ribbed decoration with colored shadings and fine colored flowers; cup, 3 inches high, saucer, 6 inches in diameter...... 2.00

No. C/240. Cup and saucer, fancy shape, fluted decoration in blue and red flowers and vines and gold band and gold handle; cup, 3 inches high, saucer, $5\frac{1}{2}$ inches in diameter..................... 2.00

No. C/241. Cup and saucer, fancy shape, with fine colored and gilt flower decorations, gold shaded band and square all gold handle; cup, 3 inches high, saucer, 6 inches in diameter.................. 2.00

No. C. 242. Cup and saucer, Japanese tea cup shape, decorated in Chinese flower decorations, cup and saucer ribbed; cup, $3\frac{1}{2}$ inches high, saucer, 6 inches in diameter 2.00

No. C/243. Cup and saucer, decoration same as 242, with gilt handle; cup, 3 inches high, saucer, 6 inches in diameter 2.00

No. C/244. Cup and saucer, Chinese tea cup shape, with fancy flower decorations; cup, 4 inches in diameter, saucer, $6\frac{1}{2}$ inches in diameter 4.50

No. C/255. Cup and saucer, new style ribbed pattern, decorations in buff, pink and blue shadings, with gold ornaments and gold stripes; cup, $3\frac{1}{2}$ inches high, saucer, $6\frac{1}{2}$ inches in diameter............. 3.75

No. C/256. Cup and saucer, ribbed pattern, all gold decorations, with underglazed blue stripes; cup, 3 inches high, saucer, 6 inches in diameter 4.00

No. C/257. Cup and saucer, fancy shape, with colored shadings and gilt ornaments and all gold and blue striped base, square all gold handle; cup, $3\frac{1}{2}$ inches high, saucer, $6\frac{1}{2}$ inches in diameter. (See cut.).. 4.00

DECORATED CHINA AFTER DINNER CUPS AND SAUCERS.

Per Dozen

No. C/230. Small cup and saucer, with gold outside decoration and all gold inside...$2.00

No. C/231. Small cup and saucer with raised all gold decoration, assorted......... .. 2.00

No. C/253. Small cup and saucer, cup decorated all gold with gold motto on white field and gold band inside.............. 2.00

DECORATED CHINA MOUSTACHE CUPS AND SAUCERS.

Per Dozen

No. M/124. Moustache cup, fancy flower and gilt decorations, with gilt mottoes; cup, $3\frac{1}{2}$ inches; saucer, 6 inches.................... $1.88

No. M/130. Assorted flower decorations; cup, 3 inches; saucer, 6 inches 1.75

No. M/140. Assorted fine large flower decorations; cup, $3\frac{1}{2}$ inches; saucer, $6\frac{1}{2}$ inches. 2.00

No. M/917. Moustache cup, fancy shape, with bright flower decorations; cup, 3 inches; saucer, $6\frac{1}{2}$ inches....................... 2.00

No. M/132. Assorted flower decorations, with colored shadings and gilt mottoes; cup, $3\frac{1}{2}$ inches; saucer, $6\frac{1}{2}$ inches............. 2.00

No. M/400, /25. Assorted flower decorations, with colored shadings; cup, $3\frac{1}{2}$ inches; saucer, $6\frac{1}{2}$ inches...................... 1.88

No. M/1020. Fine flower decorations, with mottoes in colors, assorted; cup, 3 inches; saucer, 6 inches........................ 2.00

No. M/1021. Moustache cup, with large flower decorations; cup, 3 inches; saucer, 6 inches................................ 2.00

No. M/213. Moustache cup, ribbed pattern, with large colored flower and scroll decorations; cup, $2\frac{1}{2}$ inches; saucer, $6\frac{1}{2}$ inches. 2.00

No. M/215. Moustache cup, with bright large colored flower and assorted colored shadings; cup, $3\frac{1}{2}$ inches; saucer, $6\frac{1}{2}$ inches.. 2.00

No. M/225. Moustache cup, with large colored flower decorations and colored band decoration; cup, $3\frac{1}{2}$ inches; saucer, $6\frac{1}{2}$ inches. 2.00

No. M/226. Moustache cup, extra large size, with scalloped rim, bright colored flower and gilt decorations; cup, $3\frac{1}{2}$ inches; saucer, $6\frac{1}{2}$ inches...................... 2.00

No. M/227. Moustache cup, extra large size, all colored in blue, pink and buff, with bright flower decorations, fluted Saxon pattern; cup, $3\frac{1}{2}$ inches; saucer, $6\frac{1}{2}$ inches................................ 2.00

No. M/251. Moustache cup, with new style of beaded and raised colored flower and gilt decorations; cup, $3\frac{1}{2}$ inches; saucer, $6\frac{1}{2}$ inches.............................. 4.00

DECORATED CHINA MUGS.

China mugs are all decorated with bright flowers, fancy scrolls and mottoes, and are put up in packages of one dozen, except the larger sizes, which are put up one-half dozen in a package.

Per Dozen

No. 280/5. Straight shape, assorted flower and motto decorations; $2\frac{1}{4}$ inches high...... $ .37

Per Dozen

No. 280/10. Straight shape, same style as before; 3 inches high..$ .75

No. 280/15. Straight shape, same decorations as before; $3\frac{1}{4}$ inches high.............. .88

No. 280/20. Straight shape, same decorations as before; $3\frac{1}{2}$ inches high........................ 1.00

No. 281/10. Flaring shape, with foot, assorted flower and motto decorations and colored band; 3 inches high................... .75

No. 285. Flaring shape, with fine landscape and flower decorations and gold rim; $3\frac{1}{2}$ inches high............................ 1.50

No. 286. Flaring shape, with foot, ribbed pattern, with fine raised flowers and colored shadings; $3\frac{1}{3}$ inches high 1.75

No. 287. Same shape as No. 286, colored flower decorations, with raised motto in gilt; $3\frac{1}{2}$ inches high........................... 1.75

No. 290. Flaring shape, with foot, new raised flower decorations, with gilt dots and plain gold motto; $3\frac{1}{2}$ inches high....... 2.00

DECORATED CHINA CUPS AND SAUCERS WITH PLATES.

Packed one-half dozen in a package.

Per Dozen

No. P/500. Cup, saucer and plate, assorted flower decorations; cup, $2\frac{1}{2}$ inches; saucer, 5 inches; plate, $6\frac{1}{4}$ inches..........$1.75

No. P/220. Assorted flower and motto decorations; cup, $2\frac{1}{2}$ inches; saucer, 5 inches; plate, $6\frac{1}{4}$ inches 1.75

No. P/221. Decorated the same as P/220; cup, $2\frac{3}{4}$ inches; saucer, $5\frac{1}{2}$ inches; plate, $6\frac{1}{2}$ inches 2.00

No. P/226. Fine assorted flower decorations, cup, saucer and plate with scalloped rim; cup, $3\frac{1}{2}$ inches; saucer, $6\frac{1}{2}$ inches; plate, 8 inches................................ 4.00

No. P/227. Extra large size. All colorod in pink, blue and buff, with bright flower decorations; fluted Saxon pattern; cup, $3\frac{1}{2}$ inches; saucer, $6\frac{1}{2}$ inches; plate, $8\frac{1}{4}$ inches................................ 4.00

DECORATED CHINA FRUIT PLATES.

Packed one dozen in a package.

Per Dozen

No. 275. Plate with open work rim, decorated with assorted fruits and gilt vine leaves; $7\frac{1}{2}$ inches in diameter.................$2.00

No. 276. Plate with scalloped and raised rim, fine center decoration, with Cupid and other figures; 8 inches in diameter..... 2.00

DECORATED CHINA MUSH AND MILK SETS.

Consisting of pitcher, bowl and plate; put up $\frac{1}{4}$ dozen in a package.

Per Dozen

No. B/295. Assorted fine flower decorations; pitcher, $4\frac{1}{2}$ inches; bowl, 4 inches, and plate, 6 inches........................$2.25

No. B/296. Ribbed pattern with fine assorted flowers; pitcher, 5 inches; bowl, $4\frac{1}{2}$ inches, and plate, $7\frac{1}{4}$ inches............. 3.75

No. B/297. Octagon shape, with fine large colored flower and landscape decorations; pitcher, 5 inches; bowl, $5\frac{1}{2}$ inches, and plate, 7 inches..................... 4.00

No. B/298. Fancy shape, ribbed pattern, fine flower and gilt decorations, gilt handle; pitcher, 5 inches; bowl, $5\frac{1}{2}$ inches, and plate, $7\frac{1}{2}$ inches....................... 6.00

No. B/299. Fancy shape, ribbed pattern, with colored landscape decorations and gilt handle; pitcher, 5 inches; bowl, $5\frac{1}{2}$ inches, and plate, $7\frac{1}{2}$ inches 6.00

DECORATED CHINA TOYS.

Per Gross

No. 140/4. Decorated china penny jugs, $1\frac{3}{4}$ inches high; half gross in a box....... $ .96

No. 470. Assorted penny jugs, bisque figures, vases, etc., from $1\frac{1}{2}$ to 2 inches high; one gross in a box .... .90

Per Dozen

No. B/1. Assorted bisque domestic animals; one dozen in a box ....$ .35

No. B/3. Assorted bisque birds; one dozen in a box................................. .35

No. B/4. Assorted bisque domestic birds; one dozen in a box........................ .35

No. 5. Assortment of china toys, consisting of 12 different kinds of figures, animals, mugs, cups and saucers, tea sets, wash sets, pitchers, etc.; three dozen in a wooden box............................ .38

BISQUE CHINA ANIMAL FAMILIES.

Put up one family of mother with five young ones in a box.

		Per Dozen Boxes
No. 2716.	Rabbit family	$2.00
No. 2698.	Pig family	2.00
No. 2772.	Bull-dog family	2.00
No. 2797.	Poodle-dog family	2.00
No. 2868.	Squirrel family	2.00
No. 2969.	Pug-dog family	2.00
No. 3084.	Greyhound family	2.00

DECORATED BISQUE CHINA FIGURES.

Per Dozen

No. 1491. Decorated bisque china riders, assorted; $3\frac{1}{2}$ inches high; one dozen in a package.............................$ .35

No. 500. Assorted bisque china boy and girl groups; $4\frac{1}{2}$ inches high; one dozen in a package.............................. .38

No. 505. Assorted bisque boy and girl figures, highly decorated; 6 different kinds; 5 inches high; one dozen in a package................ .75

No. 510. Assorted bisque china boy and girl groups, decorated in bright colors; $6\frac{1}{2}$ inches high; one dozen in a package.... 1.75

No. 511. Assorted bisque china boy and girl figures, brightly decorated, 6 different kinds; $7\frac{1}{2}$ inches high; one dozen in a package......... 1.75

No. 512. Fine Bisque figures, boys and girls, 6 different kinds, painted in fine colors with gold dots; $8\frac{1}{2}$ inches high; one dozen in a package............................ 2.00

No. 520. Assorted fine bisque figures, fisherman and woman, lawn tennis players, and children in winter costumes, very finely decorated; 10 inches high; $\frac{1}{2}$ doz. in a package............ .... 4.00

No. 522. Assortment and size same as No. 520, in different decorations with bronze..... 4.00

No. 524. Fine bisque boy and girl figures in grandfather and grandmother costumes, very handsomely decorated large figures; $10\frac{1}{2}$ inches high; $\frac{1}{3}$ dozen in a package............ 4.50

Per doz.

No. 531. Very fine bisque figures, assorted, page and lady and mandolin player and dancing girl with tambourine, decorated in fine blue and pink colors, with gold ornaments; 12 inches high; $\frac{1}{3}$ dozen in a package.............................. 9.00

Per Dozen

No. 532. Fine bisque boys and girls in fisherman and fisherwoman costume, highly decorated, very large and attractive; 12 inches high; $\frac{1}{3}$ dozen in a package......$9.00

No. 533. Finest bisque figures, assorted, Italian beggar boy and girl, and boy and girl eating fruit, very handsomely decorated and very ornamental; 13 inches high; $\frac{1}{3}$ dozen in a package.................. 9.00

No. 535. Fine Dresden china bisque figures, dressed in antique court costumes, highly ornamented and finely finished; 12 inches high; one-sixth dozen in a package... .12.00

No. 538. Finest bisque figures dressed in page and lady and shepherd and shepherdess costumes, finest decorations in pink and blue with gold; $13\frac{1}{2}$ inches high; one-sixth dozen in a package...............16.50

No. 540. Assortment similar to No. 538; $14\frac{1}{2}$ inches high...........................18.00

No. 545. Finest bisque figures, fisherman and woman and boy and girl in winter costume, decorated in finest colors; 14 ins. high; one-sixth dozen in a package.....21.00

No. 546. Finest bisque figures, ladies and gentlemen in 18th century costumes, highly decorated in pink and blue with gold ornaments; 15 inches high; one-sixth dozen in a package....................24.00

Besides the above line of bisque figures, a full line of finer figures, ranging in price from $2.50 to $6.00 each, will be always found in my stock.

BOHEMIAN GLASS VASES.

Per Dozen

No. 1000/5. Glass vases, assorted fancy shapes, decorated in bright colors; 5 inches high; one dozen in a package..............................$ .38

No. 1005/5. Assorted shapes and decorations, different from the previous number; $5\frac{1}{2}$ inches high; 1 dozen in package........ .40

No. 1000/10. Assorted shapes, painted alabaster color, with bright flower decorations; $8\frac{1}{2}$ inches high; 1/6 dozen in a package.... .75

No. 1005/10. Assorted shapes, ruby and painted alabaster combinations, with colored flower decorations; $9\frac{1}{2}$ inches high; 1/6 dozen in a package 1.00

Per Dozen

No. 1005/15. Assorted shapes, painted alabaster, with very bright colored flower decorations; $10\frac{1}{2}$ inches high....................$1.25

No. 1005/25. Similar assortment and same decorations as 1005/10; 12 inches high........ 1.75

No. 1010. Alabaster, with bright colored flower decorations, pink fluted bell shape top; 10 inches high.............. 1.75

No. 1015. Alabaster, with blue stripes and colored and gilt flower decorations, fluted top; $10\frac{1}{2}$ inches high.................. 2.00

No. 1020. Ivory colored vase, with bright flower and fruit decorations; $10\frac{1}{2}$ inches high.................................. 2.00

No. 1022. Fine alabaster vase, assorted shapes, with brown tinted top and large fine painted flower decorations; 10 inches high............. 4.00

No. 1024. Fine vase, decorated in fine flower and leaf decorations; 10 inches high....... 4.00

No. 1026. Fine glass vase, decorated with a new style of gold ornamentation and fine large flowers, and pink and gold tinted top; 11 inches high.... 4.00

No. 1030. Finest Bohemian glass vase, highly painted in tints and very fine apple blossom decorations; a very fine ornament for the money. 12 inches high.........9.00

No. 1031. Very fine glass vase, decorated in all gold embossed leaf and flower decoration, with brown and yellow tinted effect; 11 inches high......................... 9.00

No. 1032. Glass vase, very large shape, alabaster with blue shaded top and large fine flower decorations; 12 inches high 9.00

Per Dozen

No. 1033. Large full shape vase, gold with brown top and base and fine large chrysanthemum flower decorations ; 11 inches high... ....$9.00

BOHEMIAN GLASS VASES, FINER AND HEAVIER QUALITY.

(Small Shapes.)

Per dozen

No. 1035. Fine small vase, full shape, in yellow and brown shadings, with fine large gilt decorations ; 7 inches high..................$2.00

No. 1036/7. Fine pale blue and terra cotta glass vase, with gold and white fine flower decoration ; 7 inches high.................... 2.00

No. 1036/9. Same style as before ; 9 inches high.................... 4.00

No. 1038. Fine crystal glass vases, assorted patterns and assorted shadings, with raised crystal ornaments (new styles this season) ; 7½ inches high................ 2.00

No. 1039. Assorted crystal, colored glass vases, various shapes, ribbed patterns with fancy base and crystal leaves ; 7½ inches high................................... 2.00

No. 1040. Colored crystal glass vase with pink shadings and white crystal raised ornaments all around ; 7½ inches high 2.00

No. 1042. Fancy shapes, marbleized pink and blue colors, assorted with white raised crystal ornaments ; 8 inches high.......... 2.00

No. 1043. Pitcher shaped vase, with handle, painted in very fine tints with handsome flower decorations, handle with gold dots ; 9 inches high.................. 4.00

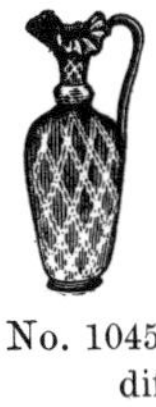

No. 1044. Fine heavy glass vase, Rose de Barry and pale blue colors, with fine gold ornaments and crystal glass handles ; 7¼ inches high. 4.00

No. 1045. Similar vase to the foregoing, but different shades, ornamented with landscape and bird decorations ; 8 inches high 4.00

Per Dozen

No. 1046. Fine, heavy, round-shape vase, with gold glass handles, assorted shadings and gilt flower and bird decorations, with raised beaded ornaments ; 6 inches high ; a very fine article.....................$9.00

No. 1047. Finest glass vase, fancy shape, with gold glass handles, assorted tints with fine gilt and colored flower decorations and raised beaded ornaments ; 9 inches high...................... 9.00

No. 1048. Very fine artistic glass vase with gold glass handles, shaded in terra cotta, pink and blue, decorated with fine gold sprigs ; 10 inches high 9.00

BOHEMIAN GLASS FLOWER AND FRUIT BASKETS.

The 25 cent sizes are packed ¼ dozen, the larger sizes ⅙ dozen in a package.

Per doz.

No. 1100. Assorted shapes and assorted colors, delicately tinted, silver speckled inside, with fluted rims ; 5 to 6 inches across ; 6 inches high $1.75

No. 1102. Assorted fancy shapes in irridescent pink, blue and opal colors ; same sizes as No. 1100 .... 2.00

No. 1103. Glass baskets with frosted crystal handles ; assorted patterns with fluted rims in blue, pink and buff colors marbleized ; from 5 to 6 inches across and 6 inches high 2.00

No. 1104. Glass baskets, new assorted styles, frosted outside, fluted rim, shaded in emerald, ruby and sapphire colors with crystal handles, from 4½ to 5 inches across, 6 inches high................... 2.00

No. 1105. Fine glass baskets, assorted shapes, (new), pink and pale blue inside and opal outside with frosted crystal handles, from 4 to 6 inches across, 6 inches high....... 2.00

No. 1106. Fine transparent glass baskets, new shapes, frosted outside with rims in assorted shaded colors, brown, blue, green, etc. with crystal handles, 5 inches across, 6 inches high........................... 2.00

Per Dozen

No. 1110. Assorted glass baskets in pink, blue and buff colored mottled glass, opal outside with frosted crystal handles, from 7½ to 9 inches across, 8 to 8½ inches high,$3.75

No. 1112. Fine crystal glass baskets (all new shapes), frosted outside and assorted colored tinted fluted rims, frosted crystal handles ; from 7½ to 8½ inches across, from 7 to 8 inches high................ 4.00

No. 1113. Fine glass baskets in irridescent colors, with colored shaded rims and frosted crystal handles, new ribbed patterns ; from 5½ to to 7 inches across, and from 6 to 7 inches high................. 4.00

No. 1146. Fine glass baskets, fancy shapes, each in two irridescent colors, with frosted tinted crystal twisted handle, new ribbed pattern ; from 6 to7½ inches across, and from 7 to 8 inches high................. 4.00

No. 1115. Finest glass baskets, assorted new very large shapes, in blue, rose and buff colors inside and opal outside, matt finish with twisted crystal handles ; from 9 to 10 inches across, and from 7 to 7½ inches high....... .. .. 4.50

No. 1120. Finest heavy glass baskets (entirely new shapes), in rose and pale blue colors, with fluted rims and raised spots, fine crystal opal glass handles ; 10 inches across and 10 inches high.............. 8.50

LAVA SMOKERS' SETS.

Per Dozen

No. 1202. Smokers' sets, assorted styles, for segars, matches, ashes ; standing horse, chamois and prancing horse, variegated bronze colors, with black base ; 6½ ins. high, 6½ inches wide....................$2.00

No. 1205. Assorted boys and girls in variegated bronze colors ; 7½ inches high, 6½ inches wide.............................

No. 1210. Assorted lion and horse design in fine variegated bronze colors ; 9 inches high, 8 inches wide.................... 4.00

No. 1220. Smokers' set with two boys smoking, or one boy figure with large broom, sweeping ; 8½ inches high, 8½ inches wide 9.00

No. 1225. Extra large size, standing and lying goat on rocks, with large receptacle for segars, ashes and matches ; 9 inches high, 9 inches wide....................10.50

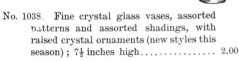

TIN TOYS.

All nicely painted, better value than ever before offered.

ASSORTED TIN ANIMALS ON PLATFORMS AND WHEELS.

Per doz.

No. 30. Six kinds, size, 4¼ inches........... $ .35
" 40. Three kinds, size, 6½ inches......... .62
" 38½. Three kinds, size, 7¼ inches........ .72
" 76. Horse, dog and sheep, (double), 6½ in. .72
" 180. Six kinds, size, 8½ inches........... 1.25
" 50. Three kinds, size, 9 inches.......... 1.38
" 51. Horse, elephant and dog, double animals, size 9¼ inches......... 1.50

TIN HORSES ON PLATFORMS AND WHEELS.

Per doz.

No. 5. Fine finish, size, 4½ inches.......... $ .35
" 10. Fine finish, larger size, 5 inches..... .40
" 11. Fine finish, larger size, 6½ inches... .62
" 12. Fine finish, larger size, 7 inches..... .70
" 25. Special, size, 9 inches............. 1.13
" 4. Trotting Horse, size, 11 inches...... 1.65
" 8. Dexter Horse, fine, size, 10 inches .. 1.87

TIN HORSES WITH RIDERS.

Per doz.

No. 199. Size, 6½ inches................... $ .70
" 200. Size, 9 inches............ .... 1.50
" 18. Dexter with rider, size, 10 inches... 2.00
" 16. Horse with rider, moving........ .... 1.75

BALANCING HORSE WITH RIDER.

No.   Per doz.
294. Balancing Horses, 6 in. $1.85
295. Balancing Horses, large, 9 inches.... 3.75
411. Balancing Animals, large, 9 inches 3.75

ASSORTED TIN WAGONS.

3 to 6 kinds in each dozen.

Per doz.

No. 133. With one horse, size, 7 inches.....$ .35
" 450. With one horse, size, 9 inches...... .67
" 336. With one large horse and driver, size, 14 inches................. 1.75
" 336½. With two horses and driver, size, 14 inches 1.87
" 352. Large Grocery Wagon, size, 17 in.. 3.50

TIN WAGONS WITH FANCY PICTURES ON SIDES.

Per doz.

No. 446. Picture Wagon, 1 horse, size, 8 inches.........$ .67
" 362. Picture Wagon, 2 horse, size, 12 inches.......... 1.75
" 142. Picture Wagon, 2 horse, size, 13 inches.......... 2.00
" 351. Picture Wagon, large, with 2 horses, size, 17 inches................. 3.50

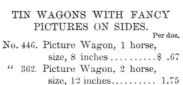

METROPOLITAN FIRE ENGINES.

Per doz.

No. 255. Fire Engine with 2 horses and driver, size, 8 inches............$ .70
No. 358. Fire Engine, large with 2 horses, driver and gong, size, 13½ inches, 1.85
No. 355. Large Fire Engine, with 2 horses, driver and gong, size, 15 inches, 3.50

TIN HOOK AND LADDER TRUCKS.

Per doz.

No. 604. With 2 horses, length, 10 inches... $ .72
No. 540. With 2 horses larger, length, 12½ in. 1.85
No. 354. With 2 horses, larger, " 18 in.. 3.50

TIN EXPRESS WAGON.

No. 353. Tin Express Wagon with two horses and driver, size, 17 in,........... $3.50

TIN CITY HORSE CARS.

No. 230. Horse Cars with 2 horses, size 10 inches ....$ .70
No. 361. Large Cars with 2 horses, size, 16 inches.......... 1.75

TIN LOCOMOTIVES.

Per doz.

No. 313½. Locomotive, size, 7 inches........ $ .72
No. 312. With Gong, size, 10 inches....... 1.85
No. 355. Larger, with Gong, size, 15 inches, 3.50

TIN TRAINS.

No. 428. Patent Galloping Goat and Boy
Leader, with chime bells, 9½
inches. One in a box..per dozen, $3.87

		Per doz.
No. 400/10.	Locomotive, tender and car, 13¼ inches	$ .75
No. 300.	Locomotive, tender and 2 cars, size, 16 inches	1.50
No. 304.	Locomotive, tender and 3 cars, size, 22 inches	1.75
No. 304½.	Locomotive and 4 cars, size 26 in.	1.87
No. 305.	Locomotive, tender and 2 larger cars, 22 inches	1.75
No. 306½.	Locomotive, tender and 4 cars, size, 39 inches	3.75
No. 308.	Large Locomotive and 2 large cars, size, 28 inches	3.88
No. 326.	Very large Excelsior Locomotive and 5 cars, size, 50 inches	7.75

TIN TOYS WITH BELL AND CHIMES.

No. 424½. Special. Extra large new chime
toys, assorted animals, 10 inches
long. Big 25c leader. Assorted
animals, elephant, goat and
horse.................per dozen, $2.00

No. 429. Patent Galloping Camel, Boy
leader and rider, with chime
bells, 9½ inches. One in a box,
per dozen, $3.87

		Per Dozen
No. 185.	Bell toy to push, horse with long stick	$ .75
No. 165.	Platform bell toy, 8 inches	1.50
No. 146.	" " " Dexter, 9½ ins..	1.88
No. 602.	" " " with moving boat, 7 inches	2.00
No. 437.	Butterfly bell toy, (new) 9 inches,	2.00
No. 405.	Double horse bell toy with two bells, 9 inches	3.50

TIN CHIME TOYS..

No. 427. Patent Galloping Elephant with
chime bells, 9½ inches. One in a
box,...............per dozen, $3.50

No. 430. Patent Galloping Horse and Drummer Boy, with chime bells, 9½
inches. One in a box..per dozen, $3.87

No. 434. Sleigh with team, driver and bell,
11 inches. One in a box,
per dozen, $3.50

**LARGE ANIMALS WITH CHIMES AND
BELLS**, on platforms, with malleable fancy wheels.
Three kinds, assorted.

		Per Dozen
No. 213.	Dogs, goats and horses, 14 inches long	$4.00
No. 288.	Large double animals, boy driving, with chime and bells, on platforms, with malleable fancy wheels, 14 inches long	4.00

No. 435. Sparring Goat and Monkey with
Bell, 10 inches. One in a box,
per dozen, $8.50

No. 431. Patent Galloping Boy, two riders
and flags, with chime bells, 9½
inches. One in a box..per dozen, $3.87

FINE MECHANICAL TIN TOYS.

No. 432.   Patent Galloping Mary and her little Lamb, with chime bells, 9½ inches.   One in a box..per dozen, $3.87

No. 433.   Patent Galloping Horse, Jockey and Bell Tree, with chime bells, 9½ inches.   One in a box........ per dozen, $3.87

No. 404.   Hurdle Race, Cantering Horse No. 2, Monkey rider and gong, movable, 12 inches.   One-half dozen in a box..............per dozen, $6.00

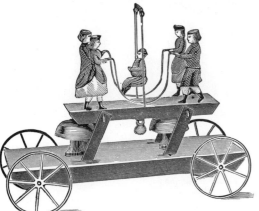

No. 423.   Patent Picnic Party, movable, striking two gongs, 12 inches. One in a box..........per dozen, $6.75

No. 534.   Santa Claus in Sleigh, drawn by two goats, 21 inches.   One in a box........per dozen, $30.00

No. 530.   Patent Mechanical Blondin Velocipede rider, dressed figure, diameter 19 inches.   One in a box...............per dozen, 39.00

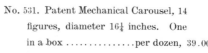

No. 531. Patent Mechanical Carousel, 14 figures, diameter 16¼ inches.   One in a box ....per dozen, 39.00

No. 532. Patent Mechanical Elevated Rail Road, consisting of dummy engine and three cars; diameter 19 inches.   One in a box, per dozen, 39.00

No. 533.   Patent Mechanical Merry-Go-Round; dressed figure turning crank; 19 inches.   One in a box.......... ....per dozen, 45.00

No. 513.   Patent Champion Velocipede Rider, dressed figure; 12 inches. One in a box.............per dozen, 18.00

FINE MECHANICAL TRAINS.

		Per Dozen
No. 22.	Painted. Locomotive, tender and one car. Size, 20 inches long.................	$4.00
No. 15.	Painted. Locomotive, tender and two cars. Size, 33 inches long...............	8.50
No. 20.	Nickel plated. Locomotive, tender and one car. Size, 23 inches long...........	8.50
No. 508/3.	Mechanical Train to run in a circle. Made extra heavy and strong...........	18 00

MECHANICAL TIN TOYS.

Best quality clock winding movements.

		Per Dozen
No. 245.	Mechanical Horse and Rider. Size, 8 inches long....................	$2.00
No. 241.	Mechanical Bakery Wagon, a new toy. Size, 18 inches long.........	4.25

MECHANICAL FIRE ENGINES.

		Per Dozen
No. 94.	With two horses. Size, 10 inches long...........................	4.00
No. 96.	Large size, with two horses. Size, 11 inches long.................	8.50

MECHANICAL LOCOMOTIVES. BEST QUALITY WORKS.

		Per Dozen
No. 89.	Painted; 6 inches long...........	$1.85
No. 90.	Painted; 8 inches long...........	3 75
No. 91.	Nickel plated; 8 inches long......	4.00
No. 92.	Nickel plated; 12 inches long......	8 00
No. 95.	Painted; large; 12 inches long....	8.00

TIN STOVES AND RANGES.

Furnished Complete.

SILVERINE TIN RANGES.

		Per Dozen
No. 8.	Silver embossed, 7 inches high......	$0.72
No. 010.	" " 8 "	1.25
No. 25.	" " 9 "	1 75
No. 50.	" " 11 "	3.75
No. 100.	" " 14 "	7.50
No. 325.	Fancy painted; 9 inches high	1.87
No. 350.	" " 11 "	4.00
No. 1½M.	" " large, "	7.50
No. 1M.	" " larger, "	10.00
No. 0M.	" very large, ...	12 00

DECORATED KITCHENS.

Printed in Bright and Beautiful Colors and in Different Designs.

		Per Dozen
Special.	Painted; 7 inches long...........	$1.87
No. 12.	Painted; large; 9 inches long.....	4.25
No. 21½.	Painted; largest; 10 inches long...	8.00

SILVERINE TIN KITCHENS.

		Per Dozen
No. 415.	Silver embossed; 9 inches long. ...	$ .72
No. 15ˢ.	" " 12 "	1.25
No. 135.	Silver embossed, with pump; 14 inches long..............	1 75
No. 405.	Silver embossed; large; 16 inches long	3.50
No. 403.	Silver embossed; extra large; 19 inches long.....................	4.25
No. 402.	Silver embossed; largest; 20 inches long	8 00

TIN KITCHEN SETS.

IN BOXES.

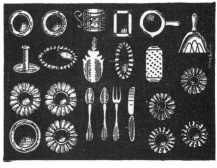

			Per Dozen
No. 4.	13 articles in set		$ .30
No. 5.	16 " "		.35
No. 10.	20 " "		.68
No. 115.	24 " "		72
No. 120.	24 " "		1.37
No. 125.	28 " "		1 50
No. 140.	32 " "		1.87
No. 50.	33 " " all large pieces.....		3.75

TIN WATERING POTS OR SPRINKLERS.

	Per Dozen
No. 1. Painted red or green,	.38
No. 3. Painted red or green,	.70
No. 6. Silverine	.70

SEA SIDE PAILS AND SHOVELS.

No.		Per Dozen
3.	Tin painted Pails and Shovels, with wood handles	.38
5.	Same as before, large size	.65

No. 16. Tin painted Pail, with japanned wood handle, and wood handle shovel .... .75

No. OO-13. Silverine Pails with shovel ..... .38

No. O-2. Same as before, larger .... .65

No. O-5. Extra large size with wooden handle and stamped Jumbo in the bottom .... .75

SEA SIDE SHOVELS.

	Per Dozen
With wooden handle, 16 inches long	.33
Galvanized Shovel, 16 " "	.37

TIN FLUTES AND FISH HORNS.

TIN FLUTES.

	Per Gross
7 inches, plain, 1 gross in a box	$ .80
10 " " ¼ " "	2.00
12 " " ⅙ " "	2.50
14 " " ⅙ " "	3.50
10 " colored, ¼ gross in a box	2.00
12 " " ⅙ " "	3.00
14 " " ⅙ " "	3.75

FINE TIN FLAGEOLETS.

Flageolets with brass tips, finely tuned, 1 dozen in a box, per dozen .... $ .70

TIN FISH HORNS.
Best Quality.

	Per Dozen
10 inches with flange	$ .20
12 " "	.30
14 " "	.35
16 " "	.40
18 " "	.50
22 " "	.85
25 " "	1.50
	Per Gross
6 " colored penny	$ .80
	Per Dozen
10 " " with flange	$ .25
12 " " "	.35
14 " " "	.40
16 " " "	.45
18 " " "	.60
22 " " "	1.00
25 " " "	1.75

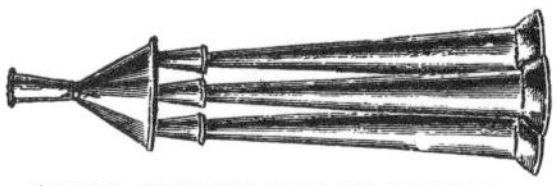

TIN JUBILEE HORNS.

	Per Dozen.
No. 38. 3 Horns connected	$2.00
No. 58. 5 "	4.00

PENNY TIN TOYS.
Extra Large.

Assorted, 1 gross in a box, per gross .... $ .90

TIN PUTTY BLOWERS.

20 inch long, 1 gross in package, per gross... $ .75

TIN KNIVES, FORKS AND SPOONS.

Assorted or separate, per gross .... $.90

TIN RATTLES.

A-B-C Tin Rattles, per gross	$1.50
Star Tin Rattles, per gross	1.75

TIN BANKS.
All Bright Colors.

Drum Bank.    Gothic Bank.

Drum Bank, per dz. 30c. Gothic Bank, per dz. $ .35
Columbus Bank, per dozen .... .35

House Bank.

House Bank, per dozen. .... $ .35

Valise Bank.

Valise Bank, per dozen	$ .35
Trunk Bank, per dozen	.35

Roaming Parrot, 7½ inches long.

Price per dozen .... $ .70

The Roaming Hippopotamus.

Pat. Aug. 16, '87. Pat. applied for

A new toy similar to the Parrot, painted in natural colors with moving jaw .... $ .70

Roaming Turtle, 7 inches long.

No. 661. Made of Tin, beautifully colored—gold, green and blue. Always on the go. Acts like a live turtle. Led by a string. No hunting the Turtle; no winding up; no stopping. With a little practice any one can guide the Turtle by the string like a pet animal; 7 inches long, packed 1 dozen in a package, per dozen .... $ .70

FINE MECHANICAL RAILWAYS.

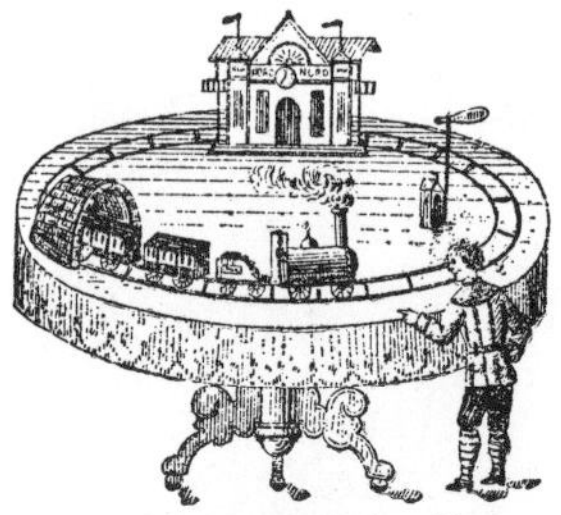

Complete with circular track. The medium and larger sizes have guard houses, stations, tunnels, bridges, etc., making a most interesting and attractive toy, each set packed complete in a box.

No. 64/1. Locomotive and 2 passenger cars, length 11 inches, with circular track 4 feet in circumference, per dozen, $9.00

No. 64/2. Locomotive, tender, 3 passenger cars, train 18 inches long, circular track 4½ feet in circumference .... per dozen, 18.00

NO. 64/3. Locomotive, 3 passenger cars, passenger station, train 18 inches long, circular track 7½ feet in circumference . ... per dozen, 36.00

No. 64/4. Locomotive, tender, 1 baggage and 2 passenger cars, with station and passengers, tunnel, signal station and guardman, circular track 8½ feet in circumference... per dozen, 48.00

No. 64/5. Locomotive, tender, 1 platform, 1 baggage, 2 passenger cars, station and passengers, 2 guard houses and men, length of train 34 inches, with circular track 8½ feet in circumference.. per dozen, 60.00

No. 64/6. Locomotive, tender, 1 baggage, 3 passenger cars, length of train 34 inches, station and passengers, 2 guard houses and men, Mt. Cenis tunnel, circular track 10 feet in circumference... per dozen, 84.00

No. 64/7. Larger and more elaborate in design than the foregoing .. each, 10.00

No. 64/8. A still larger outfit... ....each, 12.00

MECHANICAL RACE COURSES.

These fine toys are exact imitations of a race course, arranged with from 2 to 6 riders, according to size. By a simple mechanism riders are made to race round the track independent of each other, so that it is never certain to tell which one will come in first.

No. 63/1.   2   4   5   6
$9.00   18.00   30.00   42.00   60.00 per dozen

FINE FUR MECHANICAL ANIMALS.

These fine toys jump all around when wound up and afford great amusement.

Per Dozen
No. 940. Assorted Cats, Squirrels, Rabbits
and Dogs......................$ 9.00
No. 942R. Rabbits, large size................ 18.00
No. 942P. Poodle Dogs, large size 18.00

MECHANICAL SHOW PIECES.
FOR WINDOW DISPLAYS.

Per Dozen
No. 23. Skidmore Guard, named after the once famous colored regiment; all figures moving; will run from 1 to 2 hours.....................$48.00
No. 24. Monkey Band, a group of monkeys, part of whom are playing on musical instruments and the others are dancing, all moving in unison.... 48.00

MECHANICAL DANCING FIGURES.

Per Dozen
No. 98. Six different styles. Animals and figures dancing.................. $4.00
No. 99. Three different kinds. Double figures dancing....................... 9.00
No. 100. Dancing Girl..................... 9.00
No. 15. Negro Minstrel.................... 18.00
No. 42. Mechanical Musical Violin Players.
each, $4.00

MECHANICAL MUSICAL SMOKING MEN.
Each, $4.00

SMALL MECHANICAL TOYS.

Per Dozen
No. 401. Mechanical Butcher chopping meat $4.00
No. 402. Mechanical Tramp sawing wood. 4.00
No. 403. Mechanical Carpenter.......... 4.00
No. 404. Mechanical Washerwoman...... 4.00
No. 400. 3 Mechanical Figures connected: a good low price show piece... 8.00

No. 9.—SANTA CLAUS' VISIT.
BEDROOM SCENE.

Stockings on line over fireplace; child (girl) in bed, sleeping peacefully; Santa Claus (loaded with toys) appears from chimney; child is disturbed, raises herself slightly, Santa Claus steps back; child goes to sleep again; Santa Claus enters the room and makes a noise; child sits up in bed and another little girl pops out her head, with a look of delight and wonder; Santa Claus disappears. Very amusing and interesting.

This piece is not only an attraction for store windows, it will also have a large sale for Christmas presents.

No. 9. Bedroom scene. Size, 11x15..each, $3.50
No. 1. Man with Rat................each, 3.50
No. 2. Who Stole the Keyhole?......each, 3.50

No. 18.—SCHOOL.
Size, 18x14x5.   Each, $4.00

No. 14.—THE RURAL COUNTRYMAN.
STREET SCENE.   Size, 18x14x5.   Each, $4.00

This scene represents to you a countryman going along the street. Meeting a friend from the city, and while conversing with him, the bad boys think of plundering his bag, which they cut with a knife, and to their surprise out jumps a dog from the bag, which spoils their little game.

THE FATAL STOGIE.
ROOM SCENE.
Size, 18x14x5.   Each, $4.00

This scene gives to you two friends sitting at a table. One falls asleep while the other is smoking. He also gets drowsy and bobs over, and strikes his friend on the bald spot with his stogie and wakes him up, and he finds his friend sitting erect as though nothing had happened. He then proceeds to give him a piece of his mind. Suitable attraction for a cigar store.

No. 17.—RAG PICKER.
Size, 18x14x5.   Each, $4.00

No. 16.—THE EDUCATED DOG.
Size 18x14x5.   Each, $4.00

The above illustration represents our latest, a very comical show piece. A clown trying to make his poodle stand upon its hind legs, but in spite of all his efforts master poodle was in no humor to obey, until at last the clown struck on the brilliant idea to try him with a sausage, which experiment proves a perfect success.

No. 12.—THE TAILOR.

WORKSHOP SCENE. Size, 18x14x5. Each, $4.00

Fat tailor on bench, sewing; young man at bench, ironing; boy on bench, sewing. Fat tailor sews awhile, then falls asleep. Young man and boy grin and exchange glances. The boy pushes a pin forward slowly and suddenly jabs it into the fat tailor, who wakes with an exclamation of surprise and pain, only to find the young man and boy working like beavers.

This is exceedingly funny, and just the thing for a tailor's window.

STEAM TOYS.

A handsome line of new goods, neatly packed. Full directions in each box.

UPRIGHT STEAM ENGINES.

45/25.	6 in. high, per doz.	$2.00
45/50.	10 in. high with black boiler, extra large	3.75
45/65.	Square shape, 8½ in. high, Russia iron base, very substantially made, per dozen	4.00
45/100.	Same, 11½ inches, per dozen	9.00
46/100.	With brass boiler and glass water tube, 9 inches high. A handsome article, per dozen	9.00
47/50.	Steam Traction Engine, (new), per dozen	3.75
47/100.	Steam Engine with Fountain, throws water from the fountain, (new), per dozen	8.00

FAVORITE STEAM ENGINE.

The Favorite is a model steam engine, complete and perfect, and all its parts are firmly connected, so that it can be readily moved from one place to another while in operation.

The essential parts are as perfect and made as carefully as our larger and more expensive engines.

The Favorite has sufficient power to run small toys.

Richly finished in red and gold colors, per doz.   4.00

WEEDEN UPRIGHT STEAM ENGINE No. 1, NICKELED.

Every engine is thoroughly tested before packing and fully warranted by us.

Each engine is packed securely in a wooden locked corner box, suitable for mailing or expressing.

Full directions for running the engine will be found in each box, with the price of duplicate parts.

Per dozen, $9.00

WEEDEN ENGINE No. 8 (NEW).

Has highly polished brass boiler and walking beam; engine firmly fixed upon a substantial base. The engine has steam chest, cylinder, walking beam, eccentric rod and valves, balance and pulley, all carefully and accurately put together.

Price, per doz., $16.50

UPRIGHT STEAM ENGINE No. 4.

No. 4. Upright Steam Engine, similar to the No. 1, but larger size, with bronze boiler and red painted fire box, governor and fly wheel for attaching belt to, for running small machinery, height, 11 inches, per dozen.....................$15.00

No. 6. Upright Steam Engine, similar to No. 4, one size larger, finished with polished brass boiler and base, having water gauge and glass, governor and fly wheel. Height 12 inches, per doz....$24.00

DOUBLE HORIZONTAL ENGINE No. 12.

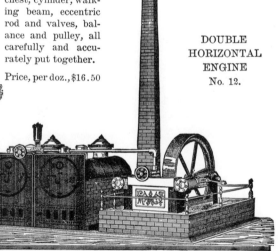

The Double Engine is made up of two complete engines. The boilers are made of polished brass. The boiler frame, engine frame and base are made of Russia iron, and are all substantially put together. The engine is so set that the piston rods and cranks work in opposite directions and furnish an interesting and entertaining illustration of the working power of the Steam Engine. All the parts are interchangeable, and we can always supply duplicate parts.

Price, per dozen $36.00

LOCOMOTIVE AND TRAIN.

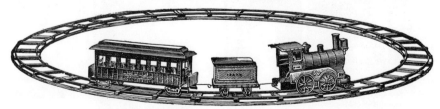

Consisting of a locomotive, tender and car, and track 3½ feet in diameter, made of steel rails and wooden sleepers. Comes in two kinds.

No. 1.	Without track, per dozen	$33.00
No. 2.	Fine with track complete	45.00

THE STEAM FORCE PUMP

is a Steam Engine and Force Pump combined, and in operation gives a good idea of how water is pumped and forced by steam pressure.
Price, per doz.
$8.50

STEAM YACHTS.

Metal Steamboats.

		Per Dozen
46/50.	Hull all nickel metal	$.25
46/100.	Hull painted in colors, with water line, black japanned boiler and awning,	48.50

ATTACHMENTS FOR STEAM TOYS.

		Per Dozen
No. 100/1.	Butcher chopping meat.	$2.00
" 100/2.	Wood sawyer..........	2.00
" 100/3.	Carpenter	2.00
" 100/4.	Washerwoman.........	2.00
No. 160.	Monkey orchestra........	6.00
" 162.	Cobler, extra large.	6.00

STEAM PILE DRIVER.

It is modeled after the Steam Pile Driving Machine, which can be constantly seen at work wherever a dock or wharf is to be built, or foundations for heavy buildings are to be put in.

Price, per dozen............................ $8.50

NEW STEAM AND MECHANICAL NOVELTIES.
Just out.
SINGLE TRACK ELEVATED RAILWAY.
Malleable Iron and Steel.

No. 3. CLOCK MOVEMENT.
Pat. April 11, 1893.

EQUIPMENT—Iron Locomotive, Tender and Passenger Car.

Circumference of track...8 feet 4 inches
Distance from floor to track.. 7½ "
" " " top of arch ....13½ "
Length of Locomotive .... 7½ "
" Tender .... 8⅓ "
" Passenger Car.. 8 "
No. 3. Price, each.. $4.50
No. 4. Double track and double trains running in opposite direction, each.............. 6 75

SINGLE TRACK ELEVATED RAILWAY.
With Trolley Wire and Poles. Malleable Iron and Steel.

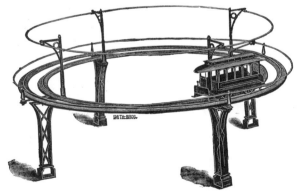

No. 25 MECHANICAL TROLLEY CAR.
Pat. April 11, 1893.

EQUIPMENT—One Model Electric Street Car, with spring motor in car, trolley on roof of car running on trolley wire.

Price, each $4.50

STEAM DERRICK.

The cut represents our new Steam Crane or Derrick, and is a model of the derrick used everywhere for lifting and placing in position heavy blocks of stone, iron, wood, or any heavy material, for loading and unloading heavy cargoes, and for many other purposes.

Price, per dozen............................$8.50

COLUMBIAN WHEEL.

Malleable Iron and Steel.

No. 5. CRANK MOVEMENT.
Pat. Applied for.

Diameter of wheel............. ...14 inches
Extreme height.................. 17 "

This is a well constructed toy throughout—strong and durable. The wheel is stamped from steel, the design of the centre being a six point star, all lines of which are heavily embossed. The axle is of steel. The columns, base, toy men and crank are of malleable iron.

The carriages which are of steel are hung on the brace pieces, and maintain a perpendicular position throughout every point of the revolution of the wheel.

The design of the star is finished in vermilion, while the circle enclosing it, as well as the columns and base are of black. The carriages in which are seated life-like miniature figures show a strong contrast in yellow.

Price, per dozen....................$12.00

No. 6. CLOCK MOVEMENT.
Pat. Applied for.
(SEE CUT ABOVE.)

Diameter of wheel... ....14 inches
Extreme height..................17 "

This toy is of the same construction as No. 5, with the exception of the propelling power, which is clockwork. The movement is very fine in quality and mechanical construction. The frame is nickel plated, thus enhancing the appearance of the toy and robbing it of the machine effect characteristic of mechanical toys.

Finished in black japan, vermilion and yellow.

Price, per dozen...... ....$21.00

No. 7. STEAM MOVEMENT.
Pat. Applied for.

Diameter of wheel...............14 inches
Extreme height..................17 "
L'gth of Horizontal Steam Engine.6 "

No. 7 is of the same construction as No. 5, with the exception of the propelling power, which is steam. The power from the Horizontal Steam Engine is transmitted to an intermediate gear which is accurately calculated to reduce the high speed of the engine to the proper speed for the wheel.

Finished in black japan, vermilion and yellow.

Price per dozen....................$27.00

IRON BANKS AND SAFES.

All the Latest Novelties and Staple Banks.

IRON BANKS.

No. 25. House Bank.............per dozen $ .37

PAVILION BANK.

No. 45. Newest 5c Bank ....per dozen $. 37

No. 225. Special 10c Bank,
per dozen, $ .75

SECURITY BANK.

CUT HALF SIZE.

No. 120. New, finished with handsome gold
top....................per dozen, $1.75

PRESTO TRICK BANK.

This bank contains the novel features of a trick drawer. Press down the button over the front door and the drawer will fly open. Put the coin in and close it. When the button is again pressed the drawer will fly open, but the coin will have mysteriously disappeared.

The money can be removed from the bottom of the bank by means of a lock and key. Handsomely decorated. Packed ½ dozen in a box.

No. 485. Size, 4½ inches high, 4 wide 2½
deep................ per dozen, $1.85

VILLA BANK.—New.

This bank is in the style of a modern country villa, and is very large and showy for the price. Handsomely painted. Packed ½ dozen in a box.

No. 98. Size, 5 inches high, 5 wide, 2¾ deep.
per dozen, $1.85

ADMINISTRATION BANK.

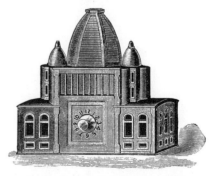

This bank is a very fair representation of the style of the Administration Building of the World's Fair. It has a first-class combination lock and is handsomely finished in white and gold. Packed one in a box.

No. 99. Size, 5¾ inches high, 6 wide, 2½
deep..................per dozen, $4.00

ORGAN BANK.

		Per Dozen.
No. 235.	Organ Banks..	$1.85
No. 116.	" " monkey, with music.................	4.00
No. 119.	Large Organ Bank, monkey, with music.................	8.00

DANCING BEAR BANK.
With Clock-work Mechanism and Chimes.
JUST OUT.

In this bank we have introduced some ingenious mechanism which produces very attractive results. It represents the front of a country house, with an Italian organ grinder and a bear on the lawn. After winding up the mechanism, place a coin in the slot and push the knob in front of the organ grinder, he will then deposit the coin and play the organ, while the bear performs his part. Handsomely painted. Packed one in a wooden box.

No. 132. Size, 6⅞ inches long, 4¾ wide, 5¼ high......per dozen, $9.00

KICKING MULE BANK.

The mule and rider being brought into position, a slight touch on a knob at the base causes the mule to kick and throw the rider over his head, when the coin is thrown from the rider's mouth into the receptacle below. One in a box.

No. 190...per dozen, $8.00

COLUMBUS BANK.—New.

Place a coin in the slot at the feet of Columbus. Press the lever, and as the coin disappears an Indian chief suddenly leaps from his place of concealment in the log, extending the pipe of peace as Columbus salutes him.

The design is of historic interest. On one side, in bold relief, is the ship of Columbus, and on the other a mounted Indian hunter in full chase of buffalo. The bank is entirely and richly finished in bronze of gold, silver and other shades. One in a box.

No. 326..per dozen, $8.00

BASE BALL BANK.

Place a coin in the hand of the pitcher, press the lever and the coin is swiftly pitched. As the batter misses, it is safely deposited by the catcher. The movements of all the figures are very lifelike. Nicely finished in fancy colors.

No. 302................................ ....per dozen, $8.00

EAGLE BANK.

Place a coin in the eagle's beak, press the lever and the eaglets rise from the nest, actually crying for food. As the eagle bends forward to feed them the coin falls into the nest and disappears in the receptacle below. One in a box.

No. 300..per dozen, $8.00

BAD ACCIDENT BANK.

Place a coin under the feet of the driver and press the lever. The boy jumps into the road, frightening the donkey, and as he rears, the cart and driver are thrown backward, when the coin falls into the body of the cart and disappears. Nicely finished in bright colors. One in a box.

No. 321............................per dozen, $8.00

FANCY BANKS AND COMBINATION SAFES.

Half size.

IRON SAFES.

No. 1. Daisy Safe, with lock and key per dozen...$ .37

NATIONAL SAFES.

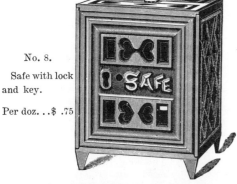

No. 8.

Safe with lock and key.

Per doz...$ .75

YOUNG AMERICA SAFE.

Our Young America is an emblematically engraved safe, representing the four seasons. It is finished in maroon color, relieved with bronze. Packed one-half dozen in a box.

No. 30 ....per dozen, $ .75

COMBINATION LOCK SAFES.
SECURITY SAFE DEPOSIT.

		Per Dozen
No. 75.	Japanned, 3 inches high..........	$1.37
No. 100.	" 4 " "	2.00
No. 200.	" 5 " "	4.00
No. 300.	" 5½ " "	6.50

SECURITY SAFE DEPOSIT.

No. 101. New, 4½ inches high .....per dozen, $1.85

SECURITY SAFE DEPOSIT TOY BANK.
With Silver Plated Combination Lock.

		Per Dozen
No. 400.	Bronzed, with inside cabinet containing two drawers, 6 inches high	$8.00
No. 500.	Large, with fine lock, 8¼ inches high, double combination, contains 3 drawers................	16.50
No. 600.	Nickel Plated Household Security Bank, contains 4 drawers, secured by Yale lock; something useful as well as ornamental....	33.00

ALL NICKEL PLATED SAFES.

With Nickel Combination Lock and Patent Money Guard.

		Per Dozen
No. 75N.	Full nickel plated, 3 inches high.	$1.85
No. 150N.	" " " 4¼ " "	3.75
No. 200N.	" " " 4¾ " "	6.75
No. 300N.	" " " 5½ " "	8.00
No. 401N.	" " " 6 " "	8.50

TRUNK REGISTERING BANK.

This well known bank has been greatly improved and reduced in price to $9.00 per dozen.

LITTLE GEM POCKET SAVINGS BANK.

Cannot be opened until full. For pennies. nickels and dimes.

Per dozen $0.65

IRON STOVES, COMPLETE.

With Stove Pipes and Cooking Utensils.

THE "O. K. No. 2" RANGE. A perfect working toy range. Nickel plated, with polished edges and ornamentation.

Length, 5¼; height, 3⅞; width, 5 inches.
Per dozen.....................$4.00

"O. K. No. 1" RANGE.

Same style as above, larger, length, 6⅝, height, 3⅞ inches, width, 5 inches.
Price, per dozen............... 6.75

THE "I. X. L." RANGE.

Nickel plated with polished edges and ornamentation.

Length, 8¼; Height, 5¼; Width, 5⅛ inches.
Cast iron, fine ground hollowware, kettle, skillet, baking pan, griddle, length of pipe and lifter included. Each range is packed in a paper box.
Price, per dozen...............$ 8.50
THE PET RANGE. 18.00

THE "BABY" RANGE.

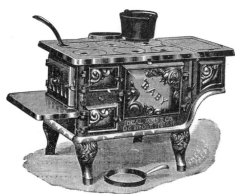

Larger than the Pet Range. Length, 16, height, 9¼, width, 8¾ inches.
Price, per dozen................$24.00

IRON TOYS.

A splendid line of strong durable toys, painted in bright oil colors, a very popular line of fast selling goods.

MODEL PONY CART,

New 25 cent toy; is very handsome and is the only iron horse toy at this price on the market.
No. 500. Price, per dozen................... $1.85
No. 140. Pony cart, larger than above size
Price, per dozen................ 4.00

No. A. Iron Sulky with horse and driver, 9 inches long.
Price, per dozen................ $4.00

No. 48. Flat Wagon with horse and driver, 12¼ inches long.
Price, per dozen................ $4.00
No. 49. Buggy with four wheels and horse and driver, 10½ inches long...... 4.00

No. D. Hansom Cab with horse and Driver, 12 inches long.
Price, per dozen................ $8.50

No. 180. Model Farm Wagon, (with load), 2 horses and driver, 14 in. long.
Price, per dozen................ $8.50

IRON LOADED TRUCKS.

No. 63. One Horse Truck. Length, 15 in.
Price, per dozen...............$ 8.50
No. 62. Two Horse Truck, larger than above.
Price, per dozen............... 12.00
No. L. Two Horse Express Wagon, loaded, large and fine.
Price, per dozen............... 19.50

No. E. English Surrey, (new), 12 in. long.
Price, per dozen................ $8.50

No. 195. Landau with two horses and drivers.
Price, per dozen................$13.50

MODEL SPRINKLING WAGON.

Sprinkles water in a very real manner.
No. 400. Price, per dozen $19.50

STREET CARS.

		Per Dozen
No. 39.	Street Car painted red with horse and driver, 13½ inches long.	$ 4.50
No. 43.	Street Car painted red, larger size, with horse and driver, 19¼ inches	8.00
No. 45.	Street Car painted red, large, with two horses and driver, 18¼ inches long	9.00
No. 46.	Street Car nickel plated, large size, with two horses and driver, 18¼ inches long	12.00

FIRE ENGINES.

		Per Dozen
No. 1000.	With fireman driving 2 running horses, 14 inches long, handsomely painted	$8.50
No. 125.	Nickel Boiler Engine, with fireman driving 2 horses, 19 inches long	18.00
No. R.	Same as No. 125, but with gong and finer finish	19.50
No. RR.	Same as R, but pumps water; is finely finished	24.00
No. RRR.	Very elaborate, with 3 galloping horses, gong, and pumps water	60.00
No. 55.	Chemical Engine, new, 19½ inches long, 2 horses and gong	21.00

HOOK AND LADDER TRUCKS.

		Per Dozen
No. 51.	With fireman driving two running horses, 22½ inches long	$8.50
No. 1010.	Same as No. 51, finer finish	9.00
No. 130.	Same as above, large size, nicely finished, 26 inches long	18.00
No. T.	Very fine finish, with striking gong	19.50

IRON HOSE CARTS.

		Per Dozen
No. 155.	With fireman and running horse, 10 inches long	$4.00
No. 1020.	With fireman and 2 horses and rubber hose	8.50
No. 135p.	Same as illustration, large new galloping horse	8.50
No. SS.	Fine finish, one large horse	13.50
No. SF.	Very elaborate, 2 galloping horses, 16½ inches long	16.50

IRON STEAMBOAT.

No. 64.	Fine Iron Steamboat, 16 inches long	per dozen, $13.50

FIRE PATROL WAGONS.

		Per Dozen
No. 60.	Fire Patrol Wagons, 2 horses, gong and 4 men	$21.00
No. 61.	Police Patrol Wagon, 2 horses, gong and 4 men	21.00

MECHANICAL IRON LOCOMOTIVES.

		Per Dozen
No. MH.	Mechanical Iron Locomotive (illustration is one-third of regular size	$8.50

IRON LOCOMOTIVE AND TENDER.
Not Mechanical.

		Per Dozen
No. 17.	Large	$4.00

LARGE IRON TRAINS AND SEPARATE CARS.

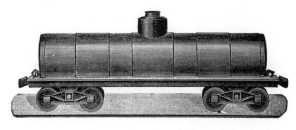

BIG TRAIN, price of each part is given separately.

				Per Dozen
No. 1.	Large Locomotive and tender, 20 inches long			$15.00
No. 2.	Combination Car, 16 inches long			10.50
No. 3.	Passenger Car,	16 "	"	10.50
No. 4.	Freight Car,	13 "	"	10.50
No. 5.	Oil Tank Car,	14 "	"	8.50
No. 6.	Platform Car,	14 "	"	8.50
No. 7.	Caboose Car,	14 "	"	8.50

IRON TRAINS.

IRON FREIGHT TRAINS.

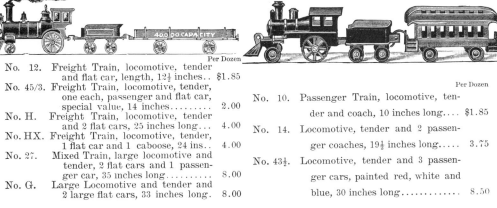

		Per Dozen
No. 12.	Freight Train, locomotive, tender and flat car, length, 12½ inches..	$1.85
No. 45/3.	Freight Train, locomotive, tender, one each, passenger and flat car, special value, 14 inches........	2.00
No. H.	Freight Train, locomotive, tender and 2 flat cars, 25 inches long...	4.00
No. HX.	Freight Train, locomotive, tender, 1 flat car and 1 caboose, 24 ins..	4.00
No. 27.	Mixed Train, large locomotive and tender, 2 flat cars and 1 passenger car, 35 inches long.........	8.00
No. G.	Large Locomotive and tender and 2 large flat cars, 33 inches long.	8.00

IRON PASSENGER TRAINS.

		Per Dozen
No. 10.	Passenger Train, locomotive, tender and coach, 10 inches long....	$1.85
No. 14.	Locomotive, tender and 2 passenger coaches, 19½ inches long.....	3.75
No. 43½.	Locomotive, tender and 3 passenger cars, painted red, white and blue, 30 inches long............	8.50

		Per Dozen
No. 28.	Large Locomotive, tender and large passenger car, size, 27 inches....................	$9.00
No. 20.	Passenger Train, locomotive, tender, baggage car and 2 coaches, length, 40 inches.....	9.00
No. FF.	Large Locomotive, tender and 2 large passenger cars, as illustrated, 44 inches long....	15.00
No. 29½.	Passenger train, locomotive, tender, baggage and 2 passenger coaches, length, 42 ins...	18.00
No. 36.	Vestibule Trains, Blue Line, handsomely painted, locomotive, tender and 2 large passenger coaches, 52 inches long....................................	27.00
No. FFF.	Extra large Vestibule train, finest finish, locomotive and tender, 1 passenger and 1 combination car, length, 60 inches..	60.00
No. 21.	Nickel Plated Passenger Train, locomotive, tender, baggage car and passenger coach, length, 31 inches..	9.00
No. 26.	Nickel Plated Passenger Train, locomotive, tender, baggage car and 2 coaches, length, 41½ inches.....................	13.50
No. 31.	Nickel Plated Passenger train, locomotive, tender, baggage car and passenger coach, larger, length, 42½ inches..	18.00

IRON TOYS.

JACK STONES.

					Per Gross
No. 0.	Jack Stones, 2 gr. in box.09c
No. 1.	"	2	"	.12c
No. 1½.	"	2	"	.14c
No. 2.	"	1	"	.18c

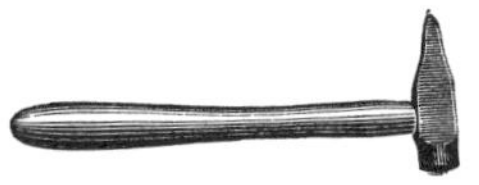

TOY HAMMERS.

		Per Dozen
No. 245.	Copper	$ .20
No. 246.	"	.30
No. 257.	"	.65
No. 15.	Tack, polished.....................	.67

TOY HATCHETS.

	Per Dozen
No. 375.....................................	$ .30
No. 400....................................	.33
No. 425....................................	.37
No. 450....................................	.63
No. 475....................................	.75

IRON PENNY TOYS.

Pick, Shovel, Hatchet, Rake and Hoe.

	Per Gross
Large (assorted, ½ gross in box).............	$ .80
Extra (with wooden handles)................	.85

TOY SAD IRONS.

		Per Dozen
No. 1.	With Stands......................	$ .33
No. 2.	"	.40
No. 4.	"	.67
No. 11.	With wooden handles and stands..	.37
No. 14.	" " " " " ..	.70
No. 25.	Polishing Iron, 1 in a box..........	2.00
No. 30.	" " " " new......	.75

CHIME TOYS.

			Per Dozen
No. 00½.	Chimes on wheels..................		$ .70
No. 1½.	"	"	1.75
No. 2½.	"	"	3.75
No. 3.	"	" very large........	6.00

REVOLVING CHIMES WITH HORSE.

		Per Dozen
No. 4.	Chimes with horse................	$1.75
No. 5½.	" " "	2.00

TUMBLER BELL TOYS, WITH HORSES.

		Per Dozen
No. 10.	Tumbler Bell Toy.................	$1.85
No. 15.	" " " with horse and rider...........................	1.85
No. 126.	Double Chime Bells, with tin horse (new)	$ .75
No. 129.	Same style, extra large...........	2.00

BELL TOYS.

PIG AND CART, with clown driver.

No. 35. Bell Toy, per dozen, $1.85

TRICK PONY BELL RINGER.

Horse swings on the pedestal and rings the bell.
No. 39.............................per dozen, $4.00

DAISY BELL TOY.

Girl with doll on sled, with chimes.
No. 37.............................per dozen, $4.00

"DING DONG BELL."

No. 29.............................per dozen, $4.00

CINDERELLA'S CHARIOT AND CHIMES.

No. 27.........................per dozen, $4.00

TRICK ELEPHANT BELL RINGER.

Half size cut.

Elephant swings on the tub and rings the bell.

No. 40 .... per dozen, $4.00

THE PIG AND COLUMBUS EGG BELL TOY.

Half size cut.

The action of the pig in trying to set the egg on end, and at the same time ring the bell, is a very attractive feature.

No. 41 .... per dozen, $4.00

MONKEY VELOCIPEDE AND CHIMES.

Painted in fancy colors. As the toy is drawn the monkey rider appears to be propelling the velocipede, each revolution of the wheels causing the bell to ring. Height, 8 in.; length, 8 in.

No. 90 .... per dozen, $4.00

CHIME RATTLES.

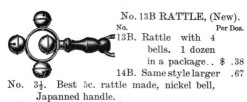

No. 13B RATTLE, (New).

No.		Per Doz.
13B.	Rattle with 4 bells. 1 dozen in a package..	$ .38
14B.	Same style larger	.67
No. 3½.	Best 5c. rattle made, nickel bell, Japanned handle.	
	Packed 1 doz. in a package................	.35

DOUBLE RATTLES.

No.		Per Doz.
6.	Japanned handle. 1 dozen in package....	$ .38
19.	Same style as No. 6, with extra large bells	.75

No.		Per Doz
8.	Double rattle, double ends. Four separate	
rattles.	Packed 1 dozen in a package.......	$ .80

BELLS.

TEA BELLS.

No.		Per Doz.
102.	White metal, black handle 1 dozen in a box........	$ .30
104.	Same style, larger........	.37
10.	Japanned handle. Packed 1 dozen in a package...	.40

NEW TEA BELLS.

No.		Per Doz
93.	Bell Metal, Japanned handle. Height, 5½ inches. The best 10c bell ever offered. Packed 1 dozen in a package........	$ .75
40.	Special Nickel Bell with japanned handle, extra size..	1.65

CALL BELLS.

No.		Per doz.
201.	New style. Nickel plated. The best 10c. call bell ever offered. Packed 1 doz. in a package.....	$ .67

No.		Per Dozen
75.	New style. Nickel Plated Metal base. The best 25c call bell on the market. Packed 6 in a package........	$2.00

BICYCLE BELLS.

No.		Per Dozen
10.	All nickel, special size for 10c....... ...	$ .75
25.	Bicycle Bells, best bell metal. All nickel large size.............................	2.00

PEWTER TOYS.

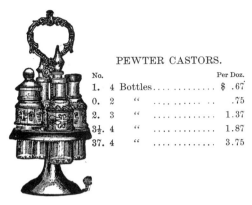

PEWTER CASTORS.

No.			Per Doz.
1.	4 Bottles	....	$ .67
0.	2 "	....	.75
2.	3 "	....	1.37
3½.	4 "	....	1.87
37.	4 "	....	3.75

LARGE PEWTER TEA SETS
in Fancy Paper Boxes.

					Per Dozen
No. 10.	Size of Boxes, 5x6¼ inches	....	$ .72
" 25.	"	"	6x9	"	.... 1.87
" 50.	"	"	8½x13	"	.... 4.00
" 100.	"	"	10½16½	"	.... 7.50
" 150.	"	"	12½x20	"	.... 8.50
" 200.	"	"	12½x20	"	.... 8.50

PEWTER PARLOR STOVES

for doll houses, per
dozen $1.88

PEWTER BASKETS.

		Per Dozen
No. 94	....	$ .20
" 93	....	.35
" 92	....	.60
" 91	....	.70

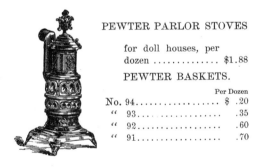

PEWTER BIRD WHISTLES.

		Per Gross
No. 228.	As'td whistles, birds, animals, etc.	$2.00
" 186¾.	Whistling Roosters	3.25
" 185.	Canary Bird whistles	3.75
" 200¾.	Cuckoo whistles	2.00
" 200.	" "	3.75
" 40.	Rooster whistles, small	2.00
" 60.	" " large	3.00

PEWTER KNIVES, FORKS AND SPOONS.

No. 8½.	Knife, fork and spoon, per gross	....	$ .65
" 5.	" " "	cards	4.00
" 52.	Knives, packed solid,	" gross	.65
" 53.	Forks, "	"	...... .65
" 54.	Spoons, "	"	...... .65

METAL WHISTLES AND DOG CALLS.

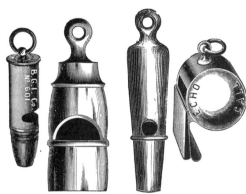

No.		Per Dozen
3.	Metal Dog Calls	$ .25
5.	" " nickel	.35
10.	" " "	.63
25.	Duplex Bicycle whistle with chain	1.25
601.	Cartridge whistle	1.25
602.	Echo whistle	1.50
2.	Universal Bicycle whistle	1.50

CELLULOID WHISTLES.

One Dozen on a Card.

	Per Dozen
Celluloid, small, very salable	$ .75
Same style, medium	1.00
Same style, large	1.50

TOOL CHESTS.

BOYS' TOOL CHESTS.

		Per Dozen
No. A.	Sliding cover box, 5 articles	$ .75
" B.	" " 10 "	1.75
" C.	Hinged " 8 "	1.87

No.		Per Dozen
No. D.	Hinged Cover Box, 10 good tools	$ 3.50
" E.	" " " with extra tray, 10 good tools	4.00
" F.	Hinged Cover Box with extra tray, 19 good tools	7.00
" G.	Hinged Cover Box with extra tray, 23 good tools	8.00
" H.	Hinged Cover Box with brace and bit, special chest, 25 good tools	9.00

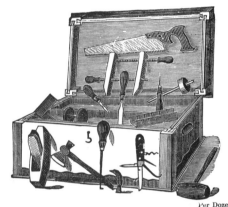

No.		Per Dozen
No. I.	Hinged Cover Box, 27 articles	$15.00
" K.	" " " larger, 28 articles	18.00
" L.	" " " " " 31 " fine tools	24.00
" M.	Hinged Cover Box, very large, 35 articles, fine tools	33.00

VERY FINE TOOL CHESTS.

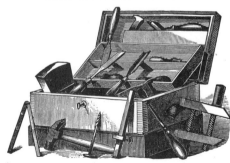

No.		Per Dozen
No. 10.	Fine Walnut Chest with lock, 22 selected tools,	each $ 5.00
" 20.	Superior Walnut Chest, elegantly finished with seperate compartments, 61 best quality tools, each.	12.00
" 30.	Same as No. 20, larger, contains 71 best quality tools	each 15.00

Can furnish finer grades up to $50.00 each.

IRON TOY PISTOLS.

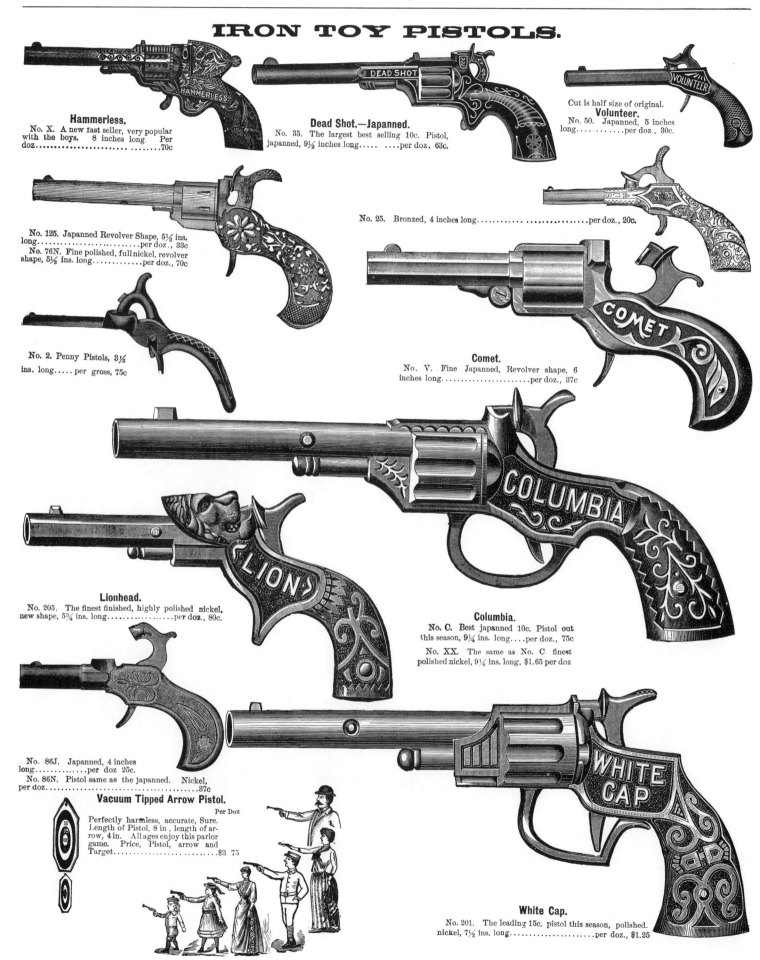

Hammerless.
No. X. A new fast seller, very popular with the boys. 8 inches long. Per doz.....................70c

Dead Shot.—Japanned.
No. 35. The largest best selling 10c. Pistol, japanned, 9½ inches long..... ....per doz. 63c.

Volunteer.
Cut is half size of original.
No. 50. Japanned, 5 inches long...........per doz., 30c.

No. 125. Japanned Revolver Shape, 5½ ins. long......................per doz., 33c
No. 76N. Fine polished, full nickel, revolver shape, 5½ ins. long............per doz., 70c

No. 25. Bronzed, 4 inches long.....................................per doz., 20c.

No. 2. Penny Pistols, 3½ ins. long..... per gross, 75c

Comet.
No. V. Fine Japanned, Revolver shape, 6 inches long......................per doz., 37c

Lionhead.
No. 205. The finest finished, highly polished nickel, new shape, 5¾ ins. long.................per doz., 80c.

Columbia.
No. C. Best japanned 10c. Pistol out this season, 9¼ ins. long....per doz., 75c
No. XX. The same as No. C finest polished nickel, 9¼ ins. long, $1.65 per doz

No. 86J. Japanned, 4 inches long.............per doz 25c.
No. 86N. Pistol same as the japanned. Nickel, per doz.....................................37c

Vacuum Tipped Arrow Pistol.
Per Doz
Perfectly harmless, accurate, Sure. Length of Pistol, 8 in , length of arrow, 4 in. All ages enjoy this parlor game. Price, Pistol, arrow and Target............................$3 75

White Cap.
No. 201. The leading 15c. pistol this season, polished. nickel, 7½ ins. long......................per doz., $1.25

Flags, Paper Lanterns, Balloons, 4th of July Goods.

American Flags.

Best Quality, Printed Muslin, Mounted on Sticks.

No.		size			Per Gross
1.	size	2x3	inches		$0 16
2.	"	2¼x4	"		25
3.	"	4x6	"		37
4.	"	4½x7½	"		50
5.	"	6x9	"		85
5½.	"	7x10½	"		1 50
6.	"	9x14	"		1 88
7.	"	12x18	"		3 00
7½.	"	12x22	"		4 00
8a.	"	14x24	"		4 50
					Per Doz
8.	"	18x27	"		60
9.	"	22x36	"		80
10.	"	27x43	"		1 25
11.	"	30x50	"		1 60
11½.	"	35x55	"		1 80
12.	"	40x66	"		3 00

Foreign Flags.

Best Quality, Printed Muslin, Mounted on Sticks

German, French and Irish.

No.		size			Per Gross
4.	size	5x8	inches		$0 80
5½.	"	7x11	"		1 80
6.	"	9x14	"		2 75
7.	"	12x18	"		4 25
					Per Doz
8.	"	18x27	"		75
9.	"	22x36	"		1 25
10.	"	27x43	"		1 75
11½.	"	35x56	"		3 00

Foreign Flags in sets, of all Nations.

Best Quality, Printed Muslin, Mounted on Sticks.

	Size 12x 8 in.	22x36 in
Per set of 12 pieces, $0 40 set.		$1 25
" 24 " 1 25 "		3 50

Grand Army Flags.

Best Quality, Printed Muslin, Mounted on Sticks.

	Per Doz
Size 24 inches long	$0 65
" 36 "	1 25

Fine Cotton Bunting Flags.

Colors warranted fast. Without Staffs.

	Per Doz
Bayonet, 16 inches long	$0 80
Battery, 3 feet long	1 65

Fine Cotton Bunting Flags,

Colors warranted fast. Mounted on Staffs.

	Per Doz
Battery. 3 feet long	$2 00
Garrison, 4 "	4 50

Sewed Muslin Flags.

Bunting Finished, Fast Colors.

These Flags are all sewed stripes. The stripes are made of fine Turkish red, bunting finished, white, and the Union is printed in fast colored blue.

The material used for these Flags is soft, the colors very brilliant, and they resemble silk flags very closely.

	Each
3 feet long	$0 50
4 "	75
5 "	1 00
6 "	1 25
7 "	1 50
8 "	1 75
10 "	2 50

Best Quality Bunting Flags.

American.

Made of the U. S. Standard Bunting. U. S. Government Regulation size and make. All flags from 6 feet up, have 44 Stars sewed on both sides.

				Each
3 feet long,	2	feet wide		$0 85
5 "	3	"		1 85
6 "	4	"		2 50
8 "	5	"		3 50
9 "	6	"		4 25
10 "	5	"		4 50
10 "	6	"		4 75
12 "	6¼	"		5 50
12 "	8	"		7 50
15 "	8	"		8 00
15 "	10	"		10 00
18 "	10	"		12 00
20 "	12	"		15 00
22 "	14	"		18 00
24 "	15	"		20 00
25 "	16	"		25 00
30 "	15	"		30 00
30 "	20	"		35 00
36 "	18	"		40 00
40 "	24	"		50 00

U. S. Pennants and Plain Burgees with Border made to order.

Estimates furnished on application.

Adjustable Flag Brackets.

Can be adjusted to any angle or position desired. Most complete and handy Flag Pole Bracket made.

No.				Per Doz
7. for Poles with 1¼ inches diameter				$ 9 00
5.	"	1½	"	10 50
3.	"	1¾	"	16 00
1.	"	2	"	18 00

Galvanized Iron Brackets.

For holding Flag Staffs and Poles. Designed for Roofs, Window Sills, Balconies, &c.

No.				Per Doz
9. for Staffs with	½	inch diameter		$ 0 75
8.	"	⅝	"	1 00
7.	"	¾	"	1 20
5.	"	1	"	1 75
4	"	1¼	"	2 00
3. for Poles with 1½		"		2 50
0. for holding 5 Flags with ½ inch diameter staffs				13 50

Flags Staffs with Gilt Spear Heads.

Staffs Blackwalnut Stained.

				Per Doz
5 feet long	⅝	inch diameter		$0 40
6 "	¾	"		50
7 "	⅞	"		75
8 "	1	"		1 00

Flag Poles, Varnished Ash Poles with Ball and Truck.

				Per Doz
8 feet long 1½ inches diameter				$ 4 50
10 "	1½	"		6 00
12 "	1½	"		7 50
14 "	1¾	"		9 00
16 "	2	"		12 00

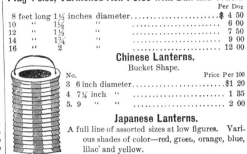

Chinese Lanterns.

Bucket Shape.

No.		Price Per 100
3 6 inch diameter		$1 20
4 7¼ inch "		1 35
5. 9 " "		2 00

Japanese Lanterns.

A full line of assorted sizes at low figures. Various shades of color—red, green, orange, blue, lilac and yellow.

Ball Shape.

	Price per 100
7 inch diameter	$3 50
8 "	4 50
10 "	5 00

Oblong Shape.

7 inch diameter	3 00
8 "	4 00
10 "	5 00
12 "	7 00

Fancy Shape, Assorted.

8 inch diameter	6 50
10 "	9 00
12 "	15 00

The New Excelsior Montgolfier Balloons.

With an entirely new device to prevent the paper from taking fire. The inflater is so arranged that it concentrates the flame to prevent its coming into contact with the paper of the Balloon. The simplest and most perfect method of protecting it from burning, requiring no adjustment. A splendid article for public and private display. Are packed assorted colors and tints, and are provided with our new Inflating Attachment, which renders them easy to fle successfully. No alchohol or other material is required to inflate them—it being only necessary to ignite the attachment

	Per Doz			Per Doz
6 feet circumference	$0 88	15 feet circumference		$3 00
8 " "	1 25	20 " "		4 00
10 " "	1 50	25 " "		6 00
12 " "	2 50	30 " "		8 00

Chinese Bombs.

For Paper Caps.

	Per Gross
Double Face	$3 75

Blank Cartridge Pistols.

	Per Doz
Magic	$1 50

Paper Caps.

One Gross small boxes in a wooden box.

	Per Gross Boxes
Best round cut, 50s	$0 16
Mammoth, 15s	45
" 50s	1 75

Iron Cannons,

Mounted on Wheels.

No.			Per Doz
20.	6 inches long		$2 00
22.	7½ "		4 00
13.	10 "		9 00
15.	12½ "		14 00
16.	15 "		20 00

Brass Cannons.

Mounted on Wheels.

No.			Per Doz
1. Artillery, 6 inches long			$4 00
2. " 8 "			8 50

Fire Cracker Cannons.

Breech Loading, Mounted on Wheels.

No.		Per Doz
1. Artillery, 6½ inches long, for No. 1 Cannon Crackers		$2 00
20-1. Artillery, 9 inches long, for No 1 Cannon Crackers		4 00
30-2. Artillery, 16 inches long, for No 2 Cannon Crackers		9 00

TORPEDOES, FIRE CRACKERS, FIREWORKS. Special Price List Mailed on Application.

MARBLES and TOPS.

BEST QUALITY AND LARGEST SIZES.

Our Marbles are full count and full sizes.—Beware of marked-up numbers and short counts.

MARBLES.

China Marbles or China Allies.

No.	WITH STRIPES.				Per 1000
oo.	painted, 100 in a Box	-			$0 35
o.	" " "			-	48
1.	" " "		-	-	70
2.	" " "		-	-	1 00
3.	" " "		-	-	1 50
4.	" " "			-	2 00
5.	" 50 "		-	-	2 50
6.	" 25 "		-	-	3 50
7.	" 25 "		-	-	5 00
8.	" 25 "		-	-	7 00
0.	glazed, 100 "		-	-	1 00
1.	" " "		-	-	1 40
2,	" " "		-	-	2 00

Common or Gray Marbles.

			Per 1000
in Bags of 1,000	-	-	$0 50

Polished or Colored Marbles.

			Per 1000
in Bags of 1,000	-	-	$0 60

Bowlers.

			Per 100
Gray, 1½ inch, in Bags of 100,	-		$0 65

Imitation or Burnt Agates.

No.				Per 1000
oo.	100 in a Box	-	-	$0 70
o.	" "	-	-	90
1.	" "	-	-	1 15
2.	" "	-	-	1 50
3.	" "	-	-	2 00

Glass Marbles.

No.	ALL FINE.		Per 1000
oo.	Fine, 100 in a Box	-	$1 50
o.	" " "		1 80
1.	" " "		2 00
2.	" " "		2 70
3.	" " "		3 70
4.	" " "	-	5 00

Glass Marbles—Continued

No.	ALL FINE.			Per dozen
6.	" 1 Doz. in a Box	-	-	$0 12
7.	" " "		-	18
8.	" " "		-	25
9.	" " "		-	35
10.	" " "		-	60
11.	" " "	-		85
12.	" " "		-	1 00

Glass Marbles with Figures.

No.			Per dozen
6.	Figures, 1 Doz. in a Box	-	$0 25
7.	" " "		30
8.	" " "		35
9.	" " "		50
10.	" " "		75

Glass Glimmers or Brandies Marbles.

No.			Per 100
o.	100 in a Box	-	$0 18
1.	" "	-	20
2.	" "	-	27

Opal Glass Marbles.

No.			Per 100
o.	100 in a Box	-	$0 24
1.	" "	-	30
2.	" "	-	45

Ballot Marbles.

			Per 100
White Glass, 100 in a Box	-	$0 25
Black Glass, "	-	25

Real Agate Marbles.

	25 IN A BOX.		Per 100
I,	Flints or gray Agates	-	$2 00
1½.	" "	-	3 00
II.	Carnelian or red Agates	-	3 00
III.	" "	-	5 00
IV.	" "	-	8 00

WOODEN TOPS AND TOP CORDS.

No. 2-0. Boxwood Top. — No. 3. Boxwood shape Top. Painted. — No. 5. Boxwood shape Polished and Striped Top. — No. 4. Lignum vitae Top. — No. 5. Whip Top Painted. — No. 7. Boxwood shape Polished, Striped and Gilded Top. — No. 4. Boxwood Top.

Bulk Peg Tops.

Stained Boxwood shape, in Bulk.

					Per gross
No. 3	-	-	-	-	$0 50
" 5					72
" 6	-	-	-	-	90

Jersey Lily Tops.

Boxwood shape, without heads, stained; in Bulk.

				Per gross
No. 3	-	-	-	$0 50
" 3 Polished	-	-	85

Polished Peg Tops.

		Assorted Colors.	Per gross
No. 3.	½ gross in a Box		$0 85

Polished and Striped Peg Tops.

Boxwood shape.   Assorted Colors.

					Per gross
No. 3.	½ gross in a Box,		-		$1 35
" 5.	¼ " "				2 25
" 6.	¼ " "		-		2 80
" 7.	¼ " "		-		4 00

Columbia Boxwood Tops.

NEW.

		Per gross
1 gross in box		$0 80

Boxwood Peg Tops.

No.	Assorted Colors.		Per gross
Special, 1 gross in a Box		-	$0 85
0	½ " "		1 50
1	½ " "		2 50
2	½ " "		3 50
3	¼ " "		4 25
4	¼ " "		7 00

Lignum vitae Peg Tops.

Boxwood Shape.

No.			Per gross
2.	½ gross in a Box	-	$4 00
3.	¼ " "		6 00
5.	¼ " "		9 00

Top Cord.

No.	1 Gross in Package.			Per gross
1.	3½ feet long	-	-	$0 20
2.	4 "	-		27
3.	4½ "	-		35
4.	5 "	-		40
5.	5 " heavy	-		50
6.	6 " extra heavy	-		55
7.	6½ "	-	-	60
8.	6½ "	-	-	70
9.	7 "	-	-	80

Whip Tops.

Assorted Colors, stained, in Bulk.

					Per gross
No. 3	-	-	-	-	$0 50
" 5	-	-	-	-	75

SPRING TOYS
AND
NOVELTIES.

Return Balls.

No. 2.
Polished and Gilded Retu·n Ball.

No. 4.
Painted Return B·ll.

No. 5.
Polished, Striped and Gilded Return Ball.

WITH RUBBER ELASTIC AND RINGS.

No.			Per gross.
2.	Painted, ⅓ gross in Box	.	$0 60
4.	" ½ "		70
2.	Mottled, ½ gross	. .	85
4.	" ½ "	.	1 55

Jumping Ropes.

No. 1.
Jute Jumping Rope.

No. 3.
Jute Jumping Rope.

No. 4.
Colored Jumping Rope.

Jute Ropes.

No.			Per doz.
1.	Stained handles, 6 ft. long	.	$0 20
2.	" " 6½ "	.	30
3.	" " 7 "	. .	40
4.	" " 7 "	.	63
5.	" " 8 "	.	70

Stained Ropes.

10.	Colored handles, 6 ft. long,	.	25
30.	" " 6½ "		37
40.	Fancy " 7 " "		70

Wire Chain Jumping Ropes (New).

			Per doz.
W 50,	With Colored handles,	- -	$0 72

HOOPS.

Packed 1 Gross of 12 different sizes.

No.			Per doz.
36.	Ash, 22 to 32 inches, .	. .	$0 35
37.	" 36 to 44 " .	.	67
38.	" 36 to 48 "	.	1 25
320.	Painted, with Bells, 28 to 36 in.		1 75

STAR HOOPS.

Star Hoop, stained, Red Star on stained wood centre, Small Bells.

No.			Per doz.
2.	Sizes 26 to 30 inches,	- -	$2 00

Princess Hoops.

Hoop is made entirely of wood, painted red, 20 inches in diameter. Two tuned gongs ring constantly as Hoop is pushed.

No.			Per doz.
3.	. . . . . .	.	$2 00
4.	. . . . .	.	4 00

Fancy Rolling Hoops.

No.			Per doz.
5.	Small, 15 inches in diameter, with 24 inch handles, . . .		$1 88

New Patent Pushing Hoop,
WITH CHIME.

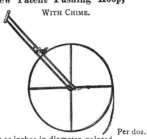

No.			Per doz.
6.	Hoop 13 inches in diameter, painted red, 24 inch Ash handle, . .		$1 88

Barnum's Calliope Cart.

A handsome 2-wheel Cart, with a set of chimes, which make a pleasant musical sound when the cart is set in motion.

No.			Per doz.
1.	. . . .	.	$2 00

Patent Roller Chime.

This is a set of chimes arranged in a finely decorated barrel with a handle, which when drawn strikes several notes, making a very good imitation of a set of chimes.
26 inches long, - - - per dozen, $4 00

Rattler Chimes (New). Per doz.

An entirely new musical toy with chimes and colored pictures, - - - - $2 00

Boys' Horse Reins.

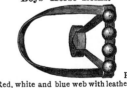

No.			Per doz.
A	Red, white and blue web with leather belt, 1 bell, - - - -		$0 37
47	Red, white and blue web, 2 large bells and leather belt, - - -		70
I U	Red, white and blue web, with 1 large chime bell, - - -		75
2 D	Fancy striped web, with 2 heavy bells, - - - -		2 00
35	Fancy striped web, with 2 heavy bells, - - - -		2 00

Boys' Horse Reins—Continued.

No.		Per doz.
25	Fine, heavy web, with leather belt and three large bells, - - -	1 88
31	Fine, heavy web, fancy leather belt, with 6 large bells, - - -	3 75
80	Fine, heavy all red web, with 3 large chime bells, - - - -	4 00
1 F	Fine, heavy fancy web, with 3 leather straps and 10 large bells (packed each in a box), - - -	8 00

Whips and Switches.

No.			Per doz.
29	Switch, Loop on handle,	- per doz.,	$0 20
33.	" with whistle,-	- - -	30
6.	" Jockey head,	- - -	33
9.	" Ring lash,	- - -	37
40.	" with handle, ring lash,	-	63
21.	Whip, leather lash,	- - -	75
22	" Straight, fine quality,	-	75
48.	" Riding, fancy,	- -	1 38
790/15	" Assorted, 12 on a card, 50 inches long,	- - -	85
790/25	" Assorted, 12 kinds on a card, 56 inches long,	- - -	1 75

Kites.

No.				Per gross.
1.	Paper, assorted colors,	-	-	$0 75
2.	" " "			80
3.	" " "			1 00
4.	" " "			1 35
5.	" " "			3 00

Japanese Bird Kites.

Small,	-	-	-	-	-	-	per 100, $
Medium,							
Large,	-	-	-	-	-	-	-

Columbia Parachute. (NEW.)

This toy can be carried in the pocket and is ready to fly at any moment.

A toy that will have an enormous sale during the coming spring and summer season.

Packed three dozen in a box, with show cards. Price, per dozen, 75 cents.

Bean Shooter.

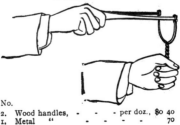

No.				Per doz.
2.	Wood handles,	-	-	$0 40
1.	Metal "	-	- -	70

CROQUET, SUMMER GAMES AND SPORTING GOODS.

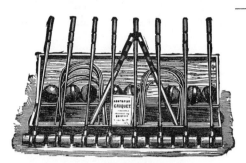

Croquet.
STANDARD SIZES, BEST QUALITY.

No.		Per Doz. Sets.
A	Eight ball, hard wood, full set, full size, in hinged covered box, 6 sets in a crate...	$ 7 50
1	Eight ball, hard wood, full set, and full size, balls and mallets varnished, in hinged covered box, packed 6 sets in crate....	9 00
3	Eight ball, hard wood, full set, balls and mallets striped and varnished, in hinged lock corner box, packed 6 sets in crate...	12 00
4	Eight ball, hard wood, full set, balls and mallets ash handles, extra striped, and varnished, fancy striped stake, packed 6 sets in crate...	18 00
5	Eight Ball, polished rock maple, ladies' set, fancy shaped mallets, ash handles, large fancy turned and striped stake, packed 6 sets in crate.....	20 00
6	Eight ball, new design, polished rock maple set, mallets 6 inches long, with ash handles. Special wickets and sockets. Large fancy stakes, painted in fine style,	24 00
8	Eight ball, patent finish set, mallet heads 7 in. long with professional handles, choice selected maple balls, large stakes patent arch sockets,	24 00
10	Eight ball, Club set, mallet heads 8 in. long, short professional ash handles, patent arch sockets, large fancy stakes. Mallets and balls made of selected rock maple—the best set that can be made of native wood,	30 00
12	Eight ball Club set. Mallet heads 8 inches long, with short professional ash handles, large fancy stakes. Mallets and balls made of selected apple wood,	36 00
15	Four ball. Club set, selected Turkey boxwood, mallet heads and balls. Painted with colors that will not fade. Elegantly finished. Tournament wickets and sockets. A fine set for presentation.	72 00

Grace Hoops.

No.		Per doz Sets.
813	Polished sticks with velvet covered Hoops, in sets of 2 Sticks and 2 Hoops, on a neat card...	$2 00

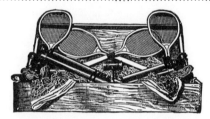

Combination Sets of Summer Games.

No.		Per Doz.
5-25	Containing Whip Top, Jumping Rope, Cup and Ball, Pop Gun, imitation rosewood...	$ 2 00
5-50	Containing Cup Ball, Whip Top, Whip, Spring Feather Ball Cup, Shuttle Cock, Jumping Rope, white enameled wood...	4 00
5-75	Containing 2 Grace Hoops and Sticks, Cup and 2 Balls, Jumping Rope, Spring Battledore. Cup and Shuttle Cock. white enameled wood, larger size...	6 00
5-100	Containing Battledore, Cup and 3 Shuttle Cocks, Jumping Rope and 2 Tennis Rackets...	8 00
5-200	Contains Jumping Rope, 2 Grace Hoops, 4 Sticks, 2 Tennis Rackets, Shuttle cocks and Cup, extra large pieces, very fine...	18 00

No.		Per Doz.
897	Battledores, Shuttle Cocks, in Sets of 2 Rackets, 2 Balls...	$2 00
898	Same as before, extra size...	3 75

Wooden Dumb Bells.
BEST QUALITY ROCK MAPLE, POLISHED.

Weight.	Per Pair.
½ lb....	$0 20
1 "	30
2 "	45
3 "	50
4 "	60

Iron Dumb Bells.
Made on most approved models, covered with black Japan. Special rates made to Gymnasiums on large orders.

Weight,	2 lbs.	3 lbs.	4 lbs.	5 lbs.	6 lbs,
Per Pair,	16c.	24c.	32c.	40c.	48c.
Weight,	7 lbs.	8 lbs.	10 lbs.		
Per Pair.	56c.	64c.	80c.		

Indian Clubs.
BEST QUALITY ROCK MAPLE, POLISHED.

Weight.		Per Pair.
1 lb....		$0 25
2 "		30
3 "		45
4 "		60
5 "		75
6 "		85

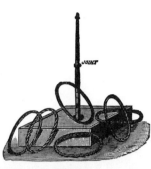

Ring Toss for Out of Doors and Indoors

No.		Per Doz.
2000.	Imitation Walnut, varnished, 3 covered rings...	$2 00
2011.	Put up in a lock corner wooden Box, with 5 posts, new style...	3 75
2012B.	Chestnut box, has 8 rattan hoops wound with fancy colored webbing...	8 00

Boxing Gloves.
STANDARD QUALITY.

No.		Per Set of 4 Gloves.
0	Boys' Chamois...	$1 00
01	" All Kid, white...	1 25
02	Men's All white Kid, in boxes...	1 63
32	" All Kid, open Finger and Pad...	1 88
42	" " with Tan Palm...	2 12
B	" " " " laced...	2 50
C	" " English, black palm...	2 75
40	" Gold Tan, Toe Pad ...	3 00
72	" Fine White Kid, gymnasium, welted all around...	3 73

Rubber Foot Balls.
BEST QUALITY—WITH BRASS KEYS.

No.			Per Dozen.
1,	6 inches in Diameter...		$ 4 50
2.	7	"	5 50
3.	8	"	7 00
4.	9	"	8 50
5.	10	"	9 00
6.	11	"	10 50
Extra Keys...			35

Rugby Foot Balls.
OVAL SHAPE, BEST INDIA RUBBER BLADDER, WITH OUTSIDE LEATHER.

Case,			Each.
No. 3	22 inches Circumference...		$2 25
" 4.	24 "	"	2 50
" 5.	27 "	"	3 00
" 6.	30 "	"	3 50
" 7.	33 "	"	3 75

American Rugby Balls. (Red Rubber.)
SOMETHING NEW—MADE ONLY IN REGULATION SIZE.

	Each.
No. 5...	$1 25

Foot Ball Inflators.

	Per Dozen.
Brass...	$8 00
Rubber...	4 00

Iron Quoits.

Weight.	Each.
1 lb...	$0 06
2 " ...	10
3 " ...	18
4 " ...	25

SAIL AND STEAM BOATS.

Imported Sloops.

No.		Per Doz.
1596-2	Painted red, with black waterline, 9 inches long	$ 37
1595-9	Same Style Boat, 11 inches long, with anchor	75
1542-1	Red Painted and varnished, carved out, with anchor, 10 inches long	75
1508-0	Red Painted Boat, carved out with seat and painted deck, 8 inches long	85
1525-2	Copper Painted Bottom, black waterline, wire rail, painted deck, metal keel and rudder, 11 inches long	1 88
1650-1	Similar Style better finished, with 3 sails, iron keel, 10½ inches long	2 00
1702-0	Fine Red Painted and Varnished, with black waterline, rudder and centerboard, 11 inches long	2 00
1702-2	Same Style as 1702-0, 14 inches long	4 00
1702-4	Same Style as before, 16 inches long	8 75
1639-2	Fine Painted Boat, Hollow, with hatch to open, railing, chain and anchor, 13 inches long	8 00
1493-3	Fine Painted and Varnished, hollow with hatch, hinged mast, 15 inches long	9 00

Imported Schooners.

No.		Per Doz
1613-1	Copper Painted, black waterline, fancy brass rail, 10 inches long	$2 00
1495-2	Fine Red Painted and Varnished, black waterline, iron keel, 11 inches long	2 00
1528-4	Same Style as before, extra size 14 inches long	4 00

American Sloops.

International and American Yacht Club Boats are made under the supervision of an experienced seaman, and their design and sailing qualities are perfect.

Inches.		Per Doz
18		$3 75
22		8 00
24		9 00
26		12 00
28		15 00

American Schooners.

Inch.		Per Doz.
18		$ 3 75
20		7 00
22		8 00
24		9 00
26		12 00
28		15 00
30		18 00
33		21 00

Three Mast Schooners, (new.)

Inch.		Per Doz
24		$12 00
26		15 00
28		18 00
30		21 00
33		30 00

Metal Steamboats.

No.		Per Doz
846-50	A Fine Nickel Boat, with painted black smoke stack, rudder, runs by steam, 12 inches long	$4 25
846-100	Fine Painted Boat, with awning on deck and all attachments, 18 inches	8 50

BASE BALLS.

Spalding's Base Balls.

BOYS' SIZE, EACH BALL IN A BOX.

No.		Per Doz.
13	Rocket	$ 45
9B	Boys' Lively	75
7B	Boys' League Junior, Horsehide	2 00
11	Boys' Bouncer, all rubber inside	2 00

REGULATION SIZES, EACH BALL IN A BOX.

| 8 | Eureka | $ 75 |
| 6 | Victor | 1 50 |

FOLLOWING ALL HORSEHIDE.

7	Boys' Favorite	2 00
5	King of the Diamond	3 75
3	Amateur	6 00
2	Professional	8 00
0	Double Seam	12 00
1	Official League	12 00

Base Ball Bats.

SPALDING'S TRADE MARKED BATS.

No.		Per Doz.
54	Maple, 26 to 28 inches	$ 38
53	" polished, 28 to 32 inches	75
56	" stained and polished, with gold stripes, 28 to 32 inches	75
2X	Antique Ash	2 00
0XB	Boys' Axle Tree	2 00
0X	Men's Axle Tree	3 75
000	Wagon Tongue Ash League Bats	8 00

Celluloid Balls.

VARIEGATED MARBLEIZED COLORS.

These handsome goods are new. They are very light and do not break. Bounce readily. Very desirable for young children, as they cannot destroy anything.

No.		Per Gross
605-1	1 inch, 1 gross in a box	$ 90

No.		Per Doz.
605-5	2 inches, 2 dozen in a box	$ 30
605-6	2¼ " 2 " " "	37
605-10	3 " 1 " " "	67
605-25	4 " ½ " " "	1 50

New Striped Celluloid Balls. (New.)

Look like billiard balls. Very bright and attractive colors.

No.		Per Doz.
606-10	2½ inches, 1 dozen in a box	$ 75
606-25	4 " ½ " " "	2 00

Columbus Celluloid Balls. (New.)

Very handsome balls in assorted colors, with pictures of the World's Fair buildings and Columbus' portrait.

No.		Per Doz.
607-20	3 inches, 1 dozen in a box	$1 50
607-25	3½ " 1 " " "	1 75

The World Celluloid Ball.

This ball has the entire map of the World on its face. It is an exact imitation of a globe, instructive as well as amusing. Entirely new.

No.		Per Doz.
608-25	3½ inches, ½ dozen in a box	$1 75

RUBBER BALLS AND TOYS.

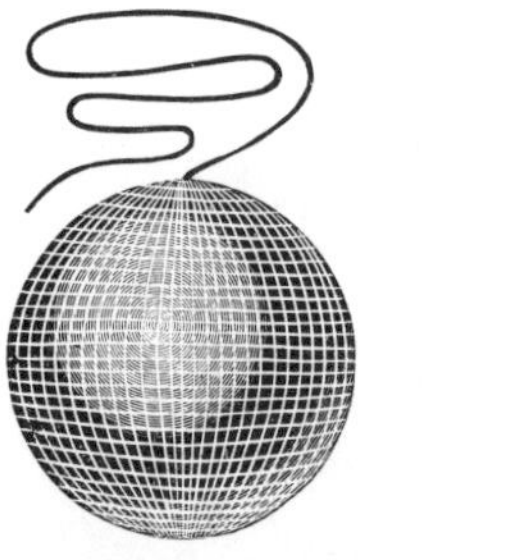

Knit Worsted Return Balls.

No.		Per Doz.
75,	Very showy toy, to each ball is attached an elastic cord. Assorted colors. 1 dozen in box.	$ 35
168,	Knit worsted balls in fancy colors. 4 inches in diameter. 1 dozen in box.	75

Kid Parlor Balls.

No.		Per Doz.
15,	The balls are covered with fine colored kid leather, stuffed with cotton, 2¼ inches in diameter. One dozen in box.	65
25,	Same as before, 4 inches in diameter. Half dozen in a box.	1 75

Newest Rubber Novelties.

Inflated Balloon Balls, entirely new.

No.		Doz.
156,	Balloon Balls, 4 inch, ½ dozen in box; colors, red and silver; bounce fully 10 feet	$1 85

Rubber Baby Rattles, with bells and with bone ring on the end of handle.

No.		Doz.
612,	1 dozen in a box	$1 85

Rubber Baby Rattle, dressed in worsted, with fancy hat and bells. A very attractive article.

No.		Doz.
613,	1 dozen in a box	$1 88

Helen's Babies. (New.)

A Rubber Baby with little doggies in its lap.

No.		Doz.
137,	½ dozen in a box	$1 88

Regular Line of Rubber Balls and Toys.

NO. 40

White Bat Balls.

No.	Diameter.	Per Doz
5	1½ inch,	$0 20
10	1⅝ "	24
15	1¾ "	30
20	1⅞ "	36
25	2 "	42
30	2¼ "	60
40	2½ "	75
45	2¾ "	1 00
5 in bulk	per gross,	2 00

White Inflated Balls.

No.	Diameter.	Doz.
105	1⅝ inch	$ 33
110	1¾	38
115	2 "	40
130	2½ "	75
155	3 "	1 50
175	4½ "	2 00

Red Inflated Balls.

132	2½ inch	$0 75

Solid Rubber Balls.

No.	Diameter.	Doz.
5	1½ inch	$0 25
10	1⅝ "	30
15	1¾ "	36
20	1⅞ "	40
25	2 "	45
30	2¼ "	70
35	2⅜ "	80
40	2½ "	1 00
45	2¾ "	1 25
Jack Stone Ball	per gross	75

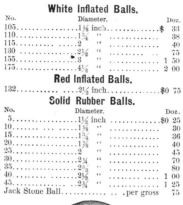

133.

Fancy Colored Inflated Balls.

No.	Diametet.	Per Doz.
113	1¾ inch	$0 40
133	2¼ "	75
149	3 "	1 25
163	4 "	2 00
193	5½ "	4 00

NO. 2

Columbia Inflated Rubber Balls.

WITH VIEWS OF WORLD'S FAIR BUILDINGS.

No.		Per Doz.
1	3½ inches,	$1 88
2	5 "	3 75
3	7 "	8 50

15

Colored Musical Fluted Balls.

No.	Diameter.	Per Doz.
15	1¾ inch	$ 38
25	2 "	50
35	2½ "	75
45	3 "	1 25
55	3½ "	2 00

Red Balloon Balls.

	Per Doz.
3½ inch diameter	$1 88
5 " "	3 50

Rubber Balloon Whistles.

No.			Per Gross.
1	Assorted colors,	small penny size	$0 85
45	" "	medium	2 50
50	" "	large	3 75
60	" "	extra large	4 25

102

No.		Per Doz.
96.	Newfoundland Dog, 8 inches long. Each one in a box	4 00
97.	Pug Dog, 7 inches long. Each one in a box	4 00
98.	Cat, 8 inches long. 1 in a box	$4 00

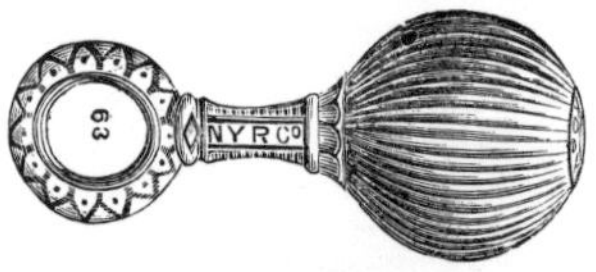

India Rubber Rattles.

No.		Per Doz.
63.	Globe shape, short ringed handle	$0 75
94.	Fancy shape, with long handle	1 00
11.	Dumb-bell shape	1 13
1 to 6.	Assorted long barrell, fancy heads, and other fancy shapes, with long ringed handles	1 12

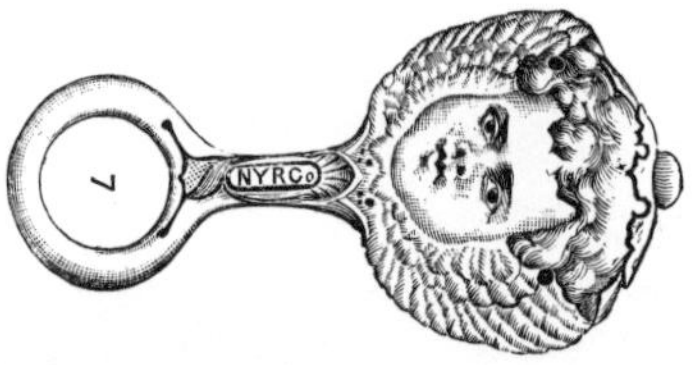

7 to 9.	Assorted Baby Faces, with short ringed handles	$1 25

83

India Rubber Toys with Voices.

No.		Doz.
00.	Assorted Boys and Girls, 3 inches long.	$0 70
8.	Assorted Animals	75
7.	" Boys and Girls. 5 inches long.	1 25
6.	Assorted Figures, 5 inches long	1 75

89

No.		Per Doz.
99.	Chickens	$0 75
54.	Assorted Soldiers, 4½ inches long	1 25
9.	Zuaves and Chinese	2 00
86.	Roly Poly Babies	1 88
10.	Assorted Animals	2 00
11.	" Cats and Dogs	2 00
106.	Cat in Boot	2 00
107.	Dog in Boot	2 00
109.	Cat in Basket	2 00
112.	Doll in Slipper	2 00
121.	Dogs, Lions, Goats, etc. ½ doz. in box	3 75

Rubber Teething Rings.

No.		Per Doz.
1.	White	$0 25

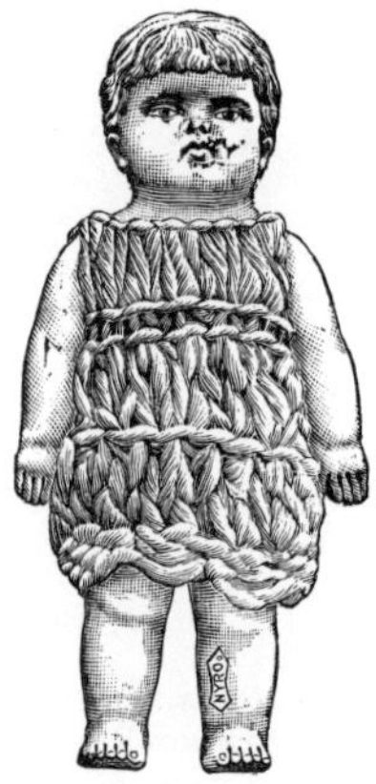

74 D

India Rubber Dolls.

No.			Per Doz.
83.	Babies, 3 inches long		$0 38
4.	" 4½ "		75
76.	" 5 "		80

N.Y.R.Co. 113.D

Rubber Dolls with Knit Worsted Dresses.

No.		Per Doz
74D.	Fat Babies, 5½ inches long	$2 00
65D.	" 7½ "	4 00
85D.	" 10½ "	8 50
113D.	Girls, 7 inches long	2 00
117D	" 9 "	4 00
118D	" 13 "	8 50

PRINTING PRESSES.

	Per Dozen
Boss, complete, with type and ink roller.....	$9.00
Pansy, " " " " " "	15.00

BALTIMOREAN PRINTING PRESSES.

All the Baltimorean Presses are put in a neat box.

No. 4. HAND INKING PRESS.

Will print a form 1½x2⅔ inches. Weight of press and outfit 4 pounds. Price of press with roller and outfit, including one font of type, 25 blank cards, ink and furniture.

Per dozen $10.00

No. 5. HAND INKING.

Will print a form 1¾x3¼ inches. Weight of press and outfit 7 pounds. Price of press with roller and outfit, including one font of type, 25 blank cards, ink and furniture.

Per dozen..........................$15.00

No. 9. SELF INKING.

Will print a form 2½x3¼ inches. Weight of press and outfit 15 pounds. Price of press with one roller and outfit of one font of type, 50 blank cards, ink and furniture.

Each................................$3.50

No. 10. SELF INKING.

Will print a form 2½x4 inches. Weight of press and outfit 18 pounds. Price of press with one roller and outfit of one font of type, 50 blank cards, ink and furniture.

Each................................$5.00

No. 11. SELF INKING.

Will print a form 2½x4 inches. Weight of press and outfit 20 pounds. This press is extra finished, with two rollers and outfit of two fonts of type, 50 blank cards, ink and furniture.

Each................................$7.00

TOY TRUNKS.

FOLIO TRUNKS.
With Trays.

			Per Dozen
No. 2.	12 inch	....	$3.88
No. 2.	14 "	....	4.75
No. 2.	16 "	....	5.00

SARATOGA TRUNKS.
With tray and hat box.

			Per Dozen
No. A.	12 inch	....	$6.00
No. A.	14 "	....	6.75
No. A.	16 "	....	7.50
No. A.	18 "	....	8.00
No. A.	20 "	....	8.50

SARATOGA TRUNKS.
Full furnished inside.

			Per Dozen
No. 12.	12 inch	....	$8.00
No. 12.	14 "	....	8.50
No. 12.	16 "	....	9.00
No. 12.	18 "	....	10.50

SARATOGA TRUNK.
Covered with crystal zinc, full finish.

ZINC (Saratoga).

			Per Dozen
17/12 inch	....		$13.50
14 "	....		15.00
16 "	....		16.50
18 "	....		18.00

WOODEN TOYS.

ALL THE LATEST AND BEST NOVELTIES,

No. 1 Piano.   No. 1 Wash Set.   No. o Log Cabin Bank.   No. 1 Churn.   No. 1 Cup & Saucer.   No. 1 Bureau.   No. 1 Pastry Set.

The above illustrations are less than one-quarter actual size.

PENNY TOYS:

No. 1 Piano.	No. 1 Wash Set.	No. 0 Log Cabin Bank.	No. 1 Churn.
No. 1 Bureau.	No. 1 Pastry Set.	No. 1 Pails.	No. 1 Baby Carriages
No. 1 Wardrobe.	No. 1 Buffet.	No. 1 Rolling Pin.	No. 1 Organ.
No. 1 Step Ladder.	No. 1 Bell Bow and Arrow.	No. 1 Wagon.	No. 1 Musket.
No. 1 Row Boat.	No. 1 Squirt.	No. 1 Sled.	No. 1 Cricket.
No. 1 Fire Engine.	No. 1 Buggy.	No. 1 Locomotive.	No. 1 Pea Shooters.
No. 1 Wm. Tell Guns.	No. 1 Louis XIV Furniture.	No. 1 Queen Anne Furniture, assorted.	

1 gross, assorted, in a box......................................	$ .90
Either of above numbers, separate..........................per gross	.90
Imported Penny Wooden Toys, 12 kinds assorted................ "	.96

LOG CABINS.

No. 5 Log Cabin.

The No. 5 and No. 10 Log Cabins are tastefully made in different colored woods.

The No. 1 comprises forty-two pieces that can be put together or taken apart at pleasure, making a very entertaining toy. Each set of the No. 1 is in a wooden packed box 9¼x7¾x2¾ inches.

	No. 5	No. 10	No. 1
Size set up......	4x4¼x3	6½x7½x5	7½ inches
	35c	72c.	$2.00 per doz.

WOOD PASTRY AND KITCHEN SETS.

No. 1 Wood Pastry Sets, board, roller and bowl.

Price, per dozen.... ....$ .35

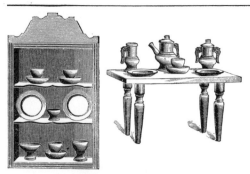

No. 1 COMBINATION WOOD TEA SET.

Nicely finished in shellac. Can all be packed in box which forms the cupboard and table. A very attractive and salable toy. Price, $1.85 per dozen.

	Per Dozen
No. 1. 7 pieces	$2.00
No. 2. 8 pieces, large set	3.75

WAGONS.

No. 2 Wagon.

No. 2	3	4
5	5¼	6 inches wide
9	10½	12 inches long
37c	60c	70c per dozen

SLEDS.

No. 2 and No. 3 Sled.

No. 2	3	4
3½	5½	8½ inches wide
11¾	15	21½ inches long
37c	70c	$1.85 per dozen

FANCY WOODEN TOYS.

All the Latest Novelties and Best Sellers.

FANCY WOODEN STEAM BOATS.

No. 71¼. "CITY OF CHICAGO."

(PATENTED.)

A complete little steamboat. Size, 13 inches long, 7¾ inches high.

Price, per dozen..................$1.85

No. 32½. "CITY OF NEW YORK."

A beautiful boat similar in design to No. 52. Has a variety cargo of freight, all parts of which pack inside of boat. Size 20 inches long, 9½ inches high.

Price, per dozen $3.75

No. 37. U. S. CRUISER.

As every one is interested in our new navy, we have selected one of the U. S. Cruisers for a model, and the boat is as exact a copy of the original as it is possible to make a toy, and cannot fail to please the boys, being finely lithographed and rigged with masts, smoke-stacks, ventilators, etc., as shown in the picture, furnished with 4 small boats, four cannon and a crew of six sailors, all packed in the body of the boat.

The circular, which accompanies the boat gives full directions for setting up, also a description of the vessels actually in commission in the United States Navy at the present time, which makes this an instructive, as well as an amusing toy. When set up, it is nearly 32 inches from stem to stern and 26 inches to top of flag-staff.

Price, per dozen.................$8.50

No. 52. STEAMBOAT "CITY OF BOSTON."

The largest of a new and handsome line of steamboats. Lithographed and ornamented in the most attractive colors. It has three decks, pilot house, walking beam, three flags, full crew, and a cargo representing the products of foreign countries, and is a marvel of beauty. All parts pack inside of boat. Size when set up, 26 inches long, 12 inches high.

Price, per dozen.................$8.50

No. 173. STEAMSHIP "NEW YORK."

This is the most elaborate toy yet made. It is as near a perfect model of the great ocean steamer whose name it bears, as it is practicable to make of wood. It is 42 inches long and the masts are 22 inches in height, and furnished with cloth sails both square and schooner rigged. It has eight small life boats which hang upon davits, and the hurricane deck is furnished with miniature ventilators, and has imitation glass skylights upon the saloon deck. Inside are packed 12 blocks with puzzle pictures representing two naval scenes. The rigging is of black cord and a diagram with printed directions for setting it up accompanies each toy, which for complete protection are packed each in a strong pasteboard box.

Price, per dozen $13.50

THE BLUE SQUADRON.

Sloop Glorianna. Schooner Marguerite. Schooner Sachem.

Three handsome full rigged boats, all with cloth sails that can be hoisted, and a full set of picture blocks in the two larger sizes. These are lithographed in a blue shade and made in a strong and substantial manner. Size of Glorianna, 21 inches long, 18 inches high; Marguerite, 29 inches long, 22 inches high; Sachem, 45 inches long, 29 inches high. Put up with full directions for setting up

		Per Dozen
No. 158.	Gloriana	$1.85
" 159.	Marguerite	3.75
" 160.	Sachem	8.50

WOODEN RAILROAD TRAINS.

No. 111. STOCK AND LUMBER TRAIN.

Lithographed to represent an ordinary freight train. One car filled with 7 alphabet blocks and the other with sticks representing lumber. Size set up, 18x3¼ inches.

Price, per dozen $1.85

No. 149. TRAIN FOR LINCOLN PARK.

A new and complete passenger train consisting of engine and a modern baggage and parlor car, lithographed in a delicate shade of blue, and contains six blocks with two puzzle pictures. Train 18 inches long. A beautiful toy and one that any child would like to run to the Exposition at Lincoln Park, as its name implies.

Price, per dozen $1.85

No. 61. N. Y. CENTRAL R. R. TRAIN.

Consists of Engine, Express and Passenger cars. Train 28 inches in length, with passenger car filled with blocks, containing the whole alphabet, with puzzle pictures on the reverse side, the whole lithographed in bright and attractive colors.

Price, per dozen..............................$4.00

No. 134. VESTIBULE TRAIN (Chicago Limited).

A very perfect model of a vestibule train of three Pullman palace coaches, containing 18 alphabet and picture blocks, and drawn by a locomotive with tender, of accurate design. All lithographed in bright colors and packed each in pasteboard box. Length of train 4 feet.

Price, per dozen $8.50

Nos. 174 and 184. THE EMPIRE STATE EXPRESS.

If the children have been pleased with our past efforts in the line of railroad trains, they certainly must be more than pleased with these two beautiful toys. We never before have made a train of so perfect a model, both as to detail and proportion as in these toys. The locomotive is patterned after one of the most modern designs and the cars are nearly a perfect imitation of the luxurious Pullman coaches now in use, both in color and shape, having the three-wheeled trucks and furnished with iron rails and imitation brakes. Are respectively 3½ and 5 feet long.

No. 174. Composed of engine, tender and one coach. Put up in a pasteboard box.
Price, per dozen $8.50

No. 184. Composed of engine tender and two coaches. Put up in a pasteboard box.
Price, per dozen..............................$13.50

No. 138. GRAVEL TRAIN.

A perfect gravel train consisting of locomotive and three cars, each manned by detachable brakemen. Size, 24 inches long.
Price, per dozen..............................1.85

No. 147. COLUMBIAN OPEN HORSE CAR.

This popular and attractive toy is nearly a perfect imitation of the open horse car, complete in all its parts. Curved dashboards front and back, imitation of striped curtains around the sides, seats with reversible backs, conductor and driver, and drawn by a span of dapple gray horses, in fact a toy that any child would prize very highly. Length 28 inches. Packed in paper box.

Price, per dozen..............................$8.50

WOODEN WASHING SETS.

LAUNDRY SETS WITH FOLDING TABLE.

Per Dozen

No. 5. Small Toy Set, with 6 inch tub, wringer, folding bench and ironing board combined, and pail.... $1.85

No. 10. (Small.) This set consists of 7 inch tub, lacquered hoops; infant pail, lacquered hoops; hardwood wringer, rub-a-dub wash board and clothes dryer, with the ironing board. Size set up, 13 in. high, 19½ in. long............. 4.00

No. 15. (Large.) This set includes 10 in. tub, lacquered hoops; toy pail, lacquered hoops; infant pail, lacquered hoops, hardwood wringer, "A-B-C" wash board, large clothes dryer and box of toy clothes pins, besides an ironing board, painted in bright red and yellow. Size set up, 16¾ in. high,9¼ in. wide, 22½ in. long........................ 8.50

No. 78¼. UNIQUE WASH SET.

This set has a new feature in clothes dryer, which is attached to tub, being quickly opened or closed. It is, like the others, the strongest and most durable wash set ever placed on the market. Size, 10 inches long, 7 inches high, 5 inches wide.

Per dozen $1.85

No. 34½. UNIQUE WASH SET.

Similar in design to No. 78¼. Consists of new style laundry tub, wringer, wash board, basket, clothes reel and pins. All parts pack inside of tub. Size, 18 inches long, 7 inches wide, 9½ inches high; reel, 11 inches high.

Per dozen $4.00

No. 56. Entirely new and original in design, consisting of latest style laundry tub, wringer, wash board, pail, basket and double line clothes reel with clothes pins. All parts pack inside of tub. Compact, attractive and strongly made. Size, 27 inches long, 13 inches high, 9 inches wide; reel, 16 inches high.

Per dozen $8.50

WASH SET.

Per Dozen

No. 25.   Wash Set, consists of wash tub, clothes wringer, clothes horse and wash board $2.00

No. 50.   Wash Set, consisting of tub, wringer, wash board, clothes horse and pail ; packed in strong paper box 4.00

No. 100. Wash Set, consisting of cedar tub, wood pail, clothes wringer, wash bench, wash board, scrub brush, rolling pin, starch bowl, pie board and clothes pins and clothes horse; packed in strong paper box 8.00

No. 2.   LAUNDRY SET.

A cute and complete little wash set, consisting of wash bench, 6 inch tub, wringer, wash board and clothes dryer. An outfit sure to please every little girl. Size of bench, 9 inches long, 4¾ inches high; nicely wrapped.

Per dozen $1.85
No. 3.   Larger size, per dozen...... 4.00

No. 141.   LADDER TRUCK.

An attractive and accurate model of our modern ladder trucks, manned by driver and steering man, drawn by two prancing horses, and containing 12 lithographed alphabet and picture blocks and two 20-inch ladders. All lithographed in bright colors. Size, 30x5½x12 inches. Each packed in paper box. This dashing toy with our fire engine and hose carriage makes a complete fire department for the boys.

Per dozen.......................... $8.50

No. 55.   SUNBEAM ALPHA-BET TOWER.

A handsome Alphabet Tower, new, this season, standing 45 in. high ; lithographed in rich designs and colors, showing pictures and the entire alphabet on its sides. It is surmounted by a Japanese lady carrying their famous parasol, which, by turning a crank, is made to revolve. At the base and in front is an opening, showing a comical picture, and by the use of a ball with rubber attached can be knocked away and another picture instantly appears. There are 12 changes. It is made in two sections, making it easy to set up. This is certainly one of the most attractive and instructive towers made.

Per dozen. $8.50

No. 70¼.   MONKEY RACE AND BLOCKS.

A very amusing toy, representing an exciting race between comical monkeys riding on the backs of dogs, mounted on wheels, and having a set of alphabet and picture blocks, the whole lithographed in handsome colors.

Per dozen $1.85

No. 69¼.   MUSICAL CART.

One of the most pleasing toys made. By simply drawing the cart beautiful musical tones are produced. Truly a marvel of melody. Simple in construction, strongly made and very handsome. Size, 6¾x5¼x5 inches.

Per dozen $1.85

No. 66¼.   MOTHER GOOSE REVOLVING TOY.

One of the latest and most attractive wood novelties of the season. By winding the cord around the spool on end of cylinder and pulling same (as in spinning a top), it causes the cylinder to revolve rapidly. The goose will then commence to walk, going quite a long distance in a lifelike and natural manner. Handsomely lithographed in colors and well made. Two securely packed in a box. Size, 14 inches long, 9 inches high.

Per dozen $1.85

No. 32¼.   LEAP FROG TARGET.

Consists of two elegant figures, one of which is hidden from view, and by hitting the target with the ball attached to the elastic is made to jump upon the shoulders of the other figure.

Sure to make everyone laugh. The bright and attractive colors and comical attitudes are sure to produce extreme merriment.

Per dozen $1.85

No. 31½.   MONKEY RACE AND BLOCKS.

A pleasing toy, similar in design to No. 70¼, and equally as handsome, but larger. Filled with alphabet and picture blocks.

Per dozen $3.75

No. 49.   MAGIC FIRE ESCAPE.

The latest novelty in the toy fire department, consisting of truck, span of horses, driver and eight firemen. By turning a crank a fireman is hoisted to a height of 38 inches from the floor. It is very attractive, and a model of ingenuity and simplicity. Would make any boy happy to possess one. Each packed in a box. Is very easy to set up. Handsomely lithographed, and is one of the leading toys of the season. Size, 34 inches long, 38 inches high.

Per dozen...... ....$8.50

No. 65¼.   FIRE ENGINE AND BLOCKS.

A neat, little fire engine, highly ornamented, having a set of picture and spelling blocks packed inside with driver and engineer, drawn by a pair of spirited horses. Length, 14 inches; height, 5 inches. Nicely wrapped.

Per dozen...............$1.85

No. 28½. FIRE ENGINE AND BLOCKS.

A handsome and perfect imitation of a modern fire engine, filled with alphabet picture and spelling blocks. An elegant pair of horses are attached, together with driver and fireman, giving it a most life like appearance. Size, 21 inches long, 7 inches high.

Per dozen.. $8.50

No. 140. WOOD STEAM FIRE ENGINE.

A perfect model of the modern steam fire engine, drawn by two life-like horses and manned by engineer and driver. The boiler contains a set of 12 alphabet and picture blocks. This toy is lithographed throughout in bright and natural colors. Size, 24x6x10 inches. Each toy packed in paper box. This excellent toy, with our ladder truck and hose cart, makes a complete fire department for any wide-awake boy.

Per dozen.. $3.75

THE WORLD'S NOAH'S ARK. (New.)
Nos. 170, 171 and 172.

The World's Noah's ark illustrated above is designed to imitate in shape the original Noah's ark, except in the fancy turn in the bow and stern. The colors, of which a rich red predominates, are so combined as to make it very attractive. Each size contains a number of animals, with Noah and family, cut out of tough fibre board and mounted on wooden bases.

			Per Dozen
No. 170.	12x5x3½ inches		$1.85
No. 171.	16x6½x4	"	3.75
No. 172.	23x7½x5	"	4.50

AMERICAN AND EUROPEAN MENAGERIE.
Nos. 167, 168, 169.

Every boy likes a caravan or menagerie, and here we have the very thing in three sizes to meet the wants of all; 2½, 3 and 5 feet long. The cages are very perfect, each having genuine wire fronts and backs, with wild animals and their keepers inside. All lithographed in attractive shades, and each packed in paper box.

					Per Dozen
No. 167.	Size,	8½x4 inches,	3 cages		$1.85
No. 168.	"	10½x5	"	3 "	3.75
No. 169.	"	14½x7½	"	4 "	8.50

No. 175. U. S. ARTILLERY.

As a companion toy to our No. 154 fort we offer our new U. S. Artillery, the two making a set that will please any boy. It is composed of a 9 inch cannon with carriage, a caisson with three artillerymen seated thereon, four wide-awake horses, two of which are mounted by a soldier each, the whole forming a perfect piece of artillery 38 inches long. Lithographed in bright colors and put up in paper box.

Per dozen... $8.50

No. 154. FORT COLUMBIA.

We offer a very attractive fort with a tower at either end and guarded by sharpshooters and gunners with several small cannons, and a large cannon 9 inches long upon a truck, with which to bombard the fort. The front of the fort is divided into three panels, which drop as soon as the towers are shot away, disclosing a fine battle scene. The whole lithographed in bright colors. Size, 20x18¼ inches.

Per dozen.. $8.50

No. 74¼. THE SOLDIER'S CAMPAIGN.

Consisting of 16 elegantly uniformed soldiers, 4 musicians and one flag, all mounted on wheels. Will march obliquely when desired.

Height of soldiers, 5 inches, full length, 13½ inches, width, 7 inches. Packed in nice box with bright label.

Per dozen.................... $1.85

No. 35¼. MILITARY PARADE.

Has a force of 28 handsome soldiers arranged in 5 companies, commander and 2 aides, and carries 6 flags, all mounted on wheels. Can be made to march obliquely when desired. Height of soldiers, 5½ inches. Comes packed in nice box, 20 inches long, 10 inches wide, with attractive label.

Per dozen.. $3.75

No. 54. ROYAL GUARDS.

A new and imposing military batalion of 33 men arranged in 5 companies, with band, 2 cannon, 2 gunners and commander, carrying 8 handsome flags, the whole mounted on wheels. The soldiers are made to march company front, or right and left oblique. The companies can be used separate or together, as desired. The soldiers are 7½ inches high, wearing rich brilliant uniforms. Full length of toy, 42 inches, width, 12¼ inches. Very easy to set up. Packed in nice box with elegant label.

Per dozen.. $8.50

No. 48. U. S. POST OFFICE.

An entirely new and original toy, affording children a most pleasing and instructive entertainment. Ten each of Toy Postal Cards and envelopes accompany P. O. It is elaborately lithographed and ornamented in handsome style and colors, has glass front and 56 letter boxes, is strongly made, and comes nearly set up. Each one carefully packed in a box. Size, 23 inches long, 19 inches high.

Price, per dozen.................$8.50

No. 31. DOLL HOUSE.

Large and elegant, finely lithographed, to represent a modern house of two rooms. Size of house, 8¾ inches long, 7 inches wide, 16 inches high, with ell 7¾ inches long, 4 inches wide, 11 inches high; or can be used as two separate houses. The ell and roof are nested in the main part and make a neat package.

Price, per dozen $8.50

No. 33. CINDERELLA COACH WITH BLOCKS.

A fine representation of an elegant Coach and Driver and Footman, drawn by a pair of Horses, all lithographed in bright colors and highly ornamented. The coach contains a set of blocks illustrating the story of Cinderella and the Glass Slipper, so familiar to all children. Length of coach, 16 inches, height, 11½ inches; Length of coach and horses 27 inches. Packed in a box.

Price, per dozen.................$8.50

No. 55¼. SANTA CLAUS AND SLEIGH.

A beautiful little team, showing Santa Claus on his annual Christmas trip. Finely lithographed in bright colors together with an elegant set of twelve alphabet picture blocks, making a most attractive toy. It is strongly made and nicely wrapped. Length 12 inches.

Price, per dozen. $1.85

No. 33½. BROWNIE BAND.

The latest style of Brownie Ten Pins, consisting of 10 musicians, with instruments, showing comical expressions and occupying laughable attitudes, each standing 8 inches high, together with three polished balls, all packed in a handsome labeled box.

Price, per dozen $3.75

No. 59. BROWNIE BAND.

A new and unique style of Brownie Ten Pins, comprising 10 grotesquely attired musicians showing the most mirth-provoking expressions and attitudes. Each standing 12 inches high, together with three handsomely striped and varnished balls, all packed in a nice box, 13 inches long, 11 inches wide, with a handsome label.

Price, per dozen $8.50

No. 34¼. "HERE YOU GO" MARBLE GAME.

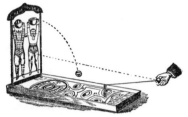

An original design for a marble Game. By drawing back the ball with elastic attached and letting it shoot forward, it strikes one of the acrobats, who immediately throws on the board the glass agate, which rolls into numbered holes. It is handsomely lithographed, printed and colored. Size when set up, 16 inches long, 5 inches wide, 11 inches high. All parts pack into base.

Price, per dozen.................$1.85

No. 22. JOLLY MARBLE GAME.

The most interesting and entertaining Marble Game yet produced. Truly a work of art and ingenuity; handsomely lithographed, nicely made and easily set up. Captivating to both old and young. It is intensely fascinating to watch the figures as they pass a marble from one to another in a very natural manner until it rolls on the board and is counted. One never tires playing the game. Nothing has been spared to make it the leading marble game. Size when set up, 19¼ inches long, 8½ inches wide, 21 inches high. Each game enclosed in a box.

Price, per dozen $8.50

No. 107. BILLY-GOAT EXPRESS.

Lithographed in bright colors. Filled with hard wood architectural building blocks with new designs. Size set up, 15x4½x4½ inches.

Price, per dozen.................$1.85

No. 108. PONY CART.

Made up and lithographed in bright colors to imitate the village cart, now so much used. Contains 12 lithographed alphabet blocks with cut up picture on the reverse side. Size set up, 14x5 inches. Retails for 25 cents.

Price, per dozen........ ....$1.85

No. 180. LUMBER WAGON.

This amusing little toy represents a perfectly proportioned low gear, such as seen upon the roads for drawing heavy loads, drawn by a pair of bay horses with driver and loaded with timber. Lithographed in bright colors, making a most desirable toy. Length 17 inches.

Price, per dozen.................$1.85

No. 51. HUMPTY DUMPTY TARGET.

A new and comical novelty, full of fun and excitement, representing a clown's head set in a base with hinged hat, ears, mouth and tongue. The object is to throw one of the rubber balls at the mouth, knocking it out and causing the tongue to appear; also to knock the ears and hat back, counting the number on part hit. Lithographed in bright colors. Comes packed one in a box. Size, 24 inches high, 13 inches wide.

Per dozen........................... $8.50

No. 52½. SPELLING ROCKER.

A new feature for chairs. A large selection of words for children to learn to spell, together with a pleasing design in rich colors. Height, 14 inches.

Per dozen............. $1.85

GRANDMA AND GRANDPA ROCKERS.
For Dolls.
No. 72¼ and No. 73¼.

An original and pleasing feature in rockers, consisting of handsomely designed chairs represented as being occupied by grandma and grandpa, who present a very lifelike appearance. They come set up and packed two in a box, one of each kind. Size, 13 inches high, 6 inches wide.

Per dozen...................... ... $1.85

No. 40¼. DOLL'S EASY ROCKER.

A large and elegant rocker, finished in handsome colors to represent rich plush upholstering. Is suitable for a very large doll. The posts have turned ornaments. Size of chair, 13 inches high, 6½ inches wide.

Per dozen........... $1.85

No. 5?. TRICK MULE.

The very latest and most pleasing novelty of the season is the famous trick mule. The performances of the clown and mule are always regarded by the children as the center of attraction in all shows. For a boy to own one and be showman would be a grand event. By rolling a ball against the bull's eye the mule instantly kicks up, throwing the clown over its head. It is very showy, strong, durable and easy to set up. It is 21 inches high, 20 inches long and mounted on wheels. Comes nicely packed, one in a box.

Per dozen........................ $8.50

No. 50¼. DOLL'S RIBBON BACK CHAIR.

Finely designed and substantially made, representing a very desirable pattern. The posts are tipped with ornaments. Comes knock-down. Size 12½ inches high, 6 inches wide.

Per dozen...... ..... $1.85

No. 60¹ DOLL'S STORY HIGH CHAIR.

A pleasing representation of rich upholstering, and on one side of back which is reversible, a picture with an appropriate story. Height, 22 inches. Packed in a neat box.

Per dozen.............. $1.85

No. 61¼. DOLL'S STORY ROCKER.

The back and seat same as the story high chair. 13½ inches high. Comes knock-down and wrapped.

Per dozen............. $1.85

No. 25¼. DOLL'S ALPHABET ROCKER.

Extra large size, pleasing and instructive. Has the alphabet lithographed in bright colors on the back and seat, together with other handsome designs, fancy turned posts, arms and legs. Suitable for a very large doll. Comes knock-down, neatly wrapped. Size of chair, 17 inches high, seat, 7½ inches square; length of rockers, 13 inches.

Per dozen..................... ..... $3.75

No. 49¼. DOLL'S ROUND BACK SETTEE.

A dainty design and a handsome piece of furniture, the seat and back representing a rich plush upholstering. The panels are connected with each other and to the corner posts by fancy turnings. Packed knock-down, but are very easily put together. Length, 11½ inches, height, 9 inches.

Per dozen........... .... $1.85

No. 24½. DOLL'S PLUSH HIGH CHAIR.

An elegant chair of extra size. The back, seat and step are lithographed in imitation of rich plush of red, blue and gold color, with a newly designed and handsome picture set in back. Has fancy turned arms and posts, tipped with pretty ornaments, and is in every respect a very strong and handsome chair. Comes knock-down, packed in a nice box.

Per dozen $3.75

No. 37¼. DOLL'S DAISY SWING.

The handsomest and most complete swing made. Is provided with reclining chair or seat in which the doll can take any position desired. It is printed, made and finished in the most attractive manner. Size when set up, 21 inches high, 9 inches wide.

Per dozen............. $1.85

FOLDING OAK BEDSTEADS.

Closed.

		Per Dozen
No. 1.	Bedstead, 20 in. long, 10½ in. wide, 12 in. high...............	$2.00
No. 2.	Bedstead, 26 in. long, 12½ in. wide, 16 in. high..........................	4.00
No. 3.	Bedstead, 26 in. long, 13 in. fancy head board.....	9.00
No. 4.	Bedstead, 28 in. long, 13 in. finely carved head board...............	15.00

FOLDING OAK CRADLES.

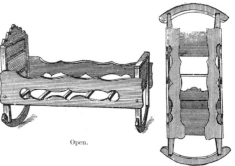

Open.

Closed.

		Per Dozen
No. 1.	Cradle, 20 in. long, 10½ in. wide, 14 in. high..........................	$4.00
No. 2.	Cradle, 26 in. long, 12½ in. wide, 18 in. high..........................	4.25
No. 1½.	Special, 20 in. long, 10½ in. wide.....	2.25

NO 47¼. CRADLE.

A handsome little cradle, with new design for head and foot, lithographed in imitation of best style of furniture. Has fancy sides with rounded tops to posts. Well made and finished. Knock-down and nicely wrapped. Size, 16 in. long, 7¼ in. wide, 9½ in. high.

Per dozen $1.85

		Per Dozen
No. 21¼.	Chestnut cradle, same style as 47¼, size, 19 in. long, 9¼ in. wide, 12 in. high	$3.75
No. 42.	Fine cradle, handsomely finished, size, 23 in. long, 12 in. wide, 16 in. high.	8.50
No. 43.	Cradle, extra fine, elegant, hard-wood finish. Just the thing that is wanted for very large dolls. Size, 28 in. long, 15 in. wide, 20 in. high.	13.50

TOY BEDSTEADS.

New and nobby. Three sizes, white and gold or colors and gold. The finest toy bedstead in the market. These goods are so different from the toy bedsteads usually found in the market, so modern in style and attractive in combination of white and gold or tasty coloring and gold, that they cannot but be welcomed by the best class of trade.

No. 221. Bedstead.

		Per Dozen
No. 220.	Small. 15¾ in. long, 8½ in. wide, 8 in. high	$2.00
No. 221.	Small Medium. 19 in. long, 10¼ in. wide, 12 in. high,	4.00
No. 222.	Medium. 25 in. long, 15½ in. wide, 16 in. high	9.00
No. 223.	Large. 30 in. long, 20 in. wide, 18 in. high, with wire foundation instead of slats	15.00

WIRE TOY BEDSTEADS.

SILVERED.

With mattresses and pillows.

	Lgth	width	height	Per Dozen
No. 1.	14 in.;	8 in.;	8½ in.	$4.00
" 24.	" 24 "	" 13 "	" 14 "	8.50
" 30.	" 30 "	" 13 "	" 12 "	11.00

" 6. Japanned Wire Bedstead, without mattress or pillows, same size as No. 0.. 2.00

No. 475. EXTENSION TABLE.

A complete extension table, made of chestnut, has a moulded edge and is finished in oil. It has one extra leaf. The legs, which are hard wood, pack inside with the leaf, making a neat shipping package. Size, 9½ inches wide, 15½ inches long, 10½ inches high.

Per dozen $1.85

		Per Dozen
No. 476.	Extension Table. Same style as 475. Size, 12x21 inches, 15½ inches high	$3.75
No. 477.	Large Medium. Height, 17¾x14¼ ins. Size without leaves, 19½x14¼ ins. Full size with leaves, 27½x14½ ins. Packed 1 dozen in a case	8.50
No. 478.	Large. Height, 21 ins. Size without extra leaves, 25x19 ins. Full size with leaves, 36x19 ins. Packed 1 dozen in a case	16.50

No. 53. DOLL'S BOUDOIR SUITE.

A new and decidedly the richest and most elaborate doll's chamber suite manufactured, representing nice carved work and handsome grained panels. The suite is composed of bedstead, dressing case, rocker, table and towel rack, all of latest patterns and well made. Comes neatly set up, nicely packed in a box. Size of bed, 18x10½ inches; dressing case, 7x9 inches; chair, 9 inches high; table, 6x4 inches.

Per dozen $8.50

No.107. THE DAISY UPRIGHT BLACKBOARD
New this Year.

A good upright blackboard at a very low price. Has the advantage of folding closely for shipping, being easily set up, having drawing lessons, the same as higher priced boards. Frame of White wood. Strong and durable. In this blackboard we are offering a great deal for a little money. Size of frame, 30x16 inches. Size of blackboard, 16x11½ inches. This blackboard is made from leatherboard same as the higher priced boards.

Per dozen $1.87

No. 45½. STANDARD FOLDING BLACKBOARD.

This is, as its name implies, really a standard blackboard, Strongly made, ornamented with latest designs in drawing, convenient to use in easel or desk form, easily opened, and when folded making a very close package; has receptacle for holding crayons. The board is of new material, warranted not to crack, and coated in a first-class manner. Height, 34 inches. Size of board, 18½x12½ inches.

Per dozen $3.75

No. 45. EXCELSIOR FOLDING BLACKBOARD.

One of the finest and most complete blackboards made. A well arranged combination of easel and desk, having a movable sawed extension with designs for drawing on either side. The board is made of new material of best quality, smooth, and warranted not to check. The desk is provided with an extra large drawer with ornamented front. The board drops forward to form the desk, showing additional designs for drawing. It is made in a substantial manner and folds very closely for shipping. Height, 48 inches. Size of board, 16x19 inches.

Per dozen $8.00

PATENT LOCK SHELF BOOK RACKS.

Patented May 17, 1881.

Capable of being taken apart and packed in a very small space. Convenient in traveling. Quickly put together or taken apart. No screws or tools required.

No. 215. Has three shelves 15 inches long, with fancy enameled tips on end of posts. Will hold 45 ordinary books . . . . Price, per dozen, 4.00

No. 222. Has three shelves 22 inches long, finished same as No. 215.

Price, per dozen, 6.00

No. 322. Has four shelves 22 inches long; finished same as No. 222.

Price, per dozen, 8.00

TEN PINS.

Packed in wooden boxes with sliding covers.

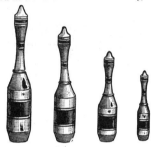

5-inch, red-stained ten pins			. . . .	$ .75
8 "	"	"	. . . .	1.75
11 "	"	"	. . . .	3.75
7 "	varnished and striped ten pins		. . . .	1.75
8 "	"	" " "	. . . .	2.75
9 "	"	" " "	. . . .	3.50
10 "	"	" " "	. . . .	4.00
12 "	"	" " "	. . . .	5.50
8 "	red and gilt striped ten pins		. . . .	3.50
9 "	" " " " "		. . . .	4.00
12 "	" " " " "		. . . .	7.00

SOLITAIRE BOARDS.

No. 1. Brown ash, plain finish, 9 inch diameter, with compartment underneath to hold the agates. Each one packed with thirty-two glass agates

Price, per dozen 4.00

No. 2. Fine brown ash, with siege polished and painted with compartment underneath to hold the agates. Each one packed with thirty-two fine glass agates.

Price, per dozen $6.00

AGATE RAILWAY.

An improvement over the old Agate Railway, in the feature of the curved bridge and silver gong bell in the tray at the end of the tracks. Made of hard wood nicely finished and packed with a set of fine glass agates.

Price, per dozen $8.00

RAQUET.

A Mechanical Game.

Front View.

No. 14.

Pat. December 15, 1891.

This game is operated by placing marbles on the top rail, the marbles descending by gravity over four sections of track, strike the trigger at the bottom and are propelled to the top rail by the action of a coiled spring, when they again begin their descent.

At each release of the trigger the carrier imparts motion to a disc which is loosely pivoted on its axle. This disc is divided into eight sections, differently colored and numbered.

The marbles quickly succeeding each other in their descent, strike the trigger and impart rapid rotary motion to the disc, a color on which stops momentarily under the index, and the number thereon is scored by the player having chosen the color indicated.

The rapidity of revolution of the disc and the minute interval of rest under the indicator, as well as the absolute uncertainty as to the winning color, renders it unquestionably the most interesting, fascinating, exciting game before the public

Price, per dozen $8.50

No. 43¼. PRIZE RING TOSS.

This is one of the most attractive toys made this season. Always a popular and entertaining game. The box and five posts are nicely printed, striped and varnished. The four rings are of rattan and strongly made. Size, 10½ inches high; box, 7¾x7¾ inches.

Price, per dozen $1.85

No. 17½. PRIZE RING TOSS

One of the prettiest designs for this popular game. Has six points all numbered, five rings wound with fancy colored material. The posts are striped and varnished. The box is well made, ornamented and highly polished. Size when set up, 19 inches high, 13 inches long, 8 inches wide

Price, per dozen $3.75

No. 28. PRIZE RING TOSS.

An ever fascinating game in improved and most attractive style. It has a center post, strongly jointed, and four corner posts, all handsomely striped and varnished. The rings, eight in number, are made of rattan, graded in size, and nicely wound with bright colored webbing, making them durable and attractive. The box is made of chestnut and has a high finish. Height when set up, 27 inches. Nicely wrapped and labeled.

Price, per dozen $8.00

No. 181. PUNCH AND JUDY TEN-PINS.

This set consists of ten lithographed *sectional* blocks representing a complete set of Punch and Judy figures, fastened to a common base, so arranged with spiral springs that when the figures are hit in the head the bodies are released and fly into the air, leaving the head to stand vibrating upon its base. For this purpose a 9-inch spring cannon is used, and the blocks are so graded in height as to present the full length of head to the front. This is decidedly a novelty, strong and not easily got out of order. Put up in paper box with showy label.

Price, per dozen $8.50

No. 182. JACK AND JILL TEN-PIN BLOCKS.

This is a novelty, being a combination of ten alphabet and picture blocks, 7x1¼x⅝ inches. This size admits of their being set up, to be knocked over by the three balls which accompany each set. Packed in fancy papered box with bright label.

Price, per dozen.................$2.00

PARLOR FLOOR CROQUET.

It consists of a full set of handsome croquet implements for a party of four, and is just the right size for in-door use and can be set up on the floor or carpet without injuring either. Packed in a neat wooden box.

No. 1. A fine set, fancy painted, extra striped and varnished.

Price, per dozen.................$8.50

No. 2. A good set, plain painted, similar to No. 1, finished in oil.

Price, per dozen.................$8.00

FINE TABLE CROQUET.

Each set with fine lithographed label.

			Per Dozen
No. 5.	4 ball set		$3.75
" 4.	6 " "		6.00
" 3.	8 " "		8.00

NEW GAMES.

No. 507. GAME OF BEAN BAG.

A very good substitute for the regular game. It answers the purpose just as well, affording endless amusement.

Price, per dozen... .... $ .75

No. 508. Same as No. 507, much larger, more attractive and altogether better.

Price, per dozen................ $2.00

THE LATEST NOVELTY.

WORLD'S FAIR PANORAMA.

Giving correct views in colors of the World's Fair Buildings.

A perfect picture of each President from Washington to Harrison, with the date and length of time when each was President.

A fine view of the Landing of Columbus.

Also a fine view of the Capitol at Washington, and of the Masonic temple at Chicago.

Price, per dozen................ $1 75

ZIMMER'S BASE BALL GAME.

Balls pitched, batted and caught! Can pitch swift and slow balls! Can pitch in and out shoots.

An opportunity for enthusiasts on the subject of the National Game to enjoy something of the excitement of an actual base ball game in their homes, is found in this miniature affair, in which the ball is pitched and batted and, if not hit safely, is instantly caught out as in the regular out-door game.

The diagram of the ball field is 22 inches square, and all the players' positions are filled with spring catches fastened to the board; these serve to stop and hold the ball, seldom failing to hold a "hot one" direct from the bat, and the chances for a safe hit are found to be about the same as in an actual game between professional nines.

Price, per dozen................ $8.00

BAGATELLE BOARDS.

Best Line Made. Handsomely Finished.

Size			Per Dozen
A.	7½x15,	1 bell	$1.75
B.	9 x17,	2 bells	3.50
C.	9 x18,	1 bell, large	4.00
D.	11 x25,	2 bells	7.00
E.	12 x28,	1 bell, large	9.00
F.	13 x31,	1 bell, large	15.00
G.	15 x33,	3 bells	22.50
H.	16½x37½,	1 bell	36.00

BAGATELLE BOARDS.

Extra Fine.

	Size		
No. 4.	36x16, 2 large bells, per dozen		$48.00
No. 3.	48x18, 2 large bells, each		7.00
No. 2.	42x27, 3 large bells, each		9.00
No. 1.	60x30, 5 large bells, extra large, each		20.00

IS MARRIAGE A FAILURE?

Large and New Board Game.

Price, per dozen........ .... $9.00

KELLY'S BABIES.

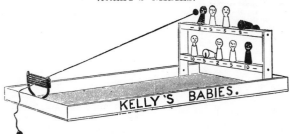

An entirely new game. The figures are knocked over by springing a ball attached to an elastic, producing a most comical effect.

Price, per dozen $2.00

COLUMBIAN BASE BALL GAME, (NEW).

Latest and Best Base Ball Game.

Price, per dozen................$13.50

CROKINOLE BOARDS.

Each

No. 2. Crokinole, varnished $2.75
No. 1. Crokinole, mahogany or antique finish, varnished, with felt cover...... 3.75

PARLOR BILLIARDS.

No. 500.

No. 500. BILLIARDS.

Mahogany, ebony or rosewood finish, or in chestnut. Bed covered with extra quality woolen cloth in
billiard green. Cloth covered elastic cushions. A1
goods every way. 32 in. long, 18 in. wide.

Per dozen....................$33.00

No. 501. BILLIARDS.

Finished in same manner as No. 500, with superior
material and workmanship. Elastic cushions, and
all the good points of No. 500. Size, 40½ in. long, 23
in. wide.

Per dozen........ ....$60.00

Furnishings: With No. 500, 2 black and 2 white
1¼-in. duranoid balls and 2 No. 1 cues. With No.
501, 2 black and 2 white 1¼-in. duranoid balls and 2
No. 2 cues.

POOL.

A Fine Line.   Mahogany Finish.

No. 513. Pool.   No. 512. Pool.   No. 511. Pool.

No. 511. POOL.

Size of table, 33x18 in. and stands 8½ in. high on
legs. Furnishings: 15 ¾-in. duranoid balls, 2 cues,
1 triangle.

Each................................$5.00

No. 512. POOL.

A larger and finer table than No. 511. Size,
41x23 in., stands 10 in. high on legs. Furnishings:
15 1-in. duranoid balls (numbered), 1 triangle, 2 cues
with leather tips. The legs screw into the table;
they can be readily removed for packing, or as con-
venience may require.

Each................................ 7.50

No. 513. POOL.

Extra Size.

50x27 in. and stands 10 in. high on legs. These
legs screw into the table and can be readily removed.
Made from selected stock. Style and workmanship
every way extra. Especial effort made to have this
table far superior to any before put upon the market.
Furnishings: 15 1¼-in. duranoid balls (numbered),
2 cues with leather tips, 1 triangle. These three pool
tables are covered with extra quality felting in billiard green, have cloth covered elastic cushions, six
knit pockets (at corners and sides), side pieces in
nickel at pockets. Extra furnishings for any of
these tables for sale on application.

Each..........................$10.00

GAME OF SHOVEL BOARD.

This is a large showy game of a novel kind, presenting many attractive features. It is one of the
best sellers ever offered.

Per Dozen

No. 519. Game of shovel board. The game
is on heavy cardboard, and comes
in box 15½ in long, with shovel
stick and 16 men............... $ .75

No. 520. Another shovel board, but larger
than the above, being 24 in. long. 1.85

No. 521. A fine game of shovel board. Comes
in wood tray 28 in. long, and
handsome throughout........... 4.00

No. 280. 9x31 inches, handsomely finished.. 8.00

THE MECHANICAL SPELLER.

Kindergarten at Home. An Educational Marvel.

Perfect in its
mechanical move-
ments. By simply
pressing the keys
any word of 2, 3,
4, or 5 letters can
be spelled.

Per dozen... $7.50

BUILDING BLOCKS.

ARCHITECTURAL BUILDING BLOCKS.

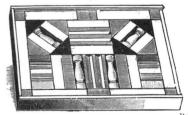

Per Dozen

No. 2/0. Size of box, 5x7 inches .... $ .35
No. 0.   "   "   "   7x9   "   .... .70
No. 1.   "   "   "   9½x12 " 1.75
No. 2. Double layer blocks, 10x16 inches... 3.75
No. 3.   "   "   "   11x16 "   ... 4.00

HARD WOOD BLOCKS.

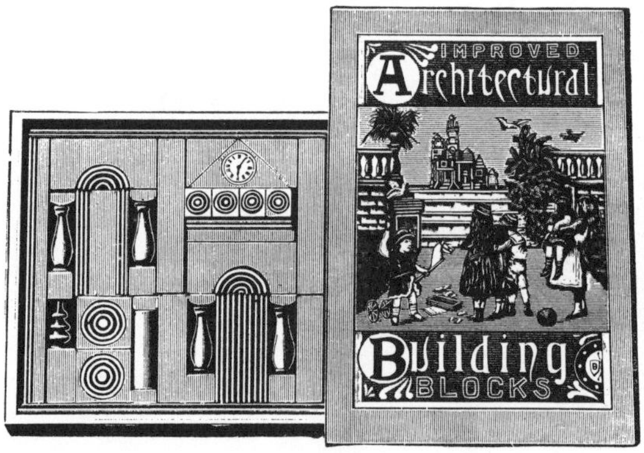

Per Dozen

No. 248. Box $9\frac{1}{4}$x7x$1\frac{5}{8}$ inches .... $ .75
No. 249. " 11x$8\frac{3}{4}$x$1\frac{1}{2}$ " 1.75
No. 250. " 15x$10\frac{1}{2}$x$1\frac{1}{2}$ " 3.50
No. 251. " 15x$10\frac{1}{2}$x$2\frac{1}{2}$ " 6.00
No. 252. " 16x$11\frac{1}{2}$x$2\frac{1}{2}$ " 8.00

WAGONS WITH HARD WOOD BLOCKS.

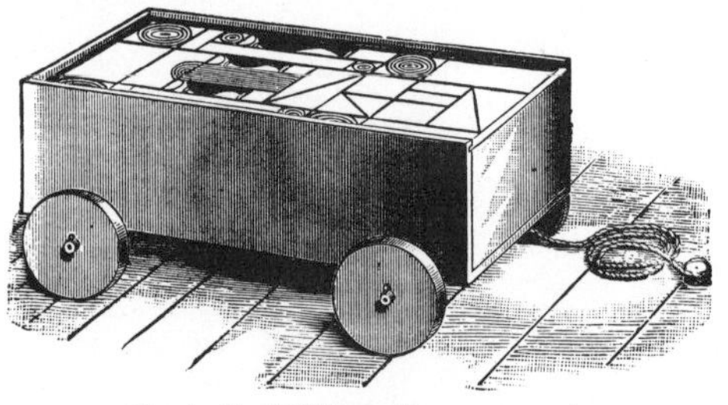

Showing No. 255 Wagon with cover removed.

Per Dozen

No. W/10. 4 wheel wagon with blocks .... $ .75
No. W/11. 4 " " " " large.. 1.75
No. W/12. 4 " " " " larger. 3.75
No. W/13. 4 " " " " " . 4.00
No. 255. Box $16\frac{5}{8}$x$9\frac{1}{2}$x$3\frac{3}{8}$ inches, contains 97 blocks 8.00
No. 256. Box 15x$8\frac{1}{2}$x$2\frac{5}{8}$ inches, contains 65 blocks 5.50
No. 257. Box 12x$7\frac{7}{8}$x$2\frac{5}{8}$ inches, contains 46 blocks 3.50
No. 258. Box $9\frac{1}{2}$x6x$2\frac{5}{8}$ inches, contains 26 blocks 1.85

U. S. MAIL A B C BLOCK WAGONS.

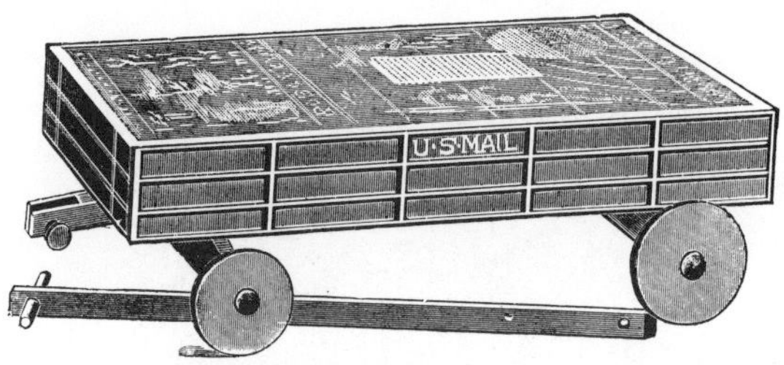

Showing No. 3 Wagon with cover removed.

Per Dozen

No. 1. U. S. box $5\frac{3}{4}$x$3\frac{3}{4}$x$2\frac{1}{8}$ inches, contains 12 lithograph blocks $1.85
No. 2. U. S. box $7\frac{5}{8}$x$5\frac{3}{4}$x$2\frac{1}{8}$ inches, contains 27 lithograph blocks 3.75
No. 3. U. S. box 11x$7\frac{5}{8}$x$2\frac{1}{4}$ inches, contains 42 lithograph blocks 8.50

UNITED STATES AND CANADA EXPRESS.

Nos. 117 and 186.

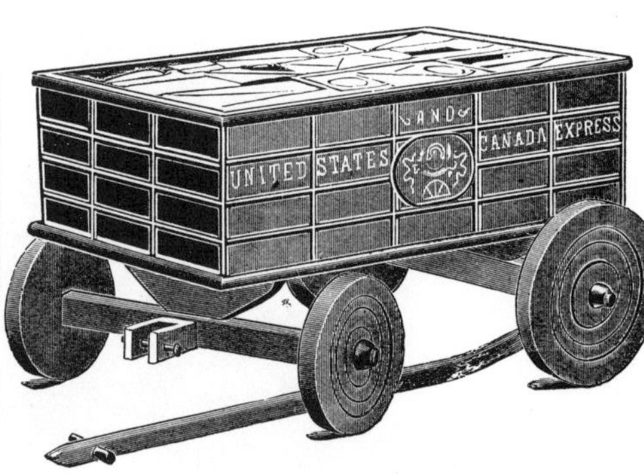

These wagons are of large size and very strongly and neatly made, having heavy hardwood running gear, finished in shellac, striped wheels, lithographed body with dark wood moulding top and bottom. Filled with hard wood building blocks.

No. 117. Size, 17x$11\frac{1}{2}$x$5\frac{1}{2}$ inches, 1 piece in a case $22.50
No. 186. Size, 15x$8\frac{1}{2}$x4 inches, 6 pieces in a case 15.00

THE EMBOSSING COMPANY A-B-C BLOCKS.

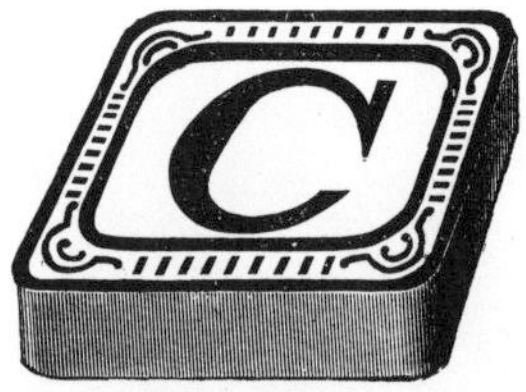

Per Dozen

No. 0. Eighteen pieces. Embossed hard wood in glazed paper boxes, with label in three colors, glossed. Bear the alphabet and numerals .... $ .75
No. 1. Twenty-five pieces. Embossed. In paper boxes, beautifully labeled. Made under a new process, giving a rich and unique effect. Letters and numerals in a variety of brilliant colors on an embossed yellow ground 1.87

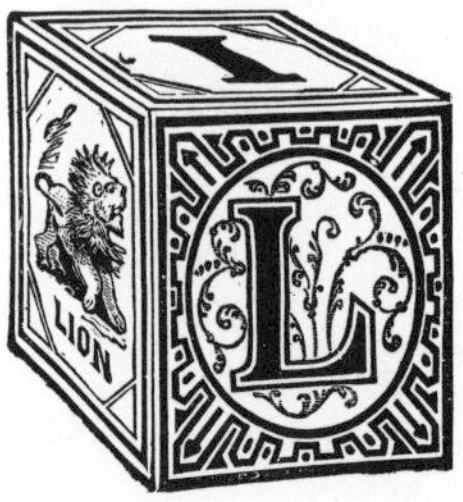

Per Dozen

No. 70A. Illustrated cubes, natural wood, embossed, and printed, 12 pieces, paper boxes, $5\frac{1}{2}$x$4\frac{1}{2}$, in $\frac{1}{2}$ dozen packages $1.25
No. 5. Quarter cubes, natural wood, 25 pieces, paper boxes, $8\frac{1}{4}$x$8\frac{1}{4}$, in $\frac{1}{2}$ dozen packages 1.60
No. 52. White wood blocks, $\frac{1}{2}$ cube size, 9 blocks in box .... .72
No. 54A. Illustrated cubes, 12 pieces, natural wood, paper boxes, $7\frac{5}{8}$x$5\frac{5}{8}$, in $\frac{1}{2}$ dozen packages 1.85

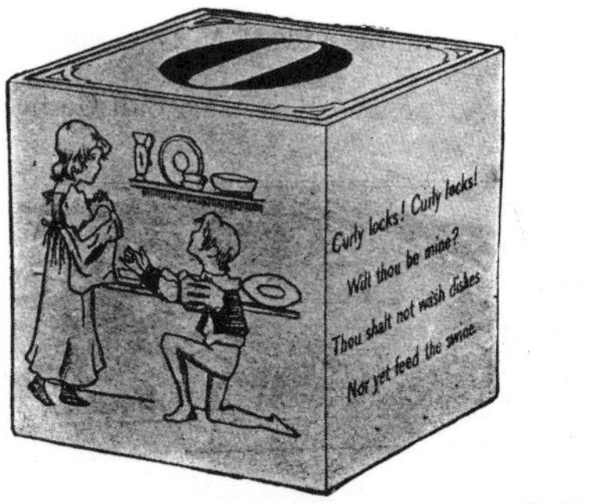

Per Dozen

No. 61A. Cubes, natural wood, 20 pieces, Special Mother Goose illustrations and rhymes, wood frame boxes, $9\frac{3}{8}$x$7\frac{5}{8}$, in $\frac{1}{4}$ dozen packages. $3.75
No. 80A. Twelve pieces. Natural wood, embossed ends, printed in colors. Twenty-four illustrations. Several impressions of each letter and the numerals. Packed in wood frame boxes with fine label...... 3.25
No. 24. Same style as 80A, but larger blocks 5.50

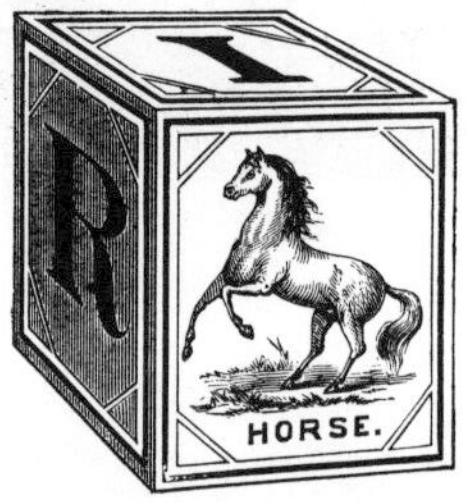

Per Dozen

No. 7. Twenty pieces. Profuse illustrations with the alphabet and numerals. Packed in paper boxes, with engraved label of special design. Painted and varnished so as to be water-proof $3.75

No. 9. ILLUSTRATED CUBES.

No. 9. Twenty pieces. Varnished and waterproof. In wood frame boxes, with fine label in five colors, glossed. Forty illustrations of animals. Several impressions of each letter of the alphabet and the numerals. Embossed gilt ends. Ornamented letters. Printed in colors......... 9.00

No. 92. MOTHER GOOSE.

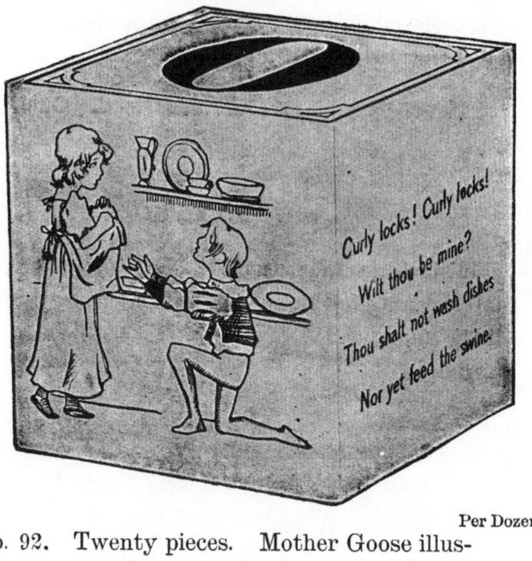

Per Dozen

No. 92. Twenty pieces. Mother Goose illustrations and rhymes, with alphabet complete. Painted and varnished, and water-proof. Wood frame box. $9.00

EMBOSSED BLOCKS.—Continued.

Per Dozen

No. 8   Twenty pieces. In wood frame boxes. Thirty-six illustrations of animals. Several impressions of each letter and all the numerals.............. $6.00

PICTURE BLOCKS.
All the Latest Novelties.

No. 176.   THE WONDER BLOCKS.

This series of blocks will be found to be very pleasing both in color and design. Each set consists of 12 alphabet and picture blocks, of ¾-inch stock, lithographed with bright colors, representing the subject designated by the label upon the box—birds, animals, circus, etc. Size of box, 12¼x8½ inches. One each of the six sets.

Per dozen....................................... $2.00

No. 177.   NURSERY BLOCKS.

There is always a demand for a nursery block, and we offer these two sets of nursery blocks as being a very desirable toy of this class. They consist of 24 well proportioned blocks of ¾-inch stock, lithographed with alphabet and pictures to correspond with respective labels on box and cut-up pictures on the edges and reverse side. Each kind.

Per dozen...................... $4.00

No. 314.   A-B-C FIRE BLOCKS.

Here we have the newest and most attractive thing in A-B-C blocks yet produced. Fire engine, hose cart, hook and ladder, and insurance patrol, besides firemen, soldiers and the alphabet illustrated.

Per dozen.....................$1.85

No. 315.   Same as above only larger and more attractive............per dozen $3.75

No. 227.   WILD WEST A-B-C BLOCKS.

Here we have a box of eight beautiful A-B-C blocks, showing life in the far west, in fine colored lithographs. Also the alphabet illustrated, soldiers and Indians. A good selling article.

Per dozen.....................$ .75

No. 78.   SUNSHINE A-B-C BLOCKS.

This handsome box contains nine hollow blocks, covered with lithographs of pleasing and beautiful designs.

Per dozen......................$1.75

No. 75.   SURPRISE A-B-C.

This is a set of fifteen hollow blocks, having designs of sheep, soldiers, cars, horse guards, circus, and the alphabet illustrated.

Per dozen........................$3.00

No. 230.   FLOWERS AND BIRDS A-B-C BLOCKS.

These beautiful blocks are the finest and most pleasing yet produced, and cannot fail to delight as well as instruct. Each box contains 18 blocks, 3¼x2¼x1.

Per dozen........................$4.00

No. 231.   BIRDS AND FLOWERS A-B-C BLOCKS.

Same style as above only put up in large cherry wood box, which contains 27 blocks.

Per dozen........................$8.50

No. 502.   THE FAIRY LAND RAILROAD A-B-C AND PICTURE BLOCKS.

6½x12½ inches.

This set contains nine blocks, each ⅞ of an inch thick, 2 inches broad and 4 inches long. Upon these blocks are an alphabet, set of numerals, Punch and Judy, a company of soldiers and a train of cars.

Per dozen........................$1.75

No. 664. ST. NICHCLAS' A-B-C AND PICTURE BLOCKS.

7½ x 12½ inches

This set is made up of 24 flat blocks. Each block is ⅜x1½x4 inches. The pictures on one side are of children at play, and on the other a large picture to be put together as a puzzle.

Per dozen........................$2.00

No. 660. THE ELF LAND RAILROAD SERIES.

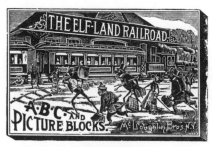

8½ x 12¼ inches.

Three kinds, put up assorted, half dozen in a package. (1) The Elf Land Railroad A-B-C and Picture Blocks. (2) Story Builder's Blocks. (3) Tommy Toddyhigh's A-B-C.

Per dozen........................$1.75

No. 655. OVERLAND RAILROAD BLOCKS.

10½x16 inches.

This is a set of twelve blocks, each 5x2½x1¼ inches. The pictures are domestic animals, a train of cars of the blue color recently adopted by an overland line, grotesque soldiers, and an alphabet.

Per dozen........................$3.75

No. 669. CHRISTMAS BLOCKS.

8x13 inches.

Per dozen........................$3.75

No. 513. GOLDENHAIR SERIES BLOCKS.

10x16½ inches. Three kinds, put up in quarter dozens, assorted. (1) Little Goldenhair's A-B-C Blocks. (2) Blocks of Delight. (3) Premium Blocks.

Per dozen........................$3.75

No. 507½. A-B-C OF FEATHERS AND SONGS. BLOCKS.

10x15 inches.

Per dozen........................$3.75

No. 534. ARTISTIC PUZZLE CUBES.

Two Kinds.

8x10½ inches.

The puzzle cubes contain 12 2½-inch cubes and make 12 different pictures, 6 cubes making a picture and six pictures appearing upon each set of six cubes.

Per dozen........................$4.50

No. 520. LITTLE FOLKS' CUBES.

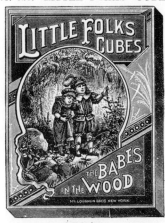

8x11 inches.

Series—6 kinds. Cinderella. Puss in Boots. Goody Two Shoes. Red Riding Hood. Jack and the Bean Stalk. The Three Bears.

Per dozen........................$6.00

PICTURE BLOCKS AND PUZZLES.

No. 546. WHITE SQUADRON PICTURE CUBES.

A full description of these ships accompanies each set of blocks, as also a set of cuts to aid in putting the blocks together properly. The ships have been selected to show best the new types of vessels being built for Uncle Sam, and cannot fail to post boys on naval matters as well as amuse them. Size, 11x21 inches.

Price, per dozen...............$12.00

No. 549. COLUMBIAN EXPOSITION CUBES.

This box of puzzle cubes contains 32 2¼ inch blocks, the box itself being 11x21 inches. The pictures on these blocks are of the buildings on the Fair Grounds at Chicago. They represent the Machinery Hall, The United States Government Building, the building of Mines and Mining, Agricultural Hall, and the Transportation Building. Size, 11x21 inches.

Price, per dozen...............$12.00

No. 579½. BABY BUNTING A-B-C AND PICTURE BLOCKS.

Nineteen inches high; 3½x3½x4 inches closed. The smallest block is 2x2x4 inches. There are five blocks in this set. The pictures do not illustrate consecutive stories but are of children fishing, riding, playing at house-keeping, dolls, etc.

Price, per dozen....$1.85

No. 509½. NESTED BLOCKS.

Thirty-two inches high; 4½x4½x5½ inches closed. The set contains six blocks, the pictures on which illustrate the "Three Bears," "Piggy," "Wandering Bunny," "Mischievous Monkey," "Humpty Dumpty," etc.

Per dozen......$3.75

No. 509. NESTED BLOCKS.

Forty-one inches high; seven inches square closed. The blocks are covered with bright colored and amusing pictures of a bolder character than the other nest, so as to be more easily made out by small children, and have an alphabet on the top.

Price, per dozen...............$7.00

No. 1S. CHAMPION A-B-C AND PICTURE BLOCKS.

Sixty-three inches high; 7¼ inches square closed. Ten blocks.

Price, per dozen............ ... $8.00

No. 571. UNITED STATES NAVAL SCROLL PUZZLES.

Six kinds, put up assorted. Box, 10½x6½ inches.

These puzzles when made up are 8½x11 inches. Each has pictures of two of the vessels of the New Navy pasted on thick straw board and cut up into irregular pieces. The box label has one of the ships upon it.

Price, per dozen............... $1.75

No. 573. WORLD'S FAIR SCROLL PUZZLES.

Six kinds put up assorted.

Price, per dozen........................... $1.75

No. 596. NEW DISSECTED MAP OF THE UNITED STATES.

Size 1.

Price, per dozen........................... $1.75

No. 597. NEW DISSECTED MAP OF THE UNITED STATES.

Size 2.

Size, 8x12 inches. Price, per dozen......... $3.75

No. 598. DISSECTED MAP OF THE UNITED STATES.

This map is a scroll puzzle, being a map of the United States mounted on board one-eighth of an inch thick and sawed into pieces on the boundaries of the states. The map when put together, measures 16x21 inches.

Price, per dozen............... $6.00

No. 599. DISSECTED MAP OF THE WORLD.

This map of the world is similar to No. 598 above, except that the map takes in the world instead of being confined to the United States. Upon the back of the map puzzle there is a picture of our National Capitol at Washington, making a second puzzle almost as interesting as the main one. The map is 16½x21½ inches.

Price, per dozen............. $8.00

No. 543. YOUNG AMERICA SCROLL PUZZLES.

Size, 9x12 inches.

Series, four kinds put up assorted.

	Per Dozen
Old Woman and her Pig	$3.75
Circus Picture Puzzle	3.75
Wild West Picture Puzzle	3.75
St. Nicholas Picture Puzzle	3.75

No. 541. BROWNIE SCROLL PUZZLE, (NEW).

Price, per dozen........................... $6.00

No. 572. WHITE SQUADRON PICTURE PUZZLE. Six Kinds.

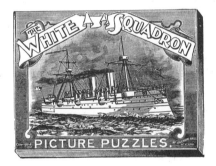

Size, 10x12 inches. Price, per dozen........$3.75

No. 527. STEAMSHIP PUZZLE, IMPROVED.

Size, 7x19 inches. Price, per dozen......... $6.00

No. 526. STEAMBOAT PICTURE PUZZLE, IMPROVED.

Price, per dozen........................... $6.00

No. 590. FIRE ENGINE PUZZLE.

9x12 inches.

In this picture puzzle the subject is a fire engine going to a fire. The size of the picture is 18x24 inches. It is carefully and accurately drawn to show all the details of a modern steam fire engine.

Price, per dozen................$6.00

No. 592. LOCOMOTIVE PUZZLE.

Size, 9x12 inches, Price, per dozen.......... $6.00

No. 574. WORLD'S COLUMBIAN EXPOSITION PICTURE PUZZLES.

Size, 10x12 inches. Price, per dozen....... $3.75

No. 537. MAGNETIC FISH POND.

14½x14½ inches.

This Fish Pond differs from the improved Fish Pond entirely. It consists of a tank or aquarium of cardboard. This is covered on the outside with pictures representing fish swimming in water, as seen through the glass of an aquarium. The fish used in the game have wire rings in their mouths. They are put out of sight on the bottom of the tank. The "hook" is a magnet on a pole and line. The magnet is drawn around the bottom of the box. When it meets a ring in a fish's mouth, the ring adheres to the magnet and the fish may be drawn out. The element of luck appertains to this game more than to the other Fish Ponds, for the reason that the fish cannot be seen at all before being caught.

It is a game for children.

Price, per dozen...............$12.00

No. 536½. FISH POND GAME, NEW AND IMPROVED.

Price, per dozen..$1.75

No. 536 is made on same plan as No. 536½, it is large and showy and very handsome, and its popular price secures for it a very large demand. No other "Fish Pond" at all approaches this. Has all the patented features.

Price, per dozen...$3.75

No. 535. IMPROVED GAME OF FISH POND.
Extra Fine Edition.

Price, per dozen...$7.50

No. 545. THE PRETTY VILLAGE.
Size 1.

This toy village is a set of ten cardboard houses, stores, churches, etc., printed to represent buildings, hinged together so that they fold up when the roofs are lifted off. They are about 6x3 inches on the ground, and high in proportion. When set up they make a pretty imitation of a village street. Some figures of the villagers are put up with them, to be cut out, to inhabit the settlement.

Price, per dozen................ $3.75

No. 547. THE PRETTY VILLAGE.
Larger than above, per doz.................$7.50

BROWNIE STAMPS.
Size, 6½x4½ inches.

These stamps are used to make figures of the celebrated Brownies of Mr. Palmer Cox. The set contains eight figures, each 1¾ inches tall, and a pad with ink. The box is of wood, with a lithographed label. These goods stand alone in the market, being reproductions of Mr. Cox's Brownie designs, so well known through his numerous works. Children who know the Brownies will not recognize any other figures than these.

No. 807.   Price, per dozen   oxes..$4.00
No. 808.   "   "   " .. 8.00

CARD GAMES,

IMMENSE VARIETY. ALL NEW AND GOOD SELLERS.

5c. AND 10c. CARD GAMES.

No. 375. PUNCH AND JUDY SERIES OF GAMES.
4 Kinds, Assorted.

Series : Old Maid ; Snap ; Punch and Judy ; Shoot that Hat.
Size, 3¼ x 4¼ inches .... per dozen, $ .35

No. 376A. OLD MAID AND BACHELOR.

2¾x4 inches.

It is the cheapest "Old Maid" game in the market.
No. 0.   Per dozen................$ .35

No. 376.   Larger than 376A.

Per dozen.........................$ .75

No. 377. MDLLE. LE NORMAND'S FORTUNE TELLING CARDS.

4x5 inches.

Per dozen.........................$ .75

No. 378. THE ELITE CONVERSATION CARDS SERIES.

Six kinds (assorted in dozens) : Love ; Marriage ; Loves and Likes ; Comical, Quizzical and Quaint: Social and Sentimental.
These games consist of fifty-two cards, upon which are printed a series of questions and answers upon subjects indicated clearly by their respective titles.
Per dozen......................$ .75

No. 374. MOTHER GOOSE GAMES SERIES.

Per dozen......................$ .75

No. 372. GAME OF AUTHORS.

Per dozen......................$ .75

No. 373. THE GOLDEN EAGLE ANAGRAMS.

3½x5 inches.

Per dozen......................$ .75

25c. CARD GAMES.

o. 379. CINDERELLA GAMES.

Handsome Revised Edition.

4½x6¼ inches.

Series—6 kinds, put up assorted in dozens: Cinderella, or Hunt the Slipper; Cock Robin; Old Mother Hubbard; House that Jack Built; Where's Johnny? Red Riding Hood. This is a series of children's games. They are as simple as their subjects indicate.

Per dozen.......................$1.75

No. 388. GRANDMA'S GAMES.

Improved.

4½x6¼ inches.

Series—6 kinds, put up assorted in dozens: Grandma's Arithmetical Games; Grandma's Geographical Games; Grandma's Game of Riddles; Grandma's Game of Useful Knowledge; Grandma's Sunday Game of Bible Questions—New Testament; Grandma's Sunday Game of Bible Questions—Old Testament. The Grandma's Games are designed for children just old enough to read easily.

Per dozen.......................$ 1.75.

No. 385. CHRISTMAS STOCKING SERIES.

Size, 4½x6¼ inches, 6 kinds, put up in assorted dozens: Christmas Stocking Game; The Judge's Game Cards; Merry Matches; Which Is It? orPay; What D'ye Buy? The Game of City Life. These games are intended for children, and are based upon subjects within their ken and suited to their taste.

Per dozen.......................$1.75

No. 382. FIRESIDE SERIES.

Size, 4½x6¼ inches. Six kinds assorted in dozens: Fox and Geese; Snip, Snap, Snorum; Dr. Fusby, M.D.; Match Making; Black Cat · Comic Conversation Cards.

Per dozen.......................$1.75

No. 392. MADAM MORROW'S FORTUNE TELLING CARDS.

4½x6¼ inches.

Per dozen.......................$1.75

No. 382½. THE GAME OF SNIP, SNAP, SNORUM.

4½x6¼ inches.

These cards are illustrated, and made up of funny characters, divided into families like those of Authors.

Per dozen.......................$1.75

No. 387. THE MERRY GAME OF OLD MAID.

5x6¼ inches.

Old Maid is one of the most popular games for children ever devised. This edition contains 42 cards, lithographed in colors.

Per dozen.......................$1.75

No. 387½. THE MERRY GAME OF OLD BACHELOR.

This is similar to No. 387.

Per dozen.......................$1.75

No. 381. POPULAR AUTHORS.

Regular Edition.

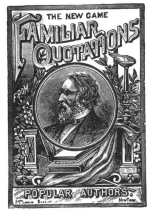

6¼x4 inches.

This game of Authors consists of cards bearing the names of authors or their works, and four selected quotations therefrom.

Per dozen.......................$1.75

No. 394. STAR AUTHORS.

Popular Edition.

Size, 6¼x4¼ inches. This game is similar in play to No. 381. It differs from it in containing cards with sixteen portraits of the various authors.

Per dozen.......................$1.75.

No. 396. IMPROVED AUTHORS.

Popular Edition.

Series—3 kinds, put ap assorted in dozens: Improved Authors—Popular Edition, size, 6¼x4½ inches; Improved Authors—Poets—Popular Edition, size, 6¼x4¼ inches; Improved Authors—Queens of Literature, size, 6¼x4½ inches.

Per dozen ....$1.87.

No. 400. BOYS IN BLUE, NEW.

5x6½ inches.................Price, per dozen, $1.85

No. 393. AVILUDE GAME.

New Popular Edition.

5x6½ inches.................Price, per dozen, $1.85

FIFTY CENT CARD GAMES.

No. 405. FLAG GAME.

This game is played with 60 cards bearing flags of all nations, brightly and correctly colored.
Price, per dozen................ $3.75

No. 416. LOGOMACHY.
Fine Edition.

This game is put up in an imitation Russia leather box handsomely stamped in gold. It is adapted to entertain a party of young people or children.
6x8½ inches....Price, per dozen, $3.75

No. 406. THE MERRY CHRISTMAS GAMES.

5¼x11 inches.............Price, per dozen, $3.75

No. 411. IMPROVED AUTHORS.

Series: Improved Authors. Improved Author-Poets. Improved Authors. Queens of Literature.

These games contain seventy-two cards, each with a lithographed portrait of some Author, Poet, Authoress or Poetess, with a fac-simile of their autograph.
Price, per dozen $3.75

No. 415. OLD MAID AND OLD BACHELOR.

Very handsome edition, containing 84 cards, large party may play.
Price, per dozen................ $3.75

TWENTY-FIVE AND FIFTY CENT BOARD GAMES.

No. 274. THE NEWPORT YACHT RACE.

This is a simple yacht race from Newport Harbor around Block Island and back.
10x10½ inches...Price, per dozen, $2.00

No. 489. THE ERRAND BOY.

The Errand Boy is a game based on the progress through life of a boy from the time he begins as errand boy till he becomes a Bank President.
10x10½ inches....Price per dozen, $2.00

No. 433. PUSSY AND THE THREE MICE.
(NEW.)

Size of box, 10x10½ inches. Board, 10x19 inches.
Price, per dozen................ $2.00

No. 551. JEROME PARK STEEPLE CHASE,
Popular Edition.

Box, 12½x16 inches. Board, 14x24 inches.

This game of horse-racing is played with **two** dice, over a board laid off in a circle imitative of a race track, and containing 100 spaces.
Price, per dozen. $3.75

No. 690. PARLOR FOOT BALL.
(NEW).

Foot Ball, like base ball, makes a good parlor game when properly adapted to the purpose.
10½x19 inches...Price, per dozen, $3.75

No. 424½. GO-BANG.
Cheap Edition.

Size, 16x16 inches.....Price, per dozen, $3.75

No. 424. GO-BANG.

Go-Bang is one of the most remarkable games published. It is a standard game for all.
10½x20 inches....Price, per dozen, $8.00

No. 550. THE WORLD'S GAME OF BASE BALL.

This Base Ball imitates in the parlor, upon the table, so far as it is possible, the great national game.

Size, 9x16 inches...Price, per dozen, $3.75

No. 452. GOLDEN LOCKS SERIES.

Three kinds assorted in quarter dozens.

Little Golden Locks. Little Red Riding Hood.
Jack the Giant Killer.

10½x20 inches....Price, per dozen $3.75

No. 692. DIAMOND SERIES, NEW.

Three kinds put up, assorted, in quarter dozens.

Cats and Mice and Tousel. Captive Princess and ambuscades. Life's Mishaps and Bobbing around the circle.

14x14 inches....Price, per dozen, $3.75

The game is designed for boys particularly, though it will be found interesting to older people also.

10½x19½ inches...Price, per dozen, $375

ONE DOLLAR BOARD GAMES.

No. 441½. TELEGRAPH BOY GAME.

9x17 inches. Board, 17x17.

The game is a race between **two, three or four** players, each using one piece. It is designed especially for boys.

Price, per dozen................ $8.00

No. 425. A TRIP AROUND THE WORLD WITH NELLIE BLY.

Fine Edition.

Nellie Bly is played on a folding board 15x17 inches when extended.

Price, per dozen............... $6.00

No. 430½. THE IMPROVED GAME OF STEEPLE CHASE.

12½x16 inches...Price, per dozen, $8.00

No. 564. KINGS AND QUEENS.

The game is fully equal, in excellence of play, to any recently published. It is intended for two players only.

Size, 12x20 inches...Price, per dozen, $6.00

No. 698. RACE AROUND THE WORLD.

Size, 14x16 ins. closed. 16x18 ins. open.

This game has its title simply in gold embossed on a background of dark imitation leather. It is intended to be of an instructive as well as amusing character. It is a game for children and young people.

Price, per dozen............... $8.00

No. 465. YACHT RACE GAME.

8½ x 16½ inches.

The yacht race is played on a board 16x32 inches. It represents a race of the New York Yacht Club, and is a game especially intended for boys, though of general interest.

Price, per dozen............... $9.00

No. 441. DISTRICT MESSENGER BOY GAME,

Size of box, 8¼x17 inches. Board 16x16 inches.

This game is said to be the most simple and complete of its kind now before the public.

Price, per dozen............... $9.00

No. 548. ARMY TENT AND SOLDIERS.

Two kinds, put up assorted.

These boxes contain sixty new paper soldiers—twenty-four kinds, ten of each kind—tin stands to make them all stand upright, and four tents. The soldiers are intended to be cut out and put on their stands, after which they may be divided into two armies, set up at a couple of yards' distance, and bowled at by their respective commanders with marbles for cannon balls. The one first bowling down all the opposition men wins the battle.

Price, per dozen............... $2.00

LOTTO GAMES.

No. 417A. No. 00 LOTTO.

This Lotto has a set of numbers on square blocks and six cards.

Size of box, 6½x3¾ inches...Price, per dozen, $ .75

No. 417B. No. 0 LOTTO.

This Lotto is put up with round counters and twelve cards, in a black box with gilt stamp.

Size of box, 6½x3¾ inches...Price, per dozen, $1.25

No. 417. TRUNK LOTTO No. 1.

This box contains twenty-four cards, a set of round men and a box of glass markers. It is put up in a wood box, covered with paper so as to represent a leather trunk.

4x6¾ inches.....Price, per dozen, $2.00

No. 418. TRUNK LOTTO No. 2.

The box of this Lotto is 4¾x8 inches. It contains twenty-four cards, a set of counters and a box of glass sufficient for the extra cards. The box is wood, covered to represent a leather trunk, and in general appearance resembles 417.

Price, per dozen............... $3.75

No. 419. TRUNK LOTTO No. 3.

The size of this box is 6x10½ inches. It contains twenty-four cards, a set of counters and a greater quantity of glass markers. The covering of the box represents a leather trunk, and resembles in general appearance the cut of No. 417.

Price, per dozen............... $7.50

No. 325. AMERICAN LOTTO.

Fancy Box.

This Lotto is the same as No. 417, above, except that the box has a lithographed label.

5x8 inches......Price, per dozen, $2.00

No. 327. AMERICAN LOTTO.

Fancy Box.

The box is of wood, covered with fancy paper, and has a lithographed label. It contains twenty-four cards, a set of counters and a box of glass sufficient for the cards.

9¾x10¾ inches................... $3.75

No. 423. PICTURE LOTTO.

The box is of wood. The set contains twelve entire cards with colored pictures, and thirty-six cards cut into slips with which to cover portions of twelve whole cards; and the usual set of counters.

9x10¼ inches.................... $6.00

TIDDLEDY WINK GAMES.

No. 851.   TIDDLEDY WINKS, No. 1.

Price, per dozen $1.85

No. 852.   TIDDLEDY WINKS, No. 2.

Price, per dozen.......................... $3.75

No. 857.   PROGRESSIVE TIDDLEDY WINKS.
Single Table Set.

This is a set of Tiddledy Winks, put up with invitation cards, score cards, markers, one set of table cards, and a single set of "Tiddledies" and "Winks." It is in all respects uniform with the four tables set above, and is intended to be used as a supplement to it when a five table party is desired.

Size, 4½x....Price, per set, each, $6.00

FIVE CENT CARD GAMES.

No. 300/5. FOX AND GEESE. OLD MAID.
PETER CODDLES. AUTHORS. SNAP.
CORDS OF FORTUNE.

A fine edition of six of the most popular card games, lithographed in five colors, and put up in neat boxes with handsome, showy labels.

Price, per dozen, assorted....... $0.32

No. 22.   GAME OF FOX AND GEESE.

This is a very interesting card game, with a tee-totum. Amusing to young and old.

Price, per dozen................. $ .67

No. 68.   GAME OF AUTHORS.

A very fine edition of this popular game.

Prices, per dozen.............. $ .67

No. 165.   RAILROAD OLD MAID.

A cheaper edition of the popular game, cards lithographed in the best style. Comes in good showy box.

Price, per dozen................ $ .67

No. 152.   'ROUND THE WORLD JOE.
No. 154.   SHOPPING.
No. 156.   TRADES.

Three newest and latest 10 cent games.

Price, per dozen.......... .... $ .75

No. 509.   PUZZLE PICTURE OF THE WHITE
SQUADRON.

Price, per dozen........................... $ .75

No. 224.   GAME OF BASE BALL,

Price, per dozen.......................... $ .75

No. 502.   GAME OF BULL.

A board game in box 7¼x7¼, with a large and novel indicator and a number of counters. A quick seller.

Price, per dozen................ $ .75

No. 25.   SNAKE GAME.

Price, per dozen .... $ .75

No. 238.   TELEGRAPH MESSENGER.
Something New.

Price, per dozen............................ $ .75

No. 223.   GAME OF MATRIMONY OR OLD
MAID.

Price, per dozen........... .... $ .75

No. 202.   HIDDEN AUTHORS.

Price, per dozen......... .... $ .71

No. 88.   COUNTRY AUCTION.

Price, per dozen....... .... $1.75

No. 82.   COUNTY FAIR.

Same series.   Price, per dozen.............. $1.75

No. 512.   GAME OF CASH.
New.   Retail 25 Cents.

Per dozen......................$1.75

No. 228.   GAME OF YACHTING.

Per dozen........... . ... $1.75

No. 513.   HOME TENNIS.

Per dozen......................$1.75

No. 29. NEW GAME OF THE GOLDEN EGG.

Per dozen.......................1.75

No. 229.   GAME OF BO-PEEP.

Per dozen......................$1.75

No. 303.   TIDDLEDY WINK TEN PINS.

Per dozen......................$1.85

No. 404.   TIDDLEDY WINK TEN PINS.
Large.

Per dozen......................$4.00

No. 304.   TETE-A-TETE.
New Game.

Per dozen......................$1.85

No. 511.   THE MYSTIC WANDERER.

Per dozen......................$2.00

No. 32.   GAME OF BELL AND HAMMER.

This is an old German game in a new dress, much more attractive and complete.

Per dozen......................$1.75

No. 321.   GAME OF CUCKOO.

Per dozen......................$1.75

RING A PEG.
The New Game.

Sells at sight. It is played upon a table, same as Tiddledy Winks, the object of the game being to snap the bone rings over the pegs. Complete game in box.

Per dozen......................$2.00

No. 179. THE FAVORITE GAMES.

Six new assorted games.

Per dozen $1.85

No. 105. PROVERBS.

An old standard game, revised and made suitable for the demands of the present day.

Per dozen......................$1.75

No. 104. PROFESSIONAL BASE BALL.

This excellent box-board game is the closest imitation of the out-door game yet produced.

Per dozen......................$1.75

No. 28. SARATOGA STEEPLE CHASE.

Per dozen......................$1.75

No. 31. STEEPLE CHASE.

A very fine edition of this popular racing game. Large board adorned with spirited pictures of the race, contained in box with brilliant label. Metal pieces for horses and riders, dice cups and directions complete.

Per dozen......................$4.00

No. 86. POPS.

A new idea in box-board games. The board represents a row of piles standing in the water. Pieces representing the players start from opposite ends of the row of piles and attempt to push each other off. No game at all like it. Played with dice.

Per dozen......................$1.75

No. 515. GAME OF TALLY HO.
New and novel.

Per dozen......................$4.00

No. 81. LUCK.
Retail Price, 25 Cents.

A most interesting box-board game of pure luck and chance. Comes with spinner or top, counters and full directions. Very exciting.

Per dozen......................$1.75

No. 402. GAME OF CHACQUE. NEW

Per dozen......................$4.00

No. 62. THE WILD FLOWER GAME.

In colors. A beautiful game in large new style box. There are over sixty cards expensively lithographed with pictures of flowers.

Per dozen......................$4.00

No. 52. GO-BANG.

This is a popular edition. Large folding board with gold squares, with a large number of wooden pieces for playing.

Per dozen......................$4.00

No. 22. THE KILKENNY CATS.

A jolly game for boys and girls.

Per dozen......................$4.00

No. 233. GAME OF MERRY CHRISTMAS.

Per dozen......................$3.75

No. 58. THE GAME OF AUTHORS.

The best edition ever made.

Per dozen......................$4.00

No. 57. LITERARY WOMEN.

A fine card game played on the Authors principle.

Per dozen......................$4.00

No. 232. GAME OF DRUMMER BOY.

This is a folding board game, size, 7x14, put up in a platform box, which contains besides, numerous drummer boys and a fine indicator. The game is new this season, and will be found highly entertaining.

Per dozen......................$3.75

No. 517. GAME OF LIFE.

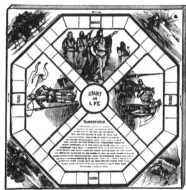

One of the finest games ever produced.

Price, per dozen............................$8.00

No. 518. GAME OF THE MERRY HUNT.

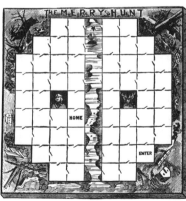

Price, per dozen.....................$8.00

No. 5. WORLD'S FAIR GAME.

The game of the season. Everybody wants one this year. Brilliantly lithographed board showing an exact reproduction of the Exposition grounds and buildings at Chicago. This is an excellent game to play. It is also a beautiful and showy article.

Price, per dozen $8.00

No. 40. CHALLENGE.
New 1893.

A new game of skill absolutely original in its process of playing. Played upon a board of new style in box about 16 inches square. A game which lovers of chess can appreciate, yet so much simpler that any child over ten years of age will enjoy it. The various pieces are numbered, and can be moved as many spaces as their numbers indicate.

Price, per dozen.................$8.00

No. 42. ZIGZAG KANGAROO.
New 1893.

A new game of skill suited for players over ten years of age. The peculiar features in the game lie in the fact that it is played upon a board covered with squares of four colors, and is played with pieces of the same color as the squares. When a piece is upon a square of its own color it is "safe;" on any other square it is liable to capture. Extremely handsome labels. Issued in a handsome box about 16 inches square, similar in general style to Challenge.

Price, per dozen.................$8.00

LARGE BOARD GAMES.

No. 7. CRAZY TRAVELER.
New.

It is the unexpected that happens in this game. It consists of a board arranged with circular pockets, combined with an apparatus which whirls a ball with great rapidity. Players count according to the numbers on the pockets in which they succeed in driving other balls with their large one, and also according to their success in making the ball knock over the tall wooden pins that rest upon the board.

Price, per dozen.................$8.00

No. 8. PRINCESS IN THE TOWER.
A Beautiful Novelty. New.

The board is 17 inches high and represents the tower where the princess is confined. The window where she is, is provided with a brass shutter, which opens and closes. Metal pieces, representing knights, climb up on a vine which runs to the top of the tower, and if captured are placed behind the brass bars of the cell at the bottom.

Per dozen...................$8.00

No. 4. PENNY POST.
New 1892.

Penny Post or the Letter Carrier's Game is novel both in its appearance and manner of playing.

Per dozen.....................$9.00

No. 164. GAME OF STANLEY IN AFRICA.
Improved.

Size, 12½ x 13½ inches. Lithographed in such harmonious colors as to make it exceedingly attractive The game is much in the form of an album, with covers of a pretty shade of clouded agate, beveled edges and nickel clasp. Two to four persons play the game. Put up with fancy papered dice cups, dart, target, etc., with full directions.

Price, per dozen.................$8.50

No. 75. JACK STRAWS.
Popular Edition.

Same as above, but fewer pieces and smaller box.

Per dozen.........................$2.00

No. 13. INNOCENCE ABROAD.

A very popular game. Comes in a large handsome box, enclosing large folding boards superbly lithographed. Innocence Abroad represents the journey of a party of people who travel by various routes toward the same destination, and who meet with various experiences and occurrences.

Per dozen..... ....$9.00

No. 183. GAME OF ARENA.

For 1893 the handsome game of Arena is offered. Not only is it attractive looking in its profuse coloring and design, but it will be found a game of merit and highly entertaining. Size, 36x9 inches. Packed with its counters and other implements in a handsome paper box, with fine label.

Per dozen..................$8.00

MAGNETIC JACK STRAWS.
Found at Last. Just the Thing for the Home Circle.

Sells at sight. Jack Straws is an old and popular game. The introduction of Magnetic Jack Straws has proven a great hit, and although but recently placed on the market, has already become popular. Two magnets go with each game. No dealer in holiday goods should be without it. Complete set in box.

Per dozen.......................$2.00

No. 165. GAME OF THE WORLD'S COLUMBIAN EXPOSITION.

In this game will be found a veritable trip through the grounds and buildings of the great Exposition at Jackson Park, Chicago The game is made up in the form of an album, with embossed covers in green, brown and maroon assorted, with beveled edges and nickeled clasps, the design being a correct representation of the principal buildings and grounds as far as practicable. The game is played by two, three or four persons, and dice are used in playing it. Put up with four leather dice cups and fancy turned men and counters with full directions, and is a decidedly interesting and ornamental game.

Per dozen.......................$8.50

No. 53. JACK STRAWS.

Fine Edition.

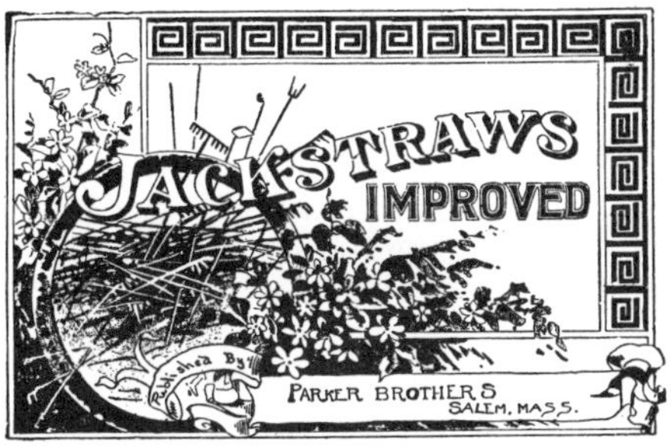

100 pieces, put up in a box with handsome label. Straws come in the shape of hoes, ladders, rakes, etc., and are numbered.

Per dozen........................$4.00

No. 500. CHESSINDIA.

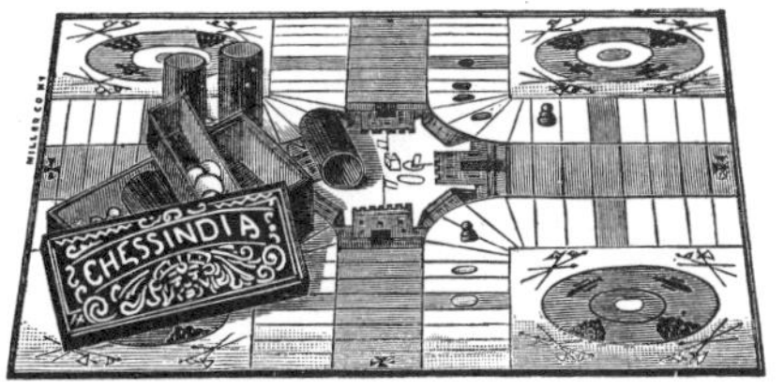

Chessindia is founded upon an ancient legend wherein four rulers combine with their armies to besiege a Fortress containing an immense treasure. There were four approaches to this Citadel, and the one who first planted his standard upon its walls was to have the largest share of the wealth it contained. The game has been designed to reproduce with its kings and knights the march of the four armies in their attack upon the Fortress. It has been called "the best of all games," and it will interest all ages.

Price, per dozen................ $7.00

GRAND RACE GAMES.

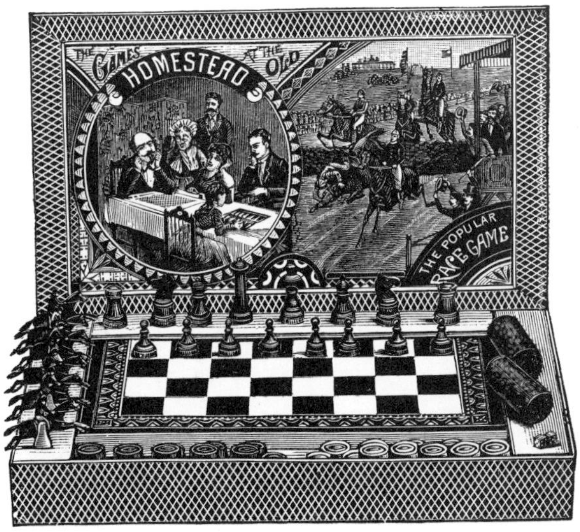

No. 1. Folding board, 12$\frac{3}{8}$x12$\frac{3}{8}$ closed, lithographed and varnished label, in five colors representing a race course, covered with fancy embossed paper. Box 5$\frac{1}{4}$x3$\frac{7}{8}$x1$\frac{1}{2}$, containing six horses and jockeys, two dice cups, dice, and directions for playing. Fancy gold top label.

Price, per dozen..$3.50

No. 2. Box 16$\frac{3}{4}$x9$\frac{1}{4}$x1$\frac{5}{8}$, covered with assorted fancy paper, with highly colored and varnished cover label, and containing a three leaf board 26$\frac{1}{2}$x14$\frac{1}{4}$ inches when open, upon which is the representation of the race course; also implements, horses, dice, etc., needed for six players, in compact and attractive form.

Price, per dozen................ $6.00

No. 3. Box 16$\frac{3}{4}$x9$\frac{1}{4}$x1$\frac{5}{8}$, covered with fancy figured paper, with lithographed and varnished cover label, depicting the scene of an exciting Hurdle Race, and containing a four leaf game board, which gives a combination of four games, viz., Chess, Checkers, Backgammon and Race Game; also compartments fitted with all the implements for each game.

Price, per dozen................ $9.00

THE STANDARD GAME OF PARCHEESI.

With Bone Counters.

PARCHEESI

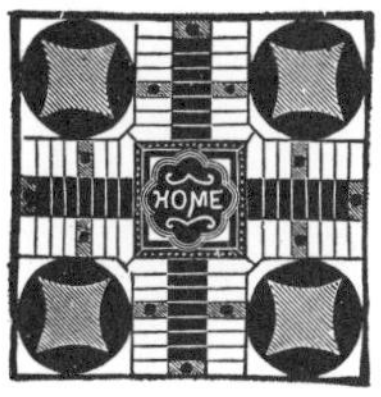

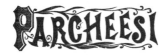

Price, per dozen........................ $8.40

BACKGAMMON BOARDS.

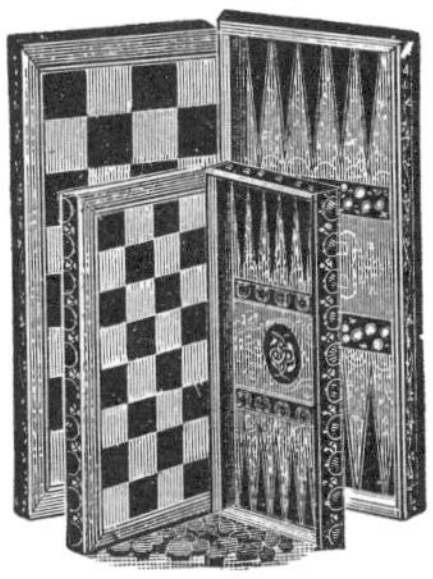

Per Dozen

No. 15. Folding board, size, 12x12x$\frac{7}{8}$ inches. Red and black 1$\frac{1}{8}$ inch squares. Fitted with dice cup and set of checkers. Border in red, black and white.................. $ .75

No. 25. Size, 12x12. Buff and black (imitation of sheep) squares 1$\frac{1}{4}$ inches, varnished. Border $\frac{3}{4}$ inches in black, buff, red and gold. Fitted with two dice cups and checkers complete 1.00

No. 30. Folding board, size, 15x15x1$\frac{1}{8}$ inches. Squares 1$\frac{1}{2}$ inches in red and black, intermediate lines in red, black and white. Border in red, black and white. Fitted complete with dice cup and checkers..... 1.50

No. 50. Size, 15x15, same style as No. 25, squares 1$\frac{1}{2}$ inches, lined off with gold and varnished. Fitted with complete set of checkers and two dice cups.............. 1.85

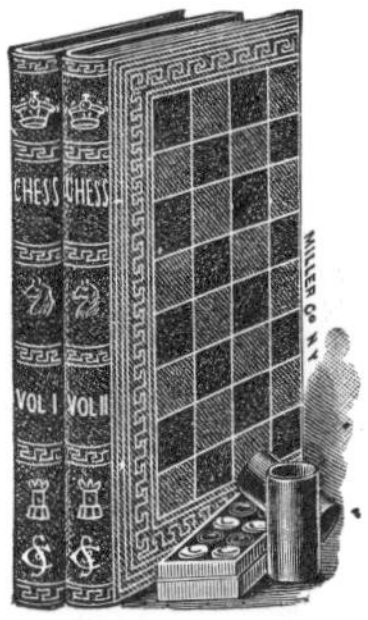

No. 75. Folding board in book form, size, 15x15. Buff and black squares 1$\frac{1}{2}$ inches. Border, 1$\frac{1}{2}$ inches wide. Finished in *durable embossed leatherette.* Two dice cups and checkers in seperate box....... 4.00

No. 200. Folding board in book form, size same as No. 75. Black and wine colored squares 1$\frac{1}{2}$ inches with gold lines. Finished in *extra quality of leatherette and embossed inside and out in gold leaf.* Complete set of implements and polished checkers in separate box. An exceedingly attractive board................................ 8.00

No. 733. Fine Leatherette................ $7.50
" 734. " " 9.00
" 718. Leather, black and red.......... 18.00
" 708. " " " finer........ 19.50
" 680. Fine leather, black and red........ 24.00
" 682. " " white " 24.00

It possesses remarkabls fascination for children as well as adults.

		Per Dozen
No. 1.	Popular Edition	$ 8.00
" 2.	Fine "	15.00
" 3.	Extra Fine Edition with Bone Men	30.00
Progressive "Halma"		Per set, 5.00

GAME OF DONKEY PARTY.

One of the most popular games ever brought on the market...............Price, per dozen, $3.75

CHESS BOARDS.

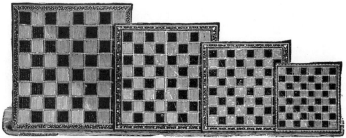

Per Dozen

No. 105. Size, 11⅝x11⅝. Squares 1¼ inches, printed in red and buff. Covered with assorted Belgian marble paper.......... $ .25

No. 106. Size, 11¾x11¾ inches. Lithographed in red and leather color with gold lines and border. Covered with morocco paper. Squares, 1³/₁₆ inches..................... .38

No. 115. Size, 14x14 inches. Squares, 1⅜ inches. Finely lithographed in red and black, with 1½ inch border in red, black and white. Varnished. Covered with imported morocco..................... .75

No. 125. Size, 16x16 inches. An extra lithographed label, varnished. Squares, 1⅝

Per Dozen

inches, in red and black with gold lines. Border 1½ inch wide in red, black and gold. Covered with best embossed morocco imported $1.50

No. 120. Size, 18½x18½ inches. Black and red squares 1½ inch with gilt lines ⅛ inch wide, border 2 inches wide in black, red and gilt. Covered with black embossed paper................................. 1.75

No. 130. Size, 18½x18½ inches. Squares 1½ inches in black and red with gilt dividing lines, and 2 inch border in red, black and gilt. Covered with fine leatherette with fancy embossed border, and title in gold leaf on cover........................... 3.50

CHESS GAME.

					Per Dozen
No. 00.	Turkey boxwood	men			$2.75
No. 0.	"	"	"		4.00
No. 4.	"	"	"	large size	6.00
No. 6.	"	"	"	largest size	8.00

CHECKERS.

Per Dozen

1 inch, Star special, 24 in a box $ .33
1⅛ and 1¼ inch, Corona embossed, 30 in a box.. .75
1⅛ and 1¼ " Crown polished, 30 " .. 1.25
1⅛ and 1¼ " King enameled, 30 " .. 1.75
1⅛ and 1¼ " Interlocking enameled, 30 in a box   1.75

BONE DOMINOES.

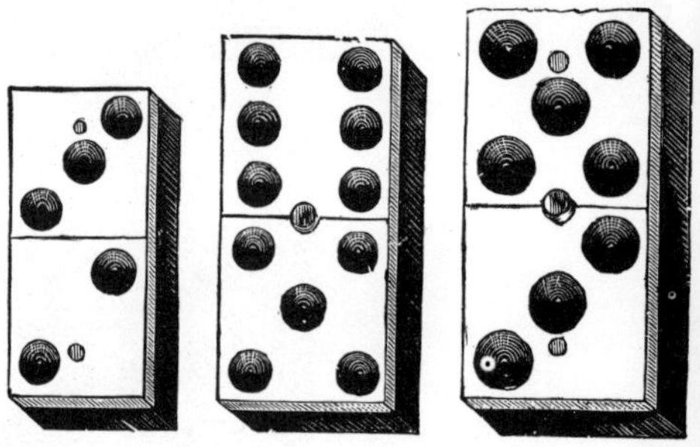

No.			Per Dozen
410/14.	In wood boxes		$2.00
410/18.	"	"	3.50
410/20.	"	"	3.75
410/22.	"	"	4.00
415/20.	"	"	4.00
415/22.	"	"	6.50
415/24.	"	"	8.50
416/24.	"	"	9.00

DOMESTIC DOMINOES.

			Per Gross
No. 5.	White wood, black spots		$4.50
No. 6.	" " in wooden boxes		4.80
No. 15.	" " red spots		8.40
No. 16.	" " in wooden boxes		9.00

					Per Dozen
American embossed	wood, red spots				.75
Quarter	"	" " "			1.20
Red	"	red " white "			1.75
Crown	"	ebony " " "			2.00
Nubian	"	" " " "			2.50
Black	"	" " " "			3.00
Arabesque	"	" " " "			3.75
Magna	"	" " " " " extra large			5.00
9–9	"	white double nine			3.75
9–9	"	black " "			7.50
12–12	"	" " twelve			12.00

CRIBBAGE BOARDS.

Complete with Pegs.

	Per Dozen
Climax, metal, nickel	$1.75
Favorite, metal and wood	2.00
Bonsilate, composition	9.00

SQUARE CORNERED BONE DICE.
Best Quality Stamped. 100 in a Box.

No.	Per 100	No.	Per 100
1	$ .30	6	$ .75
2	.35	7	1.00
3	.40	8	1.50
4	.50	9	2.00
5	.60		

BLACK DICE, ROUND CORNERED.

No.		Per 100
1.	Packed 100 in a box, ½ inch square	$1.00
2.	" 100 " ⅝ " "	2.00
3.	" 100 " ¾ " "	3.00

DICE CUPS.

No.		Per Dozen
1.	Sole leather	$ .63
2.	" "	.70
3.	" "	.80
4.	" "	.90
5.	" "	1.25
6.	" "	1.50
7.	" "	1.75

POKER CHIPS.

Prices on Poker Chips Subject to Change.

Packed 100 in a Wooden Box.

	Per M
1¼ inch composition, as'ted colors, best quality.	$2.50
1⅜ " " " " " "	2.75
1½ " " " " " "	3.00

WHIST COUNTERS.

No. 25. Nickel top, with black walnut base, finely finished...........per pair, $1.50

PLAYING CARDS.

See List on Inside Page of Back Cover. Playing Cards are sold on strictly NET 30 DAYS only.

PAPER DOLLS, SOLDIERS, AND FURNITURE.

TO BE CUT OUT.

No. 247¼. NEW SERIES—PENNY DOLLS.

The figures in this series are over 5 inches high, with 4 dresses in the latest styles. Very handsomely printed in colors. 4 kinds. Put up one gross in a package.

Per gross......................$ .90

No. 256½. AMUSEMENTS FOR CHILDREN.

12 kinds, large. Pictures of animals, etc., to be cut out. Cards, 6½x14 inches. Very handsomely printed in colors. One gross in a package, assorted.

Per gross......................$ .90

No. 259. NEW PAPER SOLDIERS AND INDIANS.
10 Kinds.

These soldiers and Indians are represented in action, running, shooting, etc. The sheets are 5¼x17 inches, with 6 and 7 on a sheet. There are 5 kinds of U. S. Regulars, 3 kinds of Zouaves, and 2 kinds of Indians. Put up assorted, one gross in a package.

Per gross......................$ .90

No. 260. PAPER SOLDIERS—INFANTRY.

Twelve kinds. They stand over five inches high, have bright and showy uniforms elegantly printed in colors on very heavy paper. United States Regulars; United States Sailors; West Point Cadets; Naval Cadets; Continentals; Grenadiers; Militia—Blue Dress; Militia—Gray Dress; Highlanders; Zouaves; German Soldiers; French Soldiers. Put up assorted, one gross in a package.

Per gross......................$ .90

No. 251. BASE BALL NINES.

Per gross......................$ .90

No. 260 A. NEW BRASS BANDS AND DRUM AND FIFE CORPS.

Four styles of uniform, making practically four bands. Like the soldiers, they are elegantly printed in bright colors and on heavy paper. Brass Band—White and Red Dress; Brass Band—Blue and White Dress; Drum and Fife Corps—Blue Dress; Drum and Fife Corps—Red and Blue Dress.

Per gross......................$ .90

No. 263. CAVALRY SOLDIERS.
The sheets are 5½x17 inches.

Per gross......................$ .90

No. 263 A. BUFFALO BILL; OR, THE WILD WEST.

Pictures of Indians, Horses, Buffalos, etc. Sheets, 4½x21 inches. Put up one gross in a package.

Per gross......................$ .90

No. 247. FRENCH PAPER DOLLS.
In Envelopes.

Six kinds. Elegantly printed in colors. Envelopes in colors and gold. Some of these have two figures. The dresses are perfectly beautiful. Marie Louise and Henri; Antoinette and Irene; Diane, the Bride; Virginie; Pauline, Baby and Annette; Eugenie and Hortense.

Price, per dozen.................$ .75

No. 248. NEW PAPER DOLLS.
Size 1. In Envelopes

Envelope 6x11 inches, printed in colors. Figures 7 inches high, all cut out of heavy cardboard. Five dresses in the modern style, with hats, etc., to match.

Price, per dozen.................$ .67

No. 249. NEW PAPER DOLLS.
Size 2. In Envelopes.

Envelope 7½x11 inches, printed in colors. Figure 9½ inches tall, already cut out of cardboard. Six dresses and six hats.

Price, per dozen.................$1.25

No. 250. PAPER FURNITURE.
Small. Four kinds, assorted.

The sets are: Parlor Set; Dining-room Set; Bedroom Set and Kitchen Set. All make up into handsome modern furniture when neatly cut out with a pair of scissors.

Price, per dozen.................$ .38

No. 255. PAPER FURNITURE.
Large. Four kinds, assorted.

The sets are: Parlor Set; Dining-room Set; Bedroom Set and Kitchen Set. When neatly cut out this furniture will fit one of our Doll Houses in perfect modern style fit for any family of Dolls in existence.

Price, per dozen.................$ .80

No. 261. LITTLE FOLKS' MENAGERIE.

A new pastime for children, consisting of animals, birds, etc., arranged especially for cutting out. Made double to enable them to stand. They are well drawn, finely printed in colors, and form a very attractive collection of animals for a nursery menagerie. Two kinds. 7x9½ inches. Package No. 1 contains 31 animals. Package No. 2 contains 33 animals. Put up in envelopes.

Price, per dozen.................$ .75

FINE PAPER DOLLS, SOLDIERS AND FURNITURE.

TO BE CUT OUT.

EMBOSSED PAPER FURNITURE.

On sheets 16x18 inches, consisting of Parlor, Bedroom and Dining-room Sets.

Price. per dozen sheets..........$ .75

EMBOSSED GERMAN PAPER DOLLS.

On sheets 12x15 inches, consisting of Boys, Girls, Babies, Nurses, Birthday Parties, etc., with complete outfits, finely printed, in very fine colors.

Price, per dozen sheets..........$ .75

No. 501. EMBOSSED PAPER DOLLS.
Cut Out.

Boys and Girls with jointed limbs, printed in fine colors.

6 inches long........Price, per dozen, $ .25

No. 502. EMBOSSED PAPER DOLLS.

Same style as No. 501. Larger.

9 inches long.......Price, per dozen, $ .35

No. 1. FINE TISSUE PAPER FAIRY DOLLS.

In 12 different colors with jointed limbs.

13 inches long.......Price, per dozen, $1.50

No. 151. FINE FAIRIES ON HALF-MOON.

Dressed in assorted color crepe tissue; with Calendar. 20 inches in circumference.

Price, per dozen.................$2.00

TOY BOOKS.

Paper, Linen and Indestructible, Half=Bound and Bound Juvenile Books.

No. 5. DAME TROT SERIES.

Six kinds. 8vo, 12 pages. Six full-page illustrations. Printed in two colors. Stories printed in large type.

Dame Trot and her Cat; Little Bo-peep; Sing-a-Song of Sixpence; The Five Little Pigs; Old Mother Goose; Old Woman who Lived in a Shoe.

Price, per gross.................$0.90

No. 8. MAY BELL SERIES.

The same size and style as No. 5, containing

The Three Bears; My First Alphabet; Three Little Pigs; Diamonds and Toads; Jack and the Bean Stalk; The Babes in the Wood.

Price, per gross.................$0.90

No. 9. ROBIN HOOD SERIES.

New, 6 kinds. Same size and style as Nos. 5 and 8, and containing

Robinson Crusoe; Story of Robin Hood; Rip Van Winkle; Aladdin, or the Wonderful Lamp; Ali Baba, or the Forty Thieves; Jack, the Giant Killer.

Price, per gross.................$0.90

No. 14. FARM YARD A-B-C.

A picture A-B-C book, showing Cattle, Poultry, Pigs, etc., 10 pages, illustrated, printed in colors.

Price per dozen.................$0.20

No. 12. PLEASEWELL SERIES.

Six kinds. Fairy and other wonderful stories. 8vo, 10 pages, 6 illustrations, printed in colors.

Three Little Kittens; The Five Little Pigs; The House that Jack Built; The Old Woman and her Pig; Dame Trot and her Cat; Mother Hubbard and her Dog.

Price, per dozen.................$0.20

No. 20. ALPHABET SERIES.
4 Kinds.

Adventures of A-B-C and Other Little People; Apple Pie A-B-C; Merry Alphabet; Jolly Animal A-B-C.

Price, per dozen.................$0.37

No. 21. WONDER STORY SERIES.

Six kinds, new. Size, 6¼ x 9¼ inches. Six full page colored illustrations, and from six to 8 plain pictures. The following are the wonderful stories:

Rip Van Winkle; Ali Baba, or the Forty Thieves; Jack, the Giant Killer; Aladdin or the Wonderful Lamp; Robin Hood; Robinson Crusoe.

Price, per dozen.................$0.33

No. 24. NOAH'S ARK A-B-C.

The animals in Noah's Ark form the basis of this book, and they are grouped in illustration of the letters in the most pleasing manner. 10 pages, six full-page and one double-page illustration, handsomely printed in colors.

Price, per dozen $0.33

No. 33. SUNSHINE SERIES.

Six kinds, size, 6½ x 9 inches.

Series:—The Three Bears; the Frog Who Would a Wooing Go; Cinderella; the Three Little Pigs; Cock Robin; the Silly Hare.

These books contain four colored pages besides the covers and three black pictures (all full page) and three pages of letterpress in good readable type.

Price, per dozen $0.37

No. 31. MAJOR'S ALPHABET.

A bright-colored Alphabet, with three illustrations on a page, prefaced by two full alphabets in black. 8vo, 12 pages. Printed in oil colors.

Price, per dozen $0.33

No. 32. NURSERY A-B-C AND SIMPLE SPELLER.

An excellent little Primer divided into easy lessons in spelling and reading, and illustrated with an object alphabet, printed in colors, 8vo, 12 pages.

Price, per dozen $0.37

No. 46. LITTLE FOLKS SERIES.

Four kinds. Newly illustrated and enlarged. Six full-page pictures, elegantly printed in colors, covers in colors and very handsome.

Package contains:—Cinderella; Jack and the Bean Stalk; Red Riding Hood; The Babes in the Wood.

Price, per dozen $0.37

No. 50. CINDERELLA SERIES.

New edition. New Covers. Six kinds. Varied contents. With two-thirds page illustrations, printed in oil colors.

Cinderella, or the Little Glass Slipper; the House that Jack Built; Alphabet and Funny Pictures; the Three Young Crows; The Babes in the Wood; Tom Thumb.

Price, per dozen $0.37

No. 51. DAME DINGLE'S SERIES.

Six kinds. Stories of Animals and Birds dressed in clothes, and given the attributes of human beings 8vo. Eight illustrations, elegantly printed in colors.

Wandering Bunny; Rich Mrs. Duck; Spoilt Piggy Wiggy; Dog's Dinner Party; Cat's Party; King Gobble's Feast.

Price, per dozen $0.37

No. 52. JOYFUL TALES.

Six kinds. New edition, new covers, the best on our list of six-cent books.

King Donkey's Doings; Queen of Hearts; Old Dame Trot; the Robber Kitten; the Butterfly's Ball; the Sad Fate of Poor Robin.

Price, per dozen $0.37

No. 55. SNOWFLAKE SERIES.

New. This is a very appropriate series for winter time, as it is made up entirely of Christmas and Winter stories.

Each book contains six elegant illustrations in colors, and several plain pictures. Very handsome covers in colors.

Santa Claus and His Works; the Robin's Christmas Eve; Frisky, the Squirrel; Hector, the Dog.

Price, per dozen $0.37

TEN CENT BOOKS.

No. 69. DARLING'S A-B-C.

With the capitals and small letters printed upon 26 half-page landscapes, showing objects whose names begin with the letters used. Descriptive lines beneath. Printed in oil colors. Showy covers. Large 8vo, 16 pages. Twenty-six half-page illustrations.

Price, per dozen................$0.70

No. 72. OUR BABY'S SERIES.

Four kinds, 7 x 10 inches in size. Fourteen pages each, all printed in full color. The pictures are made the chief feature, and the reading matter kept subordinate. Their beauty and size is marvelous for the price.

This series contains:—By Land and Water; Around the World with Santa Claus; Our Baby's A-B-C; The House that Jack Built.

Price, per dozen $0.70

No. 76. HALF-HOURS WITH THE BIBLE.

Twelve kinds, embracing a carefully written and very superior series of Bible Histories. Size, 6 x 8 inches. 32 pages. Eight to twelve illustrations. Cover in gold and colors.

Price per dozen.................$0.70

No. 78. CIRCUS AND MENAGERIE SERIES.

Four kinds. These books, for the price, far surpass anything hitherto published. They are 7 x 10 inches in size, contain fourteen pages of elegant pictures of circus tricks and performances, printed in the best style of color printing. The reading matter is in good, clear type, and will be found very entertaining. Covers elegantly printed in colors.

They are called:—Circus Sights; Circus Fun; Circus Tricks, Menagerie and Arab Show.

Price, per dozen $0.70

No. 90. THE KITTEN SERIES.

The Kitten Series consists of three books, each containing twelve pages of colored pictures and text.

The following are the titles:—The Three Little Kittens; The Three Bears; The Three Little Pigs.

Price, per dozen $0.75

No. 71. PICTURE ALPHABET.

In the time-honored style, A is for Apple, etc. One of the most elaborate of its kind. Fifteen half-page illustrations, together with spelling lessons, arranged after the best methods for teaching the young. Large 8vo, 16 pages. Fifteen illustrations in colors. Showy covers.

Price, per dozen......... ......$0.67

No. 91. MOTHER GOOSE A-B-C.

A new feature in the line of a Mother Goose book. It gives the twenty-six letters of the alphabet in their proper order, each one beginning some familiar rhyme of Mother Goose. 8¼ x 10½ inches. 14 pages every page illustrated in colors.

Price, per dozen $0.75

No. 92. THREE NEW PAINTING BOOKS.

Size 8½ x 10½ inches. Each contains 32 pages, 16 of which are illustrated, also one page of colored pictures as a guide for the children. Put up assorted one dozen in a package.

This series contains:—Domestic Animals; Playful Children; Children's Fun.

Price..........................$0.75

No. 99. CHRISTMAS EVE SERIES.

Three kinds. 8½ x 10½ inches, with eight elegant oil colored illustrations, full page, and about the same number of plain pictures.

This series is made up of:—The Robin's Christmas Eve; Hector, the Dog; Frisky, the Squirrel.

Size, 8½x10¾ inches.. Price, per dozen, $0.75

No. 100. CHILD'S FIRST BOOK.

It contains 16 pages of spelling and reading matter, in large, clear type, and illustrations in oil colors.

Price, per dozen $0.75

No. 101. CHILD'S HOME A-B-C.

New Edition.

Contains twenty-four small and six large illustrations in oil colors.

Price, per dozen.................$ .75

No. 103. MERRY ALPHABET SERIES.

Three Kinds: Put up assorted in dozens. Merry Alphabet; Apple Pie A-B-C; Jolly Animals A-B-C.

Price, per dozen..................$ .75

No. 114. ALADDIN SERIES.

Three famous fairy tales. Aladdin and Ali Baba, are from the wonderful "Arabian Nights." "Jack, the Giant Killer." Size 8½x10½, with six beautiful oil colored illustrations and several plain pictures.

Price, per dozen..................$ .75

No. 115. ROBINSON CRUSOE SERIES.

Robinson Crusoe, Robin Hood and Rip Van Winkle, comprise the series. Each of these has six colored and several plain pictures.

Price, per dozen..................$ .75

No. 116. MOTHER GOOSE IN A NEW DRESS SERIES.

Small Size.

Four kinds: Little Miss Muffet; Curly Locks; Bramble Bush; The Man in the Moon and other Rhymes. Each book contains four full-page pictures, 9½x7 inches; printed in brilliant colors, together with ten pages of smaller designs in two colors.

Price, per dozen..................$ .75

No. 117. YOUNG FOLKS' SERIES.

Six kinds. Comprising six little gems, viz.; Cinderella; Puss in Boots; The Three Bears; Red Riding-Hood; Babes in the Wood and Jack and the Bean Stalk. Pictures finely printed in colors, and six pages of stories in large type.

Price, per dozen..................$ .75

No. 120. BIRD AND ANIMAL SERIES.

Six kinds: Small Birds; Large Birds; Domestic Animals; Game Animals; Small Animals and Wild Animals. Each book contains six superb full-page illustrations of Birds or Animals. 16 pages.

Size, 10¾x9½ inches...Price per dozen, $ .75

No. 122. THE CIRCUS STORIES.

Visit to the Circus; The Wonderful Performing Dogs and the Monkey Circus, picturing in a life-like manner the wonderful performances of Men, Monkeys and Dogs. Next to the things themselves, these books will surprise and delight the little ones. Sixteen illustrations in each book. Printed handsomely in tints. 4to. 16 pages. Covers printed in colors.

Price, per dozen..................$ .75

No. 128. SUNNY HOURS SERIES.

Six kinds, new: Among the Flowers; Busy Days; By the Sea Shore; In the House, or at Home; On the Farm and With My Pets. Each book contains four handsome full-page illustrations in oil colors, and numerous plain illustrations, and pretty little stories in large type. Some of these stories place the children in the position of working people, and afford both instruction and amusement to the little folks. Size, 11x9 inches. 16 pages, with very bright covers.

Price, per dozen..................$ .75

No. 129. PALETTE PAINTING BOOKS.

Four kinds. This series of painting books contains 32 pages, on 16 of which are pictures. Eight are colored for copy and face the others, which are in black to be colored. Directions for mixing paints and coloring are printed on the inside of each cover. Put up in dozens, assorted.

Size, 7½x10 inches....Price per dozen, $1.00

No. 132. THREE LITTLE KITTENS.
Shaped.

This is a new edition of the old story. The pictures are from new designs, there being 6 full-page illustrations in colors. The book is cut out after the manner of the "Three Little Pigs" shown below.

Size, 11½x11 inches...Price per dozen, $1.00

No. 134. THE THREE BEARS.
Shaped.

This book contains the story of the Three Bears with new illustrations; it is similar to the "Three Little Kittens" and to the "Three Little Pigs" below. Put up in dozens.

Size, 8¼x11 inches...Price, per dozen, $1.00

No. 136. THE THREE LITTLE PIGS.
Shaped.

This book contains 6 full-page colored pictures from new designs. Put up in dozen packages.

Size, 8¼x11 inches...Price, per dozen, $1.00

MOTHER GOOSE.

No. 141. MOTHER GOOSE.
Square 12mo, Plain, New.

This is a very cheap edition. It contains a great variety of rhymes, and is well illustrated.

Price, per dozen.................$ .75

No. 143. MOTHER GOOSE CHIMES.

Contains one hundred and seventy-eight melodies and chimes and fifty-two illustrations. Royal, 16mo. Sixty-four pages, plain, with stiff covers, in bright colors.

Price, per dozen................ $1.25

No. 144. MOTHER GOOSE'S RHYMES.

Contains rhymes and illustrations. Royal 16mo. Sixty-four pages, plain, with stiff covers, in bright colors.

Price, per dozen................ $1.25

No. 145. OLD NURSE'S MOTHER GOOSE.

Just the book for the nursery, plenty of rhymes, and over eighty illustrations. Royal 16mo, with very showy covers.

Price, per dozen................ $1.25

No. 152. MOTHER GOOSE IN A NEW DRESS SERIES.
Large Edition.

This is a mammoth edition of Mother Goose. Size 14x11 inches. Each book contains four large illustrations, 12x9¼ inches, and ten smaller pictures. Little Miss Muffet, and other rhymes. Curly Locks, and other rhymes. Bramble Bush, and other rhymes. The Man in the Moon, and other rhymes.

Price, per dozen................$2.00

TOY BOOKS.

No. 150. BY LAND AND WATER.

This book contains pictures and verses descriptive of the characteristic modes of travel in the United States, Canada, England, Ireland, Australia, India, Egypt, and other lands where strange ways prevail.

Price, per dozen...... ....$1.87

No. 151½. A-B-C OF BIRDS.
Shaped.

The design of the cover and the shape into which this book is cut are shown in the engraving. The book is like No. 151 above, except that it is cut out as shown.

Price per dozen..................$1.87

No. 154. GREAT AMERICAN MENAGERIE.

In this book the scenes of the menagerie are represented. The pictures and text describe and illustrate snake charming, caged animals, trick seals, bears, pigs and dogs, a "happy family," goat-monkey race, dancing girls, Eastern sword contest, camel race, sham fight, juggling, etc., instead of the circus performance.

Price, per dozen..................$1.87

No. 155. A PEEP AT THE CIRCUS.

This book combines the pictures of two books. It has no text proper, only a descriptive title below the pictures.

Price, per dozen.................$1.87

No. 156. FREAKS AND FROLICS OF LITTLE GIRLS.

This book pictures little girls in all manner of sports, and also shows the mishaps that befall those who are careless.

Price, per dozen.................$1.87

No. 157. FREAKS AND FROLICS OF LITTLE BOYS.

Is the same as "Freaks and Frolics of little girls," except that the pleasures and mishaps of little boys form the subjects of its pictures.

Price, per dozen................ $1.87

No. 158. A PEEP AT BUFFALO BILL'S WILD WEST.

This book describes and pictures incidents of life in the West—such as Indian fighting, hunting, riding wild mustangs, lassoing and training them and traveling in "Prarie Schooner" to frontier homes.

Price, per dozen................ $1.87

No. 159. THE NIGHT BEFORE CHRISTMAS.

Is the "old, old story," and needs no explanation. Here we will simply say the pictures tell the story better than it was ever told before.

Price, per dozen................ $1.87

No. 161. GIRLS' AND BOYS' NAME A-B-C.

Each letter stands for a girls' or boys' name, the girls and boys being pictured in the book. The letters also stand for animals and objects, and are over three inches high.

Price, per dozen................ $1.87

No. 162. KINDERGARTEN FIRST BOOK; OR A-B-C OF OBJECTS.

Illustrates nearly three hundred different objects, including animals and birds. It will make children familiar with the names of everything they are accustomed to see in or out of the house.

Price, per dozen................ $1.87

No. 166½. OUR BABY'S A-B-C.
Shaped.

The same as No. 166, but cut out in fancy shape.
Price, per dozen................ $1.87

No. 170½. AROUND THE WORLD WITH SANTA CLAUS.
Shaped.

Cut out in fancy shape.
Price, per dozen................ $1.87

No. 177. RED RIDING HOOD PANTOMIME BOOKS.
Shaped.

Price, per dozen................ $1.87

No. 169½. A-B-C OF FUNNY ANIMALS.

Shaped.

This book is cut out, as shown in the engraving.

Price, per dozen................ $1.87

No. 172½. THE HOUSE THAT JACK BUILT.

Shaped.

Price, per dozen................ $1.87

No. 175½. FROGS AND MICE.

Shaped.

This book is cut out as shown in the picture above.

Price, per dozen................ $1.87

163A. AUNT LOUISA SERIES.

In Assorted Dozens. Twelve Kinds, or Singly as Follows in Dozens:

		Per Dozen
No. 171.	Domestic Animals................	$1.25
" 173.	Doings of the Alphabet............	1.25
" 182.	Henny Penny.....................	1.25
" 184.	Jack and the Beanstalk..........	1.25
" 198.	Red Riding-Hood................	1.25
" 199.	Robinson Crusoe.................	1.25
" 200.	Rip Van Winkle.................	1.25
" 208.	Tit, Tiny and Tittens............	1.25
" 209.	Three Little Kittens..............	1.25
" 213.	Three Christmas Boxes...........	1.25
" 216.	Visit to the Menagerie	1.25
" 222.	Yankee Doodle...................	1.25

SANTA CLAUS SERIES.

Big Picture 4to Toy Books. Six kinds are now ready.

		Per Dozen
No. 165.	Dame Trott and her Cat	$1.38
No. 168.	Cinderella	1.38
No. 174.	Beauty and the Beast...........	1.38
No. 188.	Mother Hubbard's Dog	1.38
No. 190.	Nellie's Christmas Eve	1.38
No. 202.	Santa Claus and his Works	1.38

LINEN BOOKS.

No. 265. LITTLE A-B-C BOOK.

Linen.

A showy little alphabet book at a very modest price. Each letter is illustrated with a common object, having beneath it a name for a spelling lesson. Printed on all-linen, with handsomely illustrated cover in colors.

Price, per dozen ....$ .37

No. 267. LITTLE PETS' A-B-C.

Linen.

A primer of 12 pages, printed in colors, on linen cloth. Simple lessons in large type for very small children.

Price, per dozen...$ .75

No. 267½. PLEASEWELL SERIES.

Mounted on linen.

Six kinds. A collection of fairy and other wonderful stories that have been household joys for many generations. 8vo. 10 pages and 6 illustrations in each. Printed in colors. The following books comprise the series :

The Three Little Kittens; The Five Little Pigs; The House that Jack Built; The Old Woman and her Pig; Dame Trott and her Cat; Mother Hubbard and her Dog.

Price, per dozen................$ .75

No. 268. LITTLE FOLKS' SERIES.

Linen.

Eight kinds. Favorite old nursery stories, selected for their special excellence. Newly illustrated and enlarged. Six full-page pictures, elegantly printed in colors. Covers in colors, and very handsome.

Package No. 1 contains : Cinderella ; Red Riding-Hood Babes in the Wood ; Jack and the Bean Stalk.

Package No. 2 contains ; Puss in Boots ; The Three Bears ; Tom Thumb ; Goody Two-Shoes.

Per dozen........................$1.75

No. 269. APPLE PIE A-B-C.

Mounted on Linen.

Per dozen........................$2.00

No. 273. MOTHER GOOSE SERIES.

3 Kinds. Mounted on Linen.

Per dozen........................$2.00

No. 271. YOUNG FOLKS' SERIES.

All Linen.

Six kinds, comprising six little gems from Fairy Land, illustrated by one of the best English artists. They contain six full-page pictures finely printed in colors, and six pages of stories in large type. Covers have bright pictures and are varnished. They embrace the following :

Cinderella ; Three Bears ; Babes in the Wood ; Puss in Boots ; Red Riding-Hood ; Jack and the Bean Stalk.

Per dozen......................$2.75

No. 281. MOTHER GOOSE.

All Linen.

Three kinds. Size 10½x8½ inches. The great demand for a Mother Goose in colors on linen has induced us to make these three additions to our Mother Goose literature. They contain most of the gems of the famous Nursery Rhymes, with plenty of illustrations in brilliant colors. Covers in colors and gold, making three very handsome books. They are called :

Bo-Peep, Mother Goose Melodies; Tom Tucker, Mother Goose Melodies; Old King Cole, Mother Goose Melodies.

Per dozen................. .....$2.75

No. 284. AUNT LOUISA'S BIG PICTURE BOOK.

Mounted on Linen.

These are the finest picture books printed. The kinds mounted on linen are the ones best adapted to the smaller children. The following kinds are now on hand :

Three Little Kittens ; Tit, Tiny and Tittens ; Alphabet of Country Scenes ; Visit to the Menagerie ; Santa Claus and His Works ; Mother Hubbard ; Cock Robin ; Doings of the Alphabet ; Red Riding-Hood ; Nellie's Christmas Eve.

Per dozen........................$3.75

HALF BOUND BOOKS.

No. 720. GRIMM'S FAIRY TALE SERIES.

Six kinds, assorted. In this series the Grimm collection of Fairy Tales has been divided to form six pretty, attractive books of forty-eight pages each.

Size, 8½x10¼ inches. Each contains about 16 black illustrations by Andre, has a fine colored frontispiece, and is inclosed in beautiful colored board covers. The titles of the volumes are:

The Twelve Brothers; The Enchanted Fawn; The Brave Little Tailor; The Three Golden Hairs; The Magic Mirror; The Golden Bird.

Per dozen........................$1.85

No. 726. PANTOMIME TOY BOOKS.
Half Bound.

Three kinds. Each contains five set scenes and nine trick changes, making fourteen transformations in all. Each book also contains the story of the Pantomime complete. They are elegantly printed in colors, and the transformations are the best that have ever been devised. They are very entertaining. Rich covers in colors and gold. Royal 8vo.

Aladdin; Sleeping Beauty; Blue Beard.

Price, per dozen..... .... $1.85

No. 728. LITTLE WORKERS SERIES.
Half-Bound.

Six kinds: At the Seaside; Sunny Hours; Play and Work; Dolly's Ride; Little Farmer Girl; Little Housekeeper.

Each book has four elegant illustrations in colors, and numerous pictures in black, with handsome letter-press. Size, 9x11 inches, thirty-eight pages. Showy board covers.

Price, per dozen................. $2.75

No. 744. HISTORY OF THE UNITED STATES.

A work in words of one syllable. It brings out the main points of American history, from the landing of Columbus to the present time.

Quarto. 118 pages. Board covers, with colored illustrations.

Price per dozen...................3.00

No. 746. THE PILGRIM'S PROGRESS.

This is an adaptation of Bunyan's great work, in words of one syllable, retaining the quaint style and old fashion Scriptural names of the original. Quarto. 118 pages.

Price, per dozen................ $3.00

No. 748. ROBINSON CRUSOE.

The old story written in words of one syllable. 93 pages. 4to Cap. Six full-page illustrations printed in colors.

Price, per dozen................ $3.00

No. 750. SWISS FAMILY ROBINSON.

One of the best juvenile books. 112 pages. 4to Cap. Six full-page illustrations printed in colors.

Price, per dozen............. ... $3.00

No. 752. SANDFORD AND MERTON.

A charming story. 142 pages. 4 to Cap. Six full-page illustrations printed in colors.

Price, per dozen................ $3.00

No. 778. LIFE OF WASHINGTON.

This book contains 128 pages. It is written in words of one syllable, and contains eight colored illustrations of scenes in the life of the Father of his Country. Size, 7½x9 inches.

Price, per dozen................ $3.50

ONE SYLLABLE BOOKS.
Large Size.

No. 805. CHRISTOPHER COLUMBUS.
New.

Contains 80 origiinal illustrations, 240 pages. Every boy and girl should know something of the great discoverer of America. The book will undoubtedly have a large sale.

Per dozen........................$6.00

No. 806. OUR HERO, GENERAL GRANT.
One Syllable. Plain.

86 illustrations. 170 pages. This book, being written in words which all little ones will readily understand, enables those who read it to become familiar at an early age with the prominent events in the life of this greatest of modern soldiers.

Per dozen...... .... $6.00

No. 808. SHERMAN'S LIFE AND BATTLES.
One Syllable. Plain.

96 illustrations. 158 pages. This volume portrays the triumphs of Gen. Sherman in the same simple but graphic style as is used in the history of Gen. U. S. Grant.

Per dozen........................$6.00

No. 810. OUR NAVAL HEROES.
One Syllable. Plain.

95 illustrations. 194 pages. This is a companion book to the two preceeding. It describes and illustrates the many battles in which our naval officers were engaged during our great civil war.

Per dozen........................$6.00

No. 811. LIFE AND BATTLES OF NAPOLEON BONAPARTE.
Written in Words of One Syllable.

82 illustrations. 162 pages. Next to our own national heroes there is no historical figure more likely to interest American boys and girls than that of the great military genius, Napoleon Bonaparte, nor one, a knowledge of whose acievements makes a more valuable addition to their stock of information.

Per dozen........................$6.00

No. 817. GRIMM'S HOUSEHOLD FAIRY TALES.
Half-Bound.

A large quarto of 284 pages, 8½x10¼ inches, containing over one hundred illustrations in black by that clever artist, R. Andre, together with a beautiful colored frontispiece. A new and careful translation from the original has been made of these world famous, child-delighting stories of folk lore. It is bound in elegantly colored board covers.

Price, per dozen $5.00

No. 821. HANS ANDERSEN'S HOUSEHOLD STORIES.

This book contains 316 pages of texts and cuts. The stories are too well known to require any extended description. They are the same that have delighted the children of the civilized world during the last generation in almost every language of modern times, and can only be characterized as Children's Classics. The cuts are from new designs, executed especially for this edition, and will be found appropriate as well as highly artistic. The printing is clear and neat, the type readable and the paper good. The binding is substantial and the lithographed covers handsome. The back is cloth, bearing the title and ornamentation stamped in gold. There is a colored frontispiece.

Size, 8½x10½ inches..Price, per dozen, $5.50

No. 822. SANTA CLAUS STORY BOOK.

This book contains 284 pages of well selected, simple stories, fully illustrated with appropriate and attractive pictures. It is clearly and handsomely printed on good, smooth white paper. It is bound in lithographed board covers; has a cloth back, stamped with the title and other ornamentation in gold, and a colored frontispiece.

Size, 8½x10¼ inches..Price, per dozen, $6.75

No. 829. FREAKS AND FROLICS OF LITTLE BOYS AND GIRLS.

This is made up of the two books for boys and girls heretofore described. It also contains several pages of other matter not in the other books. It has elegantly illuminated board covers. The great number and novelty of the illustrations will secure for this a large sale.

Price, per dozen $5.00

No. 768. THE MONKEY SHOW.

Half-Bound.

This is a quaint little book, quite as different in style from the usual class of toy books as it is original in illustration. The pictures are strikingly natural and brightly colored. They represent monkeys and other animals performing their funny and wonderful tricks. In fact, they are having a regular circus. As the pages are made of card-board, hinged together, they stretch out in one long panoramic view about twelve feet. The effect is wonderfully pleasing, particularly when they are stood upright. The book contains twelve pictures, 8x12, and is enclosed in handsome stiff covers.

Price, per dozen $3.75

No. 769. CIRCUS PROCESSION.

Something that every little boy and boy wants to see. This one they can see without leaving school, and may own it if they like. It gives a very accurate description of the circus going through the streets. Here can be seen elephants, camels, giraffes, horses, monkeys and other animals, with their gaily dressed attendants. A description of the procession is given on each page, making it very interesting. Like the "Monkey Show," it is twelve feet long when spread out, and is made up in the same style.

Price, per dozen $3.75

No. 770. AUTUMN SPORTS.

Twelve scenes. A panoramic book, similar in style to the "Monkey Show," but with pictures of Autumn sports.

Price, per dozen $3.75

No. 772. WINTER SPORTS.

A companion book to "Autumn Sports," but with twelve Winter scenes.

Price, per dozen $3.75

No. 773. CIRCUS SPORTS.

This book contains twelve scenes, in colors. It is the same size and style as the "Monkey Show," "Autumn" and "Winter Sports." This book shows what they do in the circus after the "Circus Procession" is over.

Price, per dozen $3.75

No. 63. PAINTING BOOKS.

Size 7½ x 8 inches. This series of painting books has 24 pages, but no colored sample page. The covers are paper, bright and attractive. Directions for mixing colors are prefixed. Put up separately in dozens.
Painting book, No. 1: Art Hours, after Kate Greenaway.
Painting book, No. 2: Steps to Art, after Kate Greenaway.
Painting book, No. 3: Young Artist.
Put up separately in dozens, price, per dozen, $0.67

No. 92. THREE NEW PAINTING BOOKS.

Size 8½ x 10½ inches. Each contains 32 pages, 16 of which are illustrated; also one page of colored pictures as a guide for the children. The covers are printed in colors, and very handsome. Put up assorted one dozen in a package.
Domestic Animals; Playful Children; Children's Fun.

Price, per dozen $0.75

No. 129. PALETTE PAINTING BOOKS.

New. Four kinds. Size 7½ x 10 inches. This series has 32 pages. The pictures are bold in design and half are colored for copy.

Price, per dozen $1.12

No. 716. LITTLE FOLKS' PAINTING BOOK.

Half-bound. 7¾ x 9½ inches. 32 pages. Similar to the foregoing in style and size, but with different subjects; 56 illustrations, after Greenaway plain, with one page in colors, for copy; neat cover in colors.

Price, per dozen $1.38

No. 180. MODEL PAINTING BOOKS.

Two kinds. New. Size, 7½ x 10 inches. These books are made up of two each of No. 129, with a new cover.

Price, per dozen $1.85

No. 183. ART PAINTING BOOKS.

New. Size, 7½ x 10 inches. This book is made up of all four of the kinds in No. 129 bound together.

Price, per dozen $3.75

No. 13. A RUN ROUND THE WORLD.

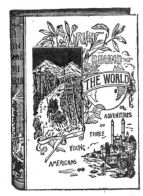

Chromo covers, 8 x 10 inches in size and 1½ inches thick. The largest book ever offered for the money In full cloth binding, handsome dies, printed on extra heavy calendered paper. 326 pages.

Price, per dozen $4.00

No. 13a. UNCLE SAM'S STORY WORLD.

A companion book to "A Run Round the World." A collection of short stories for boys and girls of all nations. Containing over 200 illustrations, with elegant colored frontispiece. 290 pages.

Price, per dozen $4.00

SPECIAL SERIES OF BOARD COVERED BOOKS.

No. 1. MOTHER HUBBARD SERIES.

Five Kinds.

Animal's A-B-C Book; Little Red Riding Hood; Jack and the Beanstalk; Old Mother Hubbard; Sing a Song of Sixpence.

Price, per dozen $0.70

No. 2. CINDERELLA SERIES.

Five Kinds.

Price, per dozen $1.25

No. 3. SUNSHINE SERIES.

Six kinds. 48 pages. Handsome cover.

Price, per doz., $1.25

No. 4. WINTER SUNSHINE SERIES.

Six kinds. 64 pages Nicely illustrated cover.

Price, per doz., $1.37

No. 5. AUNT VIRGINIA SERIES.

Five kinds.

Price, per dozen $1.50

No. 6. AFTER PLAY SERIES.

Six kinds. 112 pages. Special value.

Price, per dozen $1.75

No. 7. MERRY CHIME SERIES.

With colored frontispiece
128 pages.

Price, per doz......$1.87

No. 8. CHIT CHAT SERIES.

With colored frontispiece. 160 pages.

Price, per dozen $2.50

No. 9. RUN AND RIDE SERIES.

200 pages entirely new.

Price, per doz. $2.75

No. 10. MOTHER GOOSE'S BALL.

With five colored plates, new.

Price, per doz. $3.00

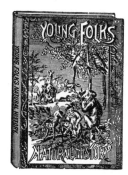

No. 11. MOTHER GOOSE SERIES.

Five kinds, new.

Price, per dozen .. $3.00

No. 12. WILD AND DOMESTIC ANIMALS.

Large and Showy Book.

Price, per dozen $3.00

No. 13. ARCTIC AND TROPICS.

Over 300 pages and cold frontispiece.

Price, per dozen $4.00

NEW LINE OF COLOR BOOKS.

Both the covers and the colored plates are printed in the highest style of lithographic art. The letterpress is on fine "ivory-finish paper" from new plates, the binding is half-cloth. We believe we can say truly that this is the finest line of juveniles ever offered to the American Public.

MISTLETOE SERIES.

Colored frontispiece. 6 vols.

Tangled Up; Hoods and Furs; In the Orchard; A Winter Frolic; Merry Coasters; Young Patriots.

Price, per dozen...... ....$3.25

SHINING HOUR SERIES.

Colored frontispiece. 6 vols.

Shining Hours; Fido and His Friends; Happy Darlings; The Magic Wand; The Fairy Circle; Sunny Days.

Price, per dozen $4.00

GOLDEN HAIR SERIES.

Golden Hair; The Morning Song; Merry Times.

Price, per dozen $4.50

IN THE SPRINGTIME SERIES.

In the Springtime ; Christmas Time.

Price, per dozen......................$6.50

HAPPY DAYS.

All fine colored pictures, a beautiful book.

Price, per dozen $9.00

FULL CLOTH BOUND BOOKS.

No. 14. PICTORIAL SERIES.

Cloth binding. 5 kinds.

Price, per dozen.................$7.00

No. 15. THE WILD WEST.

Over 700 pages, handsomely illustrated.

Price, per dozen.................$9.60

No. 16. THE LIVING WORLD.

Over 700 pages, larger than No. 15.

Price, per dozen...............$12.00

THE GEM MINIATURE BOOKS.

Bright stories for the little ones. Full of funny pictures. Each book contains four full-page colored pictures of a very pleasing design for children. Bound in half boards with handsome lithographic covers in ten colors. In neat boxes with lithographic top labels. 24 different volumes. The prettiest little books ever offered at the price.

BO PEEP LIBRARY.

5 x 6 inches, per set of 5 vols.

The Two Dicks ; Pretty Polly ; Dicky Bird, Esq.; The Cat and the Fiddle ; A Sweet Story ; A Little Blue Jacket.

Price, per set...................$0.60

POLLY'S JEWEL CASE.

5 x 6 inches, per set of 6 vols.

The New Pets ; Fireside Fancies ; Very Pretty ; Dear Little Buttercup ; Miss Mischief ; Three Little Kittens.

Price, per set...................$0.60

DOT'S CHRISTMAS BOX.

3¼ x 3½ inches, per set of 12 vols.

Miss Mistletoe ; Little Bo Peep ; Dot and Her Darlings ; Ups and Downs ; Little Play Fellows ; Apple Pie ; The Pet Puppy ; Little Love Letter ; Sand Castles ; Sugar and Spice ; Quick March ; Merry Legs.

Price, per set...................$0.60

COLUMBIAN EDITION OF THE UNITED STATES.

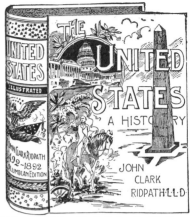

A history by John Clark Redpath, LL.D., author of the "History of the World," etc., etc. Profusely illustrated with sketches, portraits and diagrams. A handsome 8vo volume, with over 800 pages. Weight, 6 pounds ; 10¼ inches, long, 7½ inches wide, and 2¼ inches in thickness. The most complete and the most popular history of the United States of America from the aboriginal times to the present day, embracing : An account of the Aborigines ; Norsemen in the New World ; the Discoveries of the Spaniards, English and French ; the Planting of Settlements ; the Growth of the Colonies ; the Struggle for Liberty in the Revolution ; the Establishment of the Union, down to the Inauguration of President Harrison ; the Development of the Nation; the Civil War. Magnificently illustrated with flags of all Nations in colors, and numerous beautiful engravings describing the growth and development of the nation.

Price, each......................$1.30

FIFTY GLIMPSES OF NEW YORK.

An attractive work lately issued, consisting of 50 fine illustrations of New York City, made from recent photographs and handsomely bound in embossed covers. This is the best selling book of its kind issued.

Price, per dozen..................$4.00

CONTENTS OF BOOK.

1 Castle Garden and Lower End of City.
2 The Barge Office.
3 Brooklyn Bridge and East River.
4 On Brooklyn Bridge, New York side.
5 On Brooklyn Bridge, View of Cables.
6 The World, Tribune, and Times Buildings.
7 City Hall and Broadway.
8 The Post Office.
9 Wall Street and Trinity Church.
10 The Stock Exchange.
11 Washington Building, Battery Park.
12 East River, New York side.
13 Statue of Liberty.
14 The Union League Club.
15 The Cotton Exchange.
16 The Bowery, from Grand Street.
17 Washington Square and Arch.
18 Fourteenth Street, from Union Square.
19 Madison Square Garden and Park.
20 Fifth Avenue Hotel and Twenty-third Street.
21 Hoffman House, Broadway and Worth Monument.
22 Brunswick Hotel and Fifth Avenue.
23 Windsor Hotel and Fifth Avenue.
24 The Vanderbilt Residences.
25 Metropolitan Opera House and Broadway.
26 Fifty-seventh Street, near Fifth Avenue.
27 Hotel Waldorf.
28 Grand Central Depot and Grand Union Hotel.
29 The New Netherlands and Hotel Savoy.
30 The Plaza Hotel.
31 Metropolitan Museum of Art.
32 Metropolitan Museum of Art—Interior.
33 Museum of Natural History
34 A Central Park walk.
35 The Terrace, Central Park.
36 Plaza above Terrace, Central Park.
37 Belvedere, Central Park.
38 Cleopatra's Needle, Central Park.
39 Lake and view of Fifth Avenue, Central Park.
40 High Bridge, looking west.
41 Washington Bridge from High Bridge.
42 Bird's-eye View of Harlem.
43 Academy of the Sacred Heart.
44 St. Nicholas Avenue, from 129th Street.
45 Morningside Park.
46 125th St., cor. Fifth Ave.
47 "   " from Eighth Ave.
48 Seventh Ave., from 127th Street.
49 Seventh Ave., from 132d Street.
50 Elevated R. R. and 116th St., from Columbus Ave.
51 Lenox Ave. South, from 125th Street.

SCHOOL SUPPLIES AND STATIONERS' SPECIALTIES.

Slates.
Prices Subject to Change.

D. Slates,

Size			Per Doz
5x7.	18 dozen in case		$0 24
6x8.	12 " "		35
6½x10.	12 " "		37
7x11.	10 " "		40
8x12.	7 " "		45
9x13.	6 " "		55

D Slates. No. 2, Asst. in Case.

5x7	6x7	6½x10	7x11	8x12	9x15 size
2	2	2	2	½	⅓ dozen

Per case......$3 50

Bound Single Slates.

Size			Per Doz
5x7.	18 dozen in case		$0 60
6x9.	12 " "		70
7x11.	10 " "		90
8x12.	8 " "		1 15
9x13.	6 " "		1 30

Bound Double Slates.

Size			Per Doz
5x7.	9 dozen in case		$1 20
6x9.	6 " "		1 40
7x11.	5 " "		1 80
8x12.	4 " "		2 30
9x13.	3 " "		2 60

Slate Pencils.

	Per 1000
5½. in. gray pointed	$1 00
7. " "	1 30
7. " U. S. Flag pointed	1 50
7. " Gold pointed	1 75

No.		Per Gross
940.	Slate Pencils in wood, sharpened	$0 72
1946.	" " colored wood	90

Japanese Pencil Sharpener.

Per Gross

Japanese Pencil Sharpener.....................$0 80

Eagle Lead Pencils.

No.		Per Gross	No.		Per Gross
600.	Cedar	$0 30	65.	Rubber Tip	$1 00
E.	"	36	57.	Empress, rubber tips, small	1 32
140.	" with rubber top	72	50.	" " large	1 32
160.	Rosewood	84	547.	Herald " "	2 40

No.		Per Gross
321.	Mercantile	2 40
371.	Office, Rubber Tip	4 20

Lead Pencil in Boxes.

½ Gross in a Box.

No.		Per Box
80.	Assorted, rubber tips	$0 72
128.	" " "	1 32
70.	" " "	1 80

Automatic Ink Pencils.

No.		Per Doz
860.	Automatic Ink Pencils	$0 75
932.	Extra Leads, per dozen boxes	75

Penholders.

No		Per Gross
320.	Plain Cedar	$0 30
324.	Tapered Polished	50
1320.	Straight Polished	54
1324.	Tapered, assorted colors	67
1107.	Tapered Cedar, Polished, Japanned ends	1 12
1.	Crown Tapered, Polished hard rubber ends	4 25
2.	" " " hard rubber ends, larger	4 80

Penholders on Cards of Half Dozen.

No.		Per Gross
0309.	Imitation Celluloid, assorted colors, with pens	$4 00

Penholders Assorted in Cartons.

No.		Per Box
3.	Assortment, 6 Dozen of 6 kinds in a partitioned box	$0 80
6.	Assortment, 3 dozen in a box, sandlewood	87

Eagle Steel Pens.

No		Per Box
200.	Assortment box Pens, with glass cover, containing 10 boxes Pens, best variety	$2 75

No.		Per Dozen
1250.	Automatic Pen Holder	$0 75
1440.	Automatic Fountain Pen	75

No.		Per Dozen Boxes
2200.	Automatic Pocket Knife, round black handle	$2 00
2200C.	" " " oval black handle	2 00
2300.	" " " round, Celluloid	2 00
2260.	" " " with automatic reversible pencil	2 00

Colored Pastel Crayons.

No.		Per Gross Boxes
6.	Assorted colors, 6 in round box	$3 00
12.	" " 12 in round box	6 00
	Penny, 4 colored in package	75
	White Chalk Crayons, 1 gross in wood box, 8c. Price per case of 100 boxes	7 00

Pencil Boxes.

No.		Per Box
5-B.	Hard wood Pencil box, with lock and key	$0 40
368.	Imitation Inlaid Top Pencil Boxes, with lock and key	75
1.	Japanned Pencil Box, plain	90
2.	" " " with lock and key	1 20
3027.	" " " fancy picture cover, with lock and key	1 75

No.		Per Gross
11.	School Rules, 1 foot long, figured	$0 60
14.	" hardwood, 12x1¼ inches	88
30.	" " polished	1 50
35.	" maplewood, fine polished	3 00

SCHOOL SUPPLIES AND STATIONERS' SPECIALTIES, *Continued.*

Girls School Bags.

No.		Per Doz
101.	12 inch German Hemp	$0 40
226.	14 " " " with packed fringe	75

No.		Per Doz	No.		Per Doz
100.	14 inch, with draw strings, special	$2 00	125.	Macrame Bag to throw over the arm, with extra rings	$6 00
85.	Fine Woven Bag, fringed, with draw string	3 75			

Boys' School Bags.

No.		Per Doz
0.	Enameled 14 inch Leather Bags	$0 75
57.	" 14 " " " with pocket	1 75
1.	Heavy Enameled Cloth and Grained Leather, strap 14 inches	2 00
3X.	Canvas, leather bound	4 50
4X.	Alligator, leather "	4 50
6X.	Canvas, leather " finer quality	6 00
7X.	Alligator, same style as 6X	6 00
8.	Canvas, flannel lined	8 50
9.	Alligator, " "	8 50
12–14.	12 inch Hogskin, light and dark colors, very fine	16 50
13–15.	14 inch, same style	18 00

Elastic Bands Assorted.

No.		Per Doz Boxes
1.	Assorted box	$2 50
2.	" "	4 00
3.	" "	8 00
	In ¼, ½ and 1 Pound Boxes, per pound	1 85

Book Straps.

No.		Per Doz
12.	36 inch Split Leather	$0 35
10.	42 inch English grain leather	75

Shoulder Straps.

No.		Per Doz
10.	36 inch, English grain leather	$0 75
25.	42 " " " "	2 00

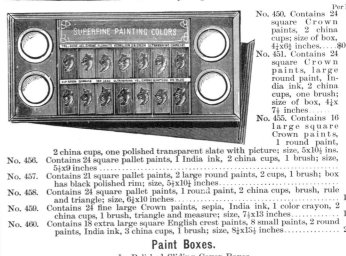

Shawl Straps.

No.		Per Doz	No.		Per Doz
13.	Split leather, 2 straps 36 in	$0 75	20.	English grain, 3 straps 36 inch	$2 00
18.	Grained leather, 3 straps 36 inch	1 50	25.	" " 2 " 42 "	2 00
15.	English grain, 2 " 36 "	1 50			

Pencil Pads.

No.		Per Gross
4100.	Special 1 cent Pad	$0 70
4000.	Large size	1 00
		Per 100
2532.	Large size, 110 sheets	$3 00
75A.	Youth series, 180 sheets	5 50
2540.	Animal series, 250 sheets	6 00

Ink Pads.

No.		Per 100
13.	Ink pads, 37 sheets	$2 50
523.	Dainty Note, 45 sheets	3 00
612A.	Dainty Note, 65 sheets	6 00
703.	Clover Leaf, 60 sheets	7 50

Blank Books.

Memorandum Books.

No.		Per Doz
314.		$0 06
510.		35
1201.	Pocket Memorandums	35
1256.	" "	75
1204.	" "	75
1130.	" "	2 00
1132.	" "	2 00

Composition Books.

No.		Per Doz
548.		$0 19
65.		35
645.		35
66.		38
634.		63
614.		68
710–20.		75

Note Books.

No.		Per Doz
62.		$0 35
145.		38
144.		63
61.		75

Paint Boxes.

Sliding covers, with bright colored pictures. One dozen in a package.

		Per Doz
No. 450.	Contains 24 square Crown paints, 2 china cups; size of box, 4¼x6¼ inches	$0 35
No. 451.	Contains 24 square Crown paints, large round paint, India ink, 2 china cups, one brush; size of box, 4¼x 7½ inches	38
No. 455.	Contains 16 large square Crown paints, 1 round paint, 2 china cups, one polished transparent slate with picture; size, 5x10¼ ins.	70
No. 456.	Contains 24 square pallet paints, 1 India ink, 2 china cups, 1 brush; size, 5½x9 inches	70
No. 457.	Contains 21 square pallet paints, 2 large round paints, 2 cups, 1 brush; box has black polished rim; size, 5½x10½ inches	75
No. 458.	Contains 24 square pallet paints, 1 round paint, 2 china cups, brush, rule and triangle; size, 6½x10 inches	1 00
No. 459.	Contains 24 fine large Crown paints, sepia, India ink, 1 color crayon, 2 china cups, 1 brush, triangle and measure; size, 7½x13 inches	1 75
No. 460.	Contains 18 extra large square English crest paints, 8 small paints, 2 round paints, India ink, 3 china cups, 1 brush; size, 8½x15½ inches	2 00

Paint Boxes.

In Polished Sliding Cover Boxes.

		Per Doz
No. 465–10.	Contains 8 fine artists paints, 2 china cups and brush; size, 3½x6 ins	75
No. 465–25.	Box polished in and outside, contains 12 very fine artists' Crown paint, 2 large china cups, 1 brush; size, 3½x9½ inches	2 00
No. 465–50.	Same style box as before, contains 20 finest artists paints, 4 large china cups with gilt bands, 1 brush; size, 4½x10 inches	3 75
No. 465–100.	Fine mahogany polished box with inside tray, 24 finest artists' colors, 4 color crayons, 2 brushes with handles, 4 large gold band cups; size, 6½x12 inches	8 50

Paint Brushes.

		Per Gross
No. A.	Assorted sizes, with wooden handles, in paper cover sliding box; 1 gross in a box	$0 75
No. B.	Fine quality, assorted sizes, with colored wooden handles, in glass covered sliding cover box; 1 gross in a box	2 00

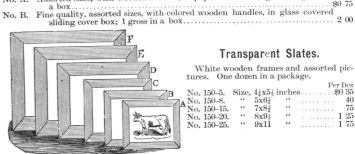

Transparent Slates.

White wooden frames and assorted pictures. One dozen in a package.

No.	Size			Per Doz
No. 150–5.	Size, 4¼x5½ inches			$0 35
No. 150–8.	" 5x6½ "			40
No. 150–15.	" 7x8¼ "			75
No. 150–20.	" 8x9½ "			1 25
No. 150–25.	" 9x11 "			1 75

Hardware Specialties for the 5 & 10c. Counter Trade.

THIS, our new department will comprise all the leading specialties. All articles in this list are of the best quality, from the most reliable factories in this country, at lowest market prices. Merchants introducing this class of goods will find them to be quick sellers at good profits, and in demand at all times of the year.

Hammers.
No.		Per Doz
245.	Coppered, with wooden handle 8½ inches long	$0 20
247.	" " " 9 " " "	27
35.	Plain Claw Hammer, 9½ inches long	38
11.	Adze Eye, full size hammer, bronze top, polished head, ½ dozen in a package	80

Carpet Tack Hammers.
No.		Per Doz
110.	All Iron, japanned and polished, 9 inches long	$0 33
255.	Polished, with claw oval hickory handle, 10 inches long, 1 dozen in a box	38
1.	Ladies Tack Hammer, polished claw, varnished oval handle, an excellent household tool	67

Tack Claws.
No.		Per Doz
150.	Bronzed, polished claw, all iron, 5½ inches long, 3 dozen in a box	$0 20
4.	Malleable Iron, black wood handle, 1 dozen in a box	35
100.	Lightning Tack Pullers, the best improvement in this line, made of solid steel with jet handle	1 00

Screw Drivers.
No.		Per Doz
10.	Cast Handle, polished steel blade, bronzed, 4½ inches long, 1 dozen in a box	$0 17
1.	Best Tool Steel, enameled handle, 1½ inch blade	22
2.	The same style, 2½ inch blade, 2 dozen in a box	35
3.	3 inch blade 1 " " " "	62
4.	4 " 1 " " " "	70
5.	5 " 1 " " " "	85

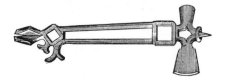

Combination Hatchet.
No.		Per Doz
300.	Coppered, 8 tools in one, 1 dozen in a box	$0 33

Combination Tool.
No.		Per Doz
8.	Consisting of can-opener, knife-sharpener, corkscrew, tack claw, hammer, glass-cutter, 1 dozen in a box	$0 50

Combination Plyers.
No.		Per Doz
2.	Consisting of plyers, wire cutter, nut cracker, glass cutter, can opener, 1 dozen in a box	$0 75

Can Openers.
No.		Per Doz
1.	American Can Opener, tuscan bronze, polished blade	$0 23
5.	Japanned Handle, steel blade	27
10.	Nickel Plated steel blade	35
3.	" " " " larger	63

Sprague Patent Can Opener.
No.		Per Doz
30.	Enameled, wood handle	$0 65

No.		Per Doz
25.	Pincers, polished japanned, 5 inches long	23
35.	Wire Nippers, same quality as No. 25, 5 inches long	23
45.	Compasses, 4½ inches long	23
55.	Pliers, 5½ inches long, japanned. 1 doz. in a box	23

Marking Awls.
No.		Per Doz
2.	Enameled Handle, warranted tempered steel blade, 4 inches long	$0 35

Brad Awls.
No.		Per Doz
110.	Wood Handle, polished blade	$0 37

Tracing Wheels.
No.		Per Doz
00.	The Favorite, jet handles, polished shanks, handle fits the hand perfectly, and is provided with a finger rest, plain wheel	$0 30
0.	Same as before, nickel plated	37
3.	Adjustable Companion Tracing Wheel, jet handle, polished steel shank blued, wheel, the most simple and neatest double tracer ever made	75

Mincing Knives.
No.		Per Doz
1.	Single Steel Blade	$0 40
2.	Double "	70

Cake Turners.
No.		Per Doz
C.	Enameled Handle, large polished steel blade	$0 60
A.	Kitchen Knives	30
B.	Shoe Knives	33

Stove Cover Lifters.
No.		Per Doz
120.	Diamond, Bright coppered, 8 inches long	$0 20
35.	Gem, nickel plated, 8 inches long	33

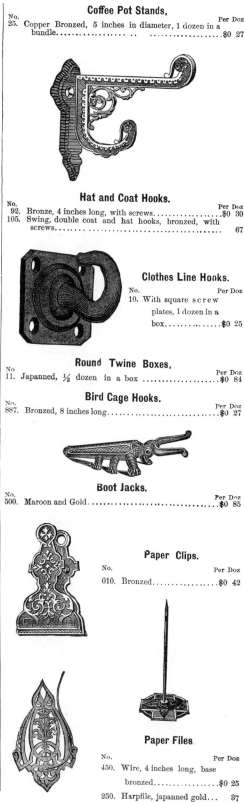

Coffee Pot Stands.
No.		Per Doz
25.	Copper Bronzed, 5 inches in diameter, 1 dozen in a bundle	$0 27

Hat and Coat Hooks.
No.		Per Doz
92.	Bronze, 4 inches long, with screws	$0 30
105.	Swing, double coat and hat hooks, bronzed, with screws	67

Clothes Line Hooks.
No.		Per Doz
10.	With square screw plates, 1 dozen in a box	$0 25

Round Twine Boxes.
No.		Per Doz
11.	Japanned, ½ dozen in a box	$0 84

Bird Cage Hooks.
No.		Per Doz
887.	Bronzed, 8 inches long	$0 27

Boot Jacks.
No.		Per Doz
500.	Maroon and Gold	$0 85

Paper Clips.
No.		Per Doz
010.	Bronzed	$0 42

Paper Files.
No.		Per Doz
450.	Wire, 4 inches long, base bronzed	$0 25
250.	Harpfile, japanned gold	37

Wire Goods Specialties for the 5 and 10 cent Counter Trade.

Tea and Coffee Pot Stands.

No.   Per Doz
3. Crown, silver luster, 6½ inches
diameter, 1 dozen in box.... $0 33

No.
1. Crown Stand, same as before
with 24 bars. 6½ inches
across.............Per doz. $0 70

Cross Toasters.

No.   Per Doz
1. The Reliable, plain toaster........................ ..$0 25
3. Our Special, with enameled handles................... 67

Bread Toasters.

No.   Per Doz
A. Size 6 x8 inches....................................$0 30
B. "   6½x9 " 38
D. "   9x11½ " 70

Potatoe Mashers.

No.   Per Doz
0. Light wire, wood
handle...... $0 20

2, The Giant, medium wire, wood handle............... 40

3. The Pride of Kitchen Masher, strong wire, wood handle. 65

3. The Kitchen Fairy, extra strong wire, with enameled
handle...... 70

Egg Beaters.

Per Doz
Spiral Egg Beater, the best and cheapest in the world......$0 35
Clipper Egg Beater, double action........................ 63

Improved Acme Egg Beater, with cog wheel movement,
quick and reliable.................................. 80
Easy Egg Beater, the best beater for the price............. 82

Spoon Egg Beaters.

No.   Per Doz
1. Red Handle, bright wire............................$0 35
2. Black Handle, better finish.......................... 40

Culinary Forks.

Patent Forks with wire handles. sharp prongs, strong
and handsome.

No.   Per Doz
2. Twisted Handle.....................................$0 25

3. Handy Cooking Fork, with wooden handles........... 38

Vegetable Skimmers.

No.   Per Doz
1. Wire Handle, an excellent skimmer..................$0 35

2. Red Handle Skimmers............................. 40
3. Enameled Handle................................. 50

Tea and Coffee Strainers.

No.   Per Doz
1. German Tea Strainers...............................$0 13
3. Best quality twilled wire cloth strainers................ 20

Enameled Handle Strainers.

No.   Per Doz
000. Finest Twilled Wire Cloth, 1¾ inches across.........$0 35
0 Same style, 2⅛ inches across......................... 72

2. Large Strainer, best corrugated wire, with tin rim
3⅛ inches across.................................. 85

Bowl Strainers.

No.   Per Doz
0. Good quality......................................$0 20
1. Same style, larger.................................. 27

2. Handle Strainer, narrow rim, 5 inches in diameter.. 42

Dish Drainer, made of bright corrugated wire, size, 12x16
inches.. 90

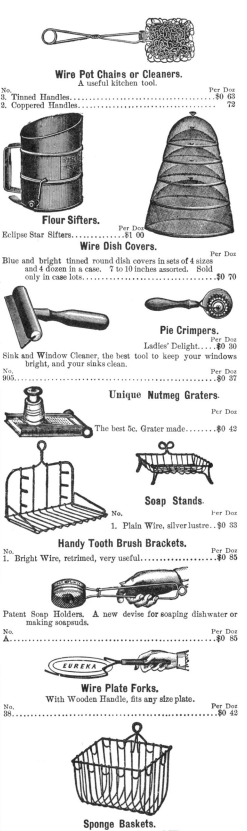

Wire Pot Chains or Cleaners.

A useful kitchen tool.

No.   Per Doz
3. Tinned Handles....................................$0 63
2. Coppered Handles.................................. 72

Flour Sifters.

Per Doz
Eclipse Star Sifters..............$1 00

Wire Dish Covers.

Per Doz
Blue and bright tinned round dish covers in sets of 4 sizes
and 4 dozen in a case. 7 to 10 inches assorted. Sold
only in case lots....................................$0 70

Pie Crimpers.

Per Doz
Ladies' Delight.....$0 30

Sink and Window Cleaner, the best tool to keep your windows
bright, and your sinks clean.
No.   Per Doz
905..$0 37

Unique Nutmeg Graters.

Per Doz
The best 5c. Grater made........$0 42

Soap Stands.

No.   Per Doz
1. Plain Wire, silver lustre..$0 33

Handy Tooth Brush Brackets.

No.   Per Doz
1. Bright Wire, retimed, very useful....................$0 85

Patent Soap Holders. A new devise for soaping dishwater or
making soapsuds.
No.   Per Doz
A..$0 85

Wire Plate Forks.

With Wooden Handle, fits any size plate.
No.   Per Doz
38..$0 42

Sponge Baskets.

Made of Silver Lustre Twisted Wire.
No.   Per Doz
00. Size, 7x4 inches..............................$0 63

Wooden and Tin, Kitchen and Household Utensils, for the 5 and 10c. Counter Trade.

Wooden Dish Mops.

No.		Per Doz
0.	White wood handle	$0 27

Polished Wooden Spoons.

No.		Per Doz
	A strong article, made of clean white wood, 12 ins. long..	$0 25
1.	Same style, 14 inch	27
3.	" " 17 "	42

Potato Mashers.

	Per Doz
Hard Maple, full shaped, good size, polished	$0 32

Enameled Handle Steak Maul.

	Per Doz
A new and handsome article, and a great seller	$0 75

Individual Butter Moulds.

	Per Doz
Assorted Prints, hand carved	$0 43
Quarter Pounds	90

Butter Spades.

	Per Doz
Plain Spades	$0 35

Rolling Pins.

	Per Doz
Solid handle, plain wood	$0 40
Revolving, flexible handles	63
Revolving, enameled handles	70

Polished Maple Bowls.

Made of best nard maple, extra deep, heavy rimmed, nicely polished

	Per Doz
11 inch, 1 dozen in a crate	$0 63
13 inch, 1 dozen in a crate	88

Wooden Family Mallet.

	Per Doz
Length, 12 inches, head 5½x2½	$0 75

Clothes Beaters.

	Per Doz
Wood handle, wire spiral beater	$0 75

Towel Racks.

	Per Doz
8 Arms, Stained wood	$0 37

Coat and Hat Racks.

	Per Doz
4 Arms, size, 4x21 inches	$0 40
6 Arms, size, 4x32	63

	Per Doz
Salt Boxes	$0 75

Towel Rollers.

	Per Doz
White wood, hard wood roller, 21x4 inches	$0 84

Splash and Table Mats.

	Per Doz
Splash Mats, white	$0 67
Splash Mats, colored	72

	Per Doz, Nests
Table Mats, oval or square shape, 6 in a nest	$4 50

	Per Doz
Sink Brooms, medium	$0 27
" " large	35
Scrub Brooms, wooden backs	37
Egg Timers	62
Straw Cuffs, in pairs	67
Putz Pomade, the best thing for cleaning all kinds of metal	40

Tin Household Utensils.

Tin Jelly Moulds.

	Per Doz
Plain Tin	$0 37

Patent O K Graters.

	Per Doz
More durable than any other grater in the market	$0 35
Victor Grater, made out of one piece of metal, with a double frame	88

Dustpans.

	Per Doz
Embossed Silver finish, half sheet	$0 40
Full Size	75

Embossed Drinking Mugs.

	Per Doz
Silver finished, 2¾x3½	$0 37

NEW! NEW! NEW!

A great want filled, something just invented to relieve the housekeepers from worry and trouble.

Imported Dust Cloths.

Made of very soft cotton material with colored border and fringe, or all colored.

No.		Per Doz
A.	16x16 inches	$0 40
B.	17x17 inches	75
C.	16x17 inches	85

Scrubbing Cloths.

Made of very heavy coarse woven Cotton Material, hemmed.

5.	23x26 inches	80
4.	23x26 inches, (better quality)	90

Round Tea Trays.

	Per Doz
12 Inches in Diameter	$0 60
13 " "	70

Oval Tea Trays.

	Per Doz
12½x16 Inches	$0 87

The W. Match Safe.

	Per Doz
Silver Finish	$0 30

HOUSEHOLD NOVELTIES.

Curling Irons

No.		Per Doz
3.	Single handle, 8 inches long	$0 35
8.	Double Black Enameled Handles, best 10c. iron	62
10.	Double handle, 6 inches long	63
6.	Same Style, 8 inches long	67
2.	Extra large, 9½ inches long	72

Comb Curlers.

No.		Per Doz
4.	Enameled, or white handle	$0 67

Tin Case Tape Measures.

No.		Per Doz
55.	1 Yard long	$0 40
100.	Better quality	70
150.	50 Feet long	2 00

Corkscrews on Cards.

No.		Per Doz
800.	Assorted, 6 wood, 6 metal handles	$0 40
500.	Same, better and larger	70

Steel Tweezers.

No.		Per Doz
3.	Assorted	$0 37
12.	Fine quality	75

FANCY GOODS DEPARTMENT.

This is one of the handsomest departments in my establishment, and embraces all the latest styles and designs of beautiful articles in plush, celluloid, wood, metal, glass and leather, and many novelties will be found in my assortment, which cannot be seen elsewhere, as I not only carry a full assortment of all the latest designs from the leading manufacturers, but also make up a number of specialties myself, and by doing so, can offer buyers good bargains at low prices.

ALBUMS.

AUTOGRAPH ALBUMS.

Per Dozen

No. 6/222½.　Embossed plush, assorted colors, with nickel word: Autographs.　Size, 3¾x6 inches............................ $1.75

No. 6/223.　Same style as before, larger size, 4x7 inches............................ 2.00

No. H.　Four assorted fancy shapes in assorted colored plush with silver flower ornaments, assorted.　Size, 5x6 inches, put up in flat boxes, four boxes in a larger box... 4.00

No. 1021.　Diamond shape; assorted, four designs in a flat box, plush, with celluloid flowers in natural colors.　Size, 5¼x5¼ inches................................. 6.00

Per Dozen

No. 1049.　Oblong shapes, four assorted designs in box, full celluloid front covers with embossed flowers, etc., in natural colors, plush backs.　Size, 4½x6¼ inches.. $8.00

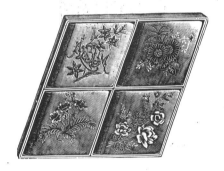

No. 1023.　Diamond shapes, four assorted designs in box, full celluloid front covers with embossed flowers, etc., in natural colors, plush backs.　Size, 5¼x5¼ inches.. 8.00

No. 1141.　Four assorted designs in box, two fancy shapes and one each harp and lyre shape, full celluloid front covers with embossed fancy designs, plush backs. Size, 5x6¼ inches 8.50

SCRAP ALBUMS.

Fine leatherette paper, assorted bright colors embossed in gilt and black with large chromo picture, assorted designs.

Per Dozen

No. 40/10.　Size, 9½ x 12..................... $ .75
No.　/25.　"　11½ x 14..................... 1.88
No.　/35.　"　13　x 17..................... 2.00

No.　/50.　"　12 x 16, finer finish 3.75
No.　/65.　"　13 x 17, "　"　.......... 4.00

PHOTOGRAPH ALBUMS.

All plush albums come assorted in the best selling and newest colors—viz., cardinal, peacock blue, old gold, orange, electric blue, olive, copper, etc.　Each album is put up in a paper box.

SMALL QUARTO SHAPE ALBUMS.

Per Dozen

No. 500.　Plush album with fancy nickel shield and nickel clasp; 6½ leaves; size, 7 x 8¾ inches $3.87

No. 490.　Silk plush, plain, with nickel clasp; 8 leaves; size, 7½ x 10 inches........... 4.00

FULL-SIZE QUARTO ALBUMS.

Per Dozen

No. 250. Silk plush with embossed flowers and the word "Portraits," nickel extension clasp; 14 tinted leaves; size, 8 x 10 inches $8.00

No. 501. Silk plush cover with embossed flowers and word "Album" in fancy letters on cover, nickel extension clasp, 12 tinted leaves arranged for 20 cabinets and 16 card pictures. Size, 8x10 inches,   8.00

No. 50. Fine silk plush, large embossed flowers and word "Album" in fancy letters on cover, nickel extension clasp, 14 tinted leaves arranged for 24 cabinets and 16 card pictures. Size, 8½x10¾ ins..   8.50

No. 252. Silk plush, embossed large fancy flowers and embossed word "Album" on cover, nickel extension clasp, 14 fancy tinted leaves, arranged as in No. 50. Size, 8½x10¾ inches...................   8.50

No. 52. Fine silk plush plain cover with nickel extension clasp, 16 tinted leaves, arranged for 28 cabinet and 16 card pictures. Size, 8¾x10¾ inches.........   9.00

No. 51. Fine silk plush with large ornamental word "Album" in celluloid on cover, nickel extension clasp tinted insides, 14 leaves for 24 cabinets, 16 card pictures. Size, same as before...................   9.00

Per Dozen

No. 53. Silk plush quarto album with bright silvered word "Album" on cover, 14 tinted leaves for 24 cabinet and 16 card pictures, nickel extension clasp. Size, 8¾ x 10¾ inches........................ $12.00

No. 508. Fine Moire plush cover with colored celluloid flowers and word "Album" in rustic letters, nickel extension clasp, colored landscape title page and 12 colored landscape, flower and bird decorated leaves for 20 cabinet and 16 card pictures. Size, 8½ x 10½ inches.................... 13.50

No. 60. Silk plush with fine large antique colored celluloid flowers and word "Album" on cover, nickel extension clasp, new style of gold and tinted flowered insides, 14 leaves. Size, 8¾ x 10¾ inches.. 15.00

No. 511. Moire silk plush cover with large oxydized silvered flower metal ornaments with word "Album," 14 tinted leaves for 24 cabinet and 16 card pictures. Size, 8½ x 10½ inches........................ 15.00

Per Dozen

No. 61. Fine silk plush with embossed borders, large word "Album" in oxydized silver, fine oxydized antique silver extension clasp, 16 leaves for 28 cabinet and 12 card pictures, inside tinted with new gold decorations. Size, 8¾ x 10¾ inches.. $18.00

No. 63. Fine silk plush album with tinted celluloid ornaments of apple blossoms, landscape and boy's head, new tinted inside with gold frame around each picture opening, nickel extension clasp. Contents and size same as before................ 18.00

No. 262. Fine silk plush cover with fancy gilt oval ornaments with gilt leaf and flowers and satin hand painted medallion. 16 leaves tinted with moss rose decorations for 28 cabinet and 8 card pictures, nickel extension clasp. Size, 9 x 10½ inches................................. 21.00

No. 5240. Silk plush full quarto album with fancy silvered metal centre piece with a Cherub and 4 silver metal fancy corners, patent silver extension clasp, 15 tinted leaves decorated with apple blossoms in gilt. Size, 8¾ x 10¾ inches.............. 22.50

Per Dozen

No. 64. Fine silk plush album, plain cover with fancy gilt shield and gilt corners, fine gilt extension clasp, new tinted insides with gilt flower decorations, 16 leaves for 28 cabinets and 12 card pictures. Size, 8¾ x 10¾...... ....$24.00

No. 264. Silk plush cover, spray of flowers and gilt medallion, fine gilt extension clasp, 16 tinted leaves with moss rose decorations for 28 cabinet and 16 card pictures . Size, 9x10½ inches........... 24.00

No. 527. Silk plush with large tinted celluloid flowers on cover, tinted inside with colored flower and butterfly decorations, gilt extension clasp, 16 leaves for 28 cabinet and 16 card pictures. Size, 8½x10½ inches...... .... 27.00

No. 528. Silk plush cover with colored celluloid flowers and bees, inside tinted and decorated with snow bells and other flowers, contents and size same as before, 27.00

No. 70. Fine extra large silk plush album with oxydized silver corner ornaments and large word "Album" in scrolls with butterfly, fancy oxydized silver extension clasp, 16 tinted leaves for 28 cabinet and 16 card pictures. Size, 9x12 inches...... 30.00

Per Dozen

No. 529. Fine extra large shape, silk plush quarto album with large colored celluloid flowers on cover, gilt inside title page, 16 leaves alternately decorated with bright gold border and colored pansies, arranged for 32 cabinet pictures. Size, 9¼x11½ inches...........................$42.00

No. 808. American quarto album holding 2 cabinets to the page, fine silk plush with celluloid word "Album" and colored celluloid flowers on cover, 16 fancy gold and marbleized decorated pages for 64 cabinet pictures, fine gilt extension clasp. Size, 9½x12 inches....................... 36.00

No. 809 American quarto Album, fine silk plush with celluloid words, "Auld Lang Syne" and colored flowers, 2 pictures to the page, 16 leaves for 64 cabinet pictures, fancy gilt flower decorated inside, fine gilt extension clasp. Size, 9¾x12 inches...... 36.00

Per Dozen

No. 5740. Large oblong shaped Album, fine silk plush with fancy silver metal centre piece with Cupid and 4 silver ornaments, silver extension clasp, 15 leaves tinted in new style for two pictures to the page holding 60 cabinet pictures. Size, 10x13 inches............ ....$33.00

LONGFELLOW SHAPE ALBUMS.

No. 2314. Longfellow shape album in silk plush with oxydized metal word, "Album" and oxydized fancy extension clasp, 16 tinted leaves for 64 cabinet pictures. Size, 7 x 16 inches....................... 24.00

No. 2315. Longfellow shape album, finest silk plush with oxydized metal corner with peacock and oxydized metal word, "Album" with butterflies and beetles, extension clasp, 16 tinted leaves decorated with palm leaves. Size same as before....... 24.00

No. 560. Longfellow shape album, fine silk plush with embossed corners and word, "Album," ornamented with embossed flowers on front cover, 16 leaves holding 96 cabinet pictures, 3 on a page, leaves decorated in new fancy flower, birds and butterfly decorations alternating with plain tints and gold lines. Size, 9 x 16 inches .$24.00

POLISHED WOOD AND CELLULOID QUARTO-ALBUMS.

No. 62. Quarto shape album with polished oakwood front cover, finely finished and ornamented with oxydized silver metal word "Album," with fuschia flower decoration, silk plush back, metal extension clasp, gold decorated new style tinted insides, 14 leaves for 24 cabinet and 16 card pictures. Size, 6¾ x 10½ inches......$18.00

No. 533. Quarto shape album, fine polished plain oakwood front cover, silk plush back, fancy silver extension clasp, 15 leaves for 26 cabinet and 16 card pictures tinted with new style gilt decorations. Size, 8½ x 10½ inches..................... 18.00

Per Dozen

No. 5220. Fine quarto-album, full celluloid front with large celluloid embossed calla and pansy flowers, silk plush back, oxydized silver extension clasp, 15 leaves with new gold and chrysanthemum decorations, arranged for 26 cabinet and 16 card pictures. Size 9 x 11 inches.............$24.00

No. 811. Fine quarto-album, celluloid cover, embossed landscape with figures and silver borders, full silk plush back, new style silver extension clasp, 12 tinted leaves decorated with gilt ornaments, arranged for 22 cabinet and 8 card pictures. Size, 8½ x 10¾ inches..................... 24.00

No. 812. Fine quarto-album with full celluloid front, assorted flower decorations in plain colors, with fancy border, silk plush back with silver rim, silver extension clasp, 12 tinted leaves decorated with assorted gold ornaments arranged for 22 cabinet and 8 card pictures. Size, 8½ x 10¾ inches.24.00

No. 228, **H.** Fine quarto album with full celluloid cover in shaded colors with embossed colored flowers and word "Portraits" and medallion with head, fine silk plush back, new style of extension clasp, 16 leaves arranged for 28 cabinet and 16 card pictures, inside decorated in new style with gold ornaments. Size, 8¾ x 10¾ inches................................... 33.00

Per Dozen

No. 227, **V.** Fine plush quarto album, full celluloid cover in colored antique with flowers and ferns, silk plush back, silver extension clasp, 16 leaves arranged for 32 cabinet pictures, imitation ivory insides. Size, same as before $33.00

No. 888. Fine quarto album with full celluloid front, cover highly embossed with landscape and mandolin player, with silver rim, fine silk plush back, silver extension clasp, 15 leaves arranged for 30 cabinet pictures, decorated in tinted grained ivory. Size 8½ x 10¾ inches...... 33.00

No. 228, **M.** Fine quarto album, full celluloid front cover in antique colors, embossed with flowers in natural colors and words "For Memory's Sake," fine silk plush back, new silver extension clasp, 16 leaves for 32 cabinet pictures, decorated with fine colored chrysanthemum and other flowers. Size, 9 x 11 inches........ 33.00

Per Dozen

No. 228, **W**. Fine quarto album, similar to No. 228, M, with decorations on front cover in Forget - Me - Nots in natural colors and words "Remember Me," new gilt extension clasp and new style of inside decoration in apple blossoms and butterflies, arranged for circular and square openings for 28 cabinet and 16 card pictures. Size, same as before............$33.00

Per Dozen

No. 962. Fine quarto album with ivory tinted celluloid full front, highly embossed with allegorical figure representing music with Cupid, silver rim, fine silk plush back, extension silver clasp, 15 ivory tinted leaves, arranged for 30 pictures. Size, 8½ x 10¾ inches....................$39.00

Per Dozen

No. 5254, **L**. Fine quarto album, Aluminum metal front cover with embossed centre panel, word "Album" in gilt wire, silk plush back, silver extension clasp, 15 tinted leaves with new gilt square and medallion decoration, arranged for 26 cabinet and 16 card pictures. Size, 9 x 11 inches...................... ....$33.00

No. 930. Fine quarto album with full white celluloid cover decorated with hand painted bouquet of Violets, Snow Bells and other flowers in natural colors with silver rim all around, silk plush back, new style of silver extension clasp, 15 tinted leaves arranged for 26 cabinet and 16 card pictures. Size, 8½ x 10¾ inches... 33.00

No. 226, **G**. Fine quarto album with fine celluloid front and back covers, front decorated in embossed large flowers with word "Album," 16 ivory tinted inside leaves arranged for 28 cabinet and 16 card pictures, new style clasp. Size, 9 x 11 inches 39.00

No. 5252, **B**. Fine quarto album, full metal front cover, lower corner silver finish engraved with word "Album" and flowers, upper corner copper finish engraved with ornaments and flowers, diagonal band in gilt, silk plush back, silver extension clasp, size and contents same as before, leaves decorated in apple blossoms, tinted gilt decoration................... 36.00

No. 538. Fine quarto album full celluloid front cover with highly embossed flowers in natural colors, silk plush back, 16 leaves with new style of flower decorations arranged for 28 cabinet and 16 card pictures, large silver extension clasp. Size, 8½ x 10¾ inches..................... 33.00

No. 226, **C**. Fine quarto album full celluloid front and back covers, embossed word "Cabinets," large flowers, ferns, pinks, etc., fine silver extension clasp, 16 ivory tinted leaves for 28 cabinet and 16 card pictures. Size 9 x 11 inches............. 39.00

No. 1613. Easel stand album, drop front, plush cover with large fancy word "Album" in celluloid on front cover, silver extension clasp, 15 leaves for 30 cabinet pictures, leaves tinted with gold flowers and medallion, drawer in base. Size, 7 x 10½ x 13 inches........................ 33.00

Per Dozen

No. 1647, **C.** Easel stand album, drop front, front cover full celluloid with edged flowers and ferns and large word "Cabinets" embossed in fancy scrolls, plush base with drawer, silver extension clasp, 16½ leaves arranged for 33 cabinet pictures, decorated in a new style of gilt tinted flowers. Size, 7 x 11 x 13 . . . .$45.00

TOILET CASES.

Per Dozen

No. 175. 3 piece case, wood box with metal ornament on top, silesia lining $8.50

PLUSH TOILET CASES.

No. 2987. Embossed plush, silesia lining 8.00
No. 2998. Embossed plush, silesia lining, larger size 9.00

No. 100. Special, silk plush, silesia lining . . . 9.00
No. 2925. Silk plush, silesia lining, large size, 16.50

Per Dozen

No. 7364. Silk plush, celluloid ornament on top, bevel edge mirror $16.50
No. 7351. Silk plush, celluloid ornament on top, bevel edge mirror with 4 manicure tools 20.00

No. 137. Silk plush, fancy shape box, 3 piece fittings 21.00

No. 7339. Silk plush, fancy shape, celluloid ornament on top, 3 piece toilet and 3 piece manicure tools 27.00
No. 7367. Silk plush, celluloid and gilt ornament on top, 3 piece toilet and 3 piece manicure tools, fine 33.00

No. 89. Silk plush, fancy shape, gilt ornament on top, 3 piece toilet, very fine 36.00

No. 2913. Silk plush, large square shape, plain top, 5 piece toilet, square mirror . . . 27.00

Per Dozen

No. 98. Silk plush, silvered ornament on top, fancy shape case, square mirror, 3 piece toilet, 7 piece manicure $36.00

No. 105. Silk plush, large square shape silvered ornament on top, 5 piece toilet, 4 piece manicure 42.00

No. 133. Silk plush, fancy shape, ornaments on top, fancy shape mirror, best quality. 48.00

CELLULOID TOILET SETS.

Per Dozen

No. 1934. 3-piece set, silesia lining $9.00

No. 1976. Silvered ornaments on top and silvered trimmings, silesia lined 16.50

No. 1978. 3-piece set, gilt ornaments and trimmings on top, selisia lined, larger case 18.00

No. 1978½. Same style as before with 3-piece toilet in silver fittings 22.50

Per Dozen

No. 1981. Gilt trimmings, 3-piece toilet, 5-piece manicure, white fittings........$25.50

No. 1979. Same style case as before with 3-piece toilet, gold and silver finished fittings.................................... 30.00

No. 1982. Celluloid case with gilt ornaments and trimmings. 3-piece fancy shaped white toilet fittings and 5-piece white manicure fittings...................... 30.00

No. 1982½. Same case as before with all silvered fittings.......................... 39.00

No. 1983. Large shape celluloid case, with ornaments and trimmings in gilt, 3-piece toilet, 7-piece manicure, fittings in silver. 45.00

MANICURE SETS.

No. 6857. Silk plush case, satin lined 5-piece fittings.. 9.00

No. 283. Wood case, 4-piece silvered fitting......... 9 00

Per Dozen

No. 255. Celluloid case with gilt trimmings, 4-piece fittings, new $9.00

No. 251. Celluloid case with gilt trimmings and ornament on top, satin lined, 6-piece silvered fittings......................... 20.00

No. 2928. Silk plush case with 3-piece small toilet and 5-piece manicure.............18.00

No. 6955. Silk plush, fancy shaped case with silvered ornament on top, mirror in cover, 7-piece fittings......................... 19.50

WORK BOXES.

PLUSH WORK BOXES.

Per Dozen

No. 300. Embossed plush, silesia lined. Size of box, 4¼ x 5¼ inches, 5 tools $4.00

No. 302. Embossed plush, silesia lined. Size of box, 5 x 6 inches, 7 tools.............. 4.50

No. 6154. Embossed plush with full mirror in cover. Size of box, 6 x 8 inches, 5 tools, 8.50

No. 308. Embossed plush with smaller mirror in cover. Size of box, 7 x 9 inches, 7 tools... 9.00

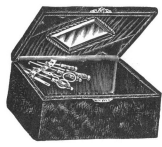

Per Dozen

No. 6027. Silk plush case with small bevel edge mirror in cover, satin lined. Size of box, 7½ x 9½ inches, 6 tools...............$18.00

No. 6120. Silk plush fancy shape box, with mirror (painted with flowers) in cover and bound with a silk cord, satin lined. Size of box, 7 x 9 inches, 6 tools.......... 18.00

No. 230. Silk plush with silvered ornaments and silvered border, inside cover finished with hand painted satin, size 6x8½ inches, 6 fine tools.... .... 33.00

No. 231. Same style as before with bevel edge mirror in cover. Size of box, 8 x 9½ inches................................... 39.00

No. 232. Same style as before with large bevel edge mirror in cover. Size of box, 8 x 10¼ inches.......................... 45.00

No. 3265. Fine silk plush fancy shape case with fancy celluloid top, padded silk and satin fancy finish inside. Size of box, 8 x 13 inches........................... 42.00

No. 3260. All celluloid case, finished in antique with fine leather trimmings, fancy bevel edge mirror in cover, satin lined. Size of box, 7½ x 8½ inches........ 45.00

Per Dozen

No. 3139. Fine celluloid case, antique finish with silk plush trimmings, fine fancy bevel edge mirror in cover. Size of box, 8 x 11, 8 fine tools......................$48.00

No. 3243. Silk plush with silvered ornaments, fancy shape case, 7 tools in cover, partition for jewelry......................... 18 00

No. 3257. Silk plush, fancy shape case with fancy celluloid cover, 7 pieces and inside box for jewelry......................... 27.00

WORK BOXES, POLISHED OAK WOOD COVERS.

Per Dozen

No. 42. Leatherette sides, mirror in cover, satin lined, 5 tools......................$9.00

No. 48. Silk plush, silver trimmed sides, bevel edge mirror in cover, fine satin finish inside, 5 tools...................... 22.50

Per Dozen

No. 49. Same style as before with gilt trimmings on sides, 6 tools, finished in gilt...$27.00

No. 50. Same style as before, larger size with silvered ornaments and silvered, trimmed sides, bevel edge mirror in cover, 6 silver tools...........................40.00

No. 3266. Celluloid case with gilt trimmings and ornament, bevel edge mirror in cover, satin lined, 8 tools. Per dozen....$18.00

No. 165. Celluloid case with gilt trimmings, satin lined, large bevel edge mirror in cover, 8 tools...........................$20.00

No. 64. All celluloid with silvered trimmings on silvered feet, round bevel edge mirror in cover, 6 silvered tools................. 24.00

No. 3275. Fine all celluloid embossed case, fine satin finish inside, fancy bevel edge mirror in cover, 7 fine bone-handled tools, 45.00

Per Dozen

No. 3277. Same as before, larger, with 8 tools................................$50.00

PLUSH GLOVE AND HANDKERCHIEF BOXES.

Sold in Sets only.

Per Dozen Sets

No. 1065/66. Embossed plush, silesia lining.. $9.00

No. 1008/9. Silk plush, satin lined.......... 9.00

No. 6730/80. Fine silk plush, satin lined with glove stretcher, larger size box.......... 18.00

No. 6731/81. Fine silk plush with embossed celluloid ornament, silvered trimmings, satin lined and glove stretcher 24.00

PLUSH JEWELRY CASES.

No. 405. Silk plush satin lined with separate tray. Size of box, 5x7 inches.

Per dozen.. $9.00

No. 406. Same style as before with lock and key. Size of box, 5½x7¾.................. 16.50

No. 418. Same style as before. Size of box, 6¼x9 inches...........................$20.00

No. 3432. Silk plush fancy shape with celluloid flower ornament on top, bevel edge mirror in cover, silesia lined, lock and key 15.00

No. 3462. Fancy shape with large celluloid ornament on top, round bevel edge mirror in cover, lock and key........... 21.00

PLUSH ODOR STANDS.

Per Dozen
No. 2. Stand with mirror in back, silesia lining, gilt paper ornaments, bottle of perfume...... $ .75

No. Star F. Embossed plush stand with two mirrors, satin lined base, silvered metal border, one bottle perfume................ 2.00

No. 16. Silk plush stand, satin lined base, silvered metal border, 2 large mirrors in box, 2 imitation cut glass bottles, not filled..... 4.00

No. 34. Embossed plush stand with canopy top, satin lined base, large mirror in box, drawer in base, 2 imitation cut glass bottles, not filled........ 9.00

Per Dozen
No. 45. Fancy shape stand, silk plush with large mirror in back, satin base and embossed silver metal ornaments, two imitation cut glass bottles, not filled............ $9.00

No. 32. Fine silk plush stand with 6 reflecting mirrors, gilt handle and gilt metal ornaments, satin lined base, 2 large and one small bottle of perfumery.............. 9.00

No. 30. Fine silk plush stand with canopy top, 3 large reflecting mirrors, silver wire handle and silvered ornamented base, 2 imitation cut glass fancy bottles filled with perfumery........................ 9.00

SHAVING SETS.

No. 4. Folding paper box with embossed silver cup, Badger hair nickel handled brush.. 9.00

No. 23. Paper box with embossed silver cup, Badger hair embossed silver handled brush, bevel edge embossed silver hand mirror............................... 18.00

No. 2413½. Silk plush box, satin lined, with embossed silver sides, embossed silver cup and silvered brush..................... 24.00

No. 737. Plush box, satin lined, decorated china cup, nickel handle brush and nickel handle razor.... .... 9.00

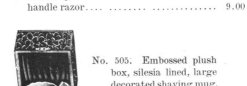

No. 505. Embossed plush box, silesia lined, large decorated shaving mug, nickel handle brush and nickel handle razor.... 13.50

Per Dozen

No. 504. Silk plush box, satin lined, patent flat decorated china shaving mug, nickel handle brush and nickel handle razor....$15.00

No. 512. Embossed plush, silesia lined with folding stand-mirror on top, decorated patent china shaving mug.......... 18.00

No. 535. Celluloid case with gilt trimmings, satin lined, flat patent decorated china shaving mug, gilt handle brush and bone handle razor........................... 27.00

No. 537. Fine celluloid case with gilt trimmings, bevel edge stand-mirror (folds flat in top of cover) satin lined, contents same as before...... 36.00

WHISK BROOM HOLDERS.

PLUSH WHISK BROOM HOLDERS.

Per Dozen
No. 4194. Diamond shape, embossed silver frame, silk plush centre with silvered ornament (Cupid) enameled whisk broom............... $4.00

Per Dozen

No. 4197. Long shape embossed plush with silver frame and bevel edge oblong mirror, whisk same as before. $4.50

No. 4235. Diamond shape figured silk plush with oxydized frame and bevel edge mirror, gilt handle whisk................. 9.00

No. 4265. Fancy shape silk plush with round celluloid embossed ornament in gilt embossed frame, gilt handle whisk......... 9.00

POLISHED WOOD WHISK BROOM HOLDERS.

Per Dozen

No. 4230. Polished oak, fancy shape with frame, diamond shape bevel edge mirror, oxydized gilt handle whisk............$8.50

Per Dozen

No. 4228. Fancy shape oak polished, diamond shape, oxydized gilt frame around embossed celluloid ornament fine large gilt handle broom......................$9.00

No. 5406. Polished oak, oblong shape with bevel edge mirror (round) in beaded gilt frame, 2 oxydized ox-horn hat holders, gilt handle whisk...................... 9.00

No. 5405. Fancy shape polished oak with 2 ox-horn hat holders, diamond shape bevel edge mirror in embossed gilt frame, gilt handle whisk..........................13.50

FANCY WOOD WALL CABINETS.

Per Dozen

No. 2022. Fancy wood, salmon color and gilt, decorated carved wood frame with fine hand painted flower celluloid panel in back.................................$12.00

No. 2023. Polished oak with carved ornaments in natural wood color, large decorated celluloid panel in back........... 13.50

MUSIC WRAPPERS AND CASES.

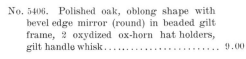

Per Dozen

No. 729. Leatherette imitation seal with strap...................................$3.75
No. 426. Sole leather one piece with strap....6.50

Per Dozen

No. 722. Imitation seal lined with leather, with pocket and strap...................$9.00
No. 718. Solid calf skin, black Japanned with heavy strap and heavy handle....... 8.50
No. 711. Leatherette round box shape with nickel ring ornament.................... 4.00
No. 714. Silk plush, same shape as before.... 7.00
No. 728. Sole leather, same shape as before.. 8.50

LAP TABLETS.

Per Dozen

No. 76. Imitation seal skin square shape with metal screw top ink, and partition for pens, etc.. $4.50

No. 2332. Imitation seal skin leather cover with patent oxydized silver spring cover ink and pen holder.... 6.50

No. 69. Imitation seal skin leather cover, square shape with oxydized silver patent spring cover ink and covered partition for pens, etc....... 9.00

No. 194/2. Fancy embossed leather (flower decor.) with oxydized silver cover, patent spring ink and covered partition for pens, etc................................. 9.00

Per Dozen
No. 80. Imitation seal skin leather, silvered bow knot ornaments, lock and key, leather covered patent spring ink, partition for pens, etc..$13.50

No. 198/3. Fine imitation seal skin leather cover with silvered ornaments, leather covered patent spring ink, and covered partition for pens, etc., inside pockets (cloth lined).......................... 16.50

No. 58/3. Fine imitation seal skin leather with inside pockets (leather lined) covered patent spring ink, and partition for pens, etc.................................... 18.00

SOLE LEATHER COLLAR AND CUFF BOXES.

Per Dozen
No. 433L. One box partitioned for collars and cuffs........... $8.50

No. 467. Same style as before, larger........... 16.50

No. 439. Oblong shape box, partitioned off for collars and cuffs with leather strap and buckle.............. 16.50

No. 434. 2 piece set, consisting of collar box and cuff box........................... 8.50

LEATHER TRAVELING DRESSING CASES.

Per Dozen
No. 420½. Oblong shape seal leather sliding case, containing wood handle brush, comb and tooth brush $4.50

No. 468½. Square shape sole leather with oxydized silver spring clasp, containing brush, comb and tooth brush..................... 4.50

No. 460. Oval shape sole leather sliding case, containing brush, comb, tooth brush and nail brush............................ 8.50

No. 469. Same style as 468½, larger case, containing brush, comb, tooth brush and nail brush............................ 9.00

No. 457. Square shape sole leather sliding case containing fine brush (French hair), comb, tooth brush and nail brush............. ... 13.50

No. 980. Sole leather folding shape (cloth lined), containing French brush, comb, tooth brush, nail brush and nickel soap box........ 18.00

No. 462. Square shape sole leather case with leather strap and buckle, containing French hair brush, celluloid comb, nail brush and tooth brush, nickel engraved soap box, bone handle razor and bone handle shaving brush................................ .... 24.00

Per Dozen
No. 605. Embossed leather sliding case, oval shape, containing brush, comb, tooth and nail brush.... $9.00

No. 607. Same style as before with oxydized silver covered partition for collar and cuff buttons at the end................ 13.50

No. 620. Fancy embossed leather sliding case, square shape with mirror inside, containing brush, comb, tooth brush and nail brush............................ 12.00

No. 951. Imitation seal skin folding case (leather lined) containing brush, comb, tooth brush, nail brush, nickel engraved soap-box, screw top perfume bottle, bone handle shoe-hook and shears........... 24.00

KNIFE, FORK AND SPOON SETS IN BOXES.

Per Dozen
No. 1880. Silver plated 3-piece set in satin lined box................................$1.75

No. K/25. 3-piece set heavier plated fancy pattern in fancy paper box.............. 2.00

No. K/50. Plush case silesia lined, heavy plated 3-piece set, fancy pattern........ 4.50

Per Dozen

No. K/100. Fine silk plush case silesia lined with fine heavy plated knife, fork, tea spoon, dessert spoon and napkin ring.....$9.00

No. 500. Paper box, satin lined containing heavy plated knife, fork, spoon, napkin ring and child's mug................... 8.50

IMPORTED WOOD WORK BOXES.

Per Dozen

No. 406/25. Polished wood box, lock and key, with imitation inlaid cover, size of box 4¾ x 7, furnished with 4 tools........$2.00

No. 406/50. Fine polished wood box with lock and key, size of box 6½ x 8½ with imitation inlaid cover with large mirror inside, satin pin cushion, 4 tools.......... 4.50

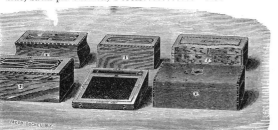

WRITING DESKS.

IMPORTED WOODEN WRITING DESKS.

Per Dozen

No. 80/1. Polished case, lock and key, size of box 6½ x 10, fancy cover, velvet lined and ink with metal screw top............... $5.00

No. 80/2. Same style as before, size of box 7½ x 11½..................... .... 8.00

No. 80/5. Same as before with 2 inks, size of box 10 x 14........................... 18.00

N 80/6. Polished antique oak with fine metal trimmings, velvet lined, with one ink, size of box 9 x 14.................. 18.00

DOMESTIC WOODEN WRITING DESKS.

Per Dozen

No. 108. 12 inches long, 8 inches wide, 3½ inches deep. French Burl desk, bevel edge, black and gilt ornaments, nice flowered finish outside; inside fitted with walnut, and lined with colored flannel....... $9.00

Per Dozen

No. 175. 12 inches long, 8 inches wide, 3½ inches deep. Walnut stained top, gilt ornaments, outside well filled and varnished, inside neatly fitted with walnut, and lined with colored flannel $9.00

No. 70. 12 inches long, 8 inches wide, 3½ inches deep. Walnut Desk, gilt ornaments, outside well filled and varnished, inside neatly fitted with walnut and lined with colored flannel.... .... 12.00

No. 299. Oakwood, ornamented with black and gilt band, and lined with colored flannel, 8 x 12 inches....................... 12.00

No. 126. 13 inches long, 9 inches wide, 4¾ deep. Veneered with oak, bevel edge, black and gilt ornaments, flowed varnish finish outside, inside fitted with reeded folds, lined with colored flannel......... 16.50

No. 196. 13 inches long, 9 inches wide, 4½ inches deep. Walnut desk, bevel edge, polished outside, fitted with walnut reeded folds and lined with colored velvet 16.50

METAL AND WOODEN INK STANDS.

Per Dozen

No. 52/5. Ink stand, round nickel case, round ink well with metal cover.............. $0.40

No. 52/10. Ink-stand with polished wood, round base, bronzed metal ink rack and nickel covered glass ink well.... .... .75

No. 02178. Silvered metal ink stand, horse shoe shape base with square ink well, heavy silvered fancy cover... 2.00

No. 2177. Silvered metal ink stand, fan shape base with square ink well, heavy silvered cover...... 2.00

No. 01667½. Silvered metal ink stand, oval base with fancy scalloped edge large square ink well with fine heavy silvered cover................................... 4.00

No. 01. Heavy silvered metal ink stand, oval shape fancy tray, one large square ink well with a metal silvered cover...... 4.00

No. 021. Metal ink stand, same style as No. 01, double size sith two ink wells........ 9.00

No. 02159. Large square silvered fancy tray with perforated border, 2 large square ink wells with heavy silvered fancy covers.. 8.50

No. 177. Polished oak wood library ink stand, square shape with two large square ink wells with glass tops................ 8.00

No. 180. Polished oak wood square shape library ink stand, finer finish than No. 177, 9.00

PICTURE FRAMES.

POLISHED WOOD, AND PLUSH PICTURE FRAMES.

(All frames are for Cabinet picture.)

Per Dozen

No. 2803. Wood square frame 6 x 8 inches, painted in white with gilt embossed lattice work..............$2.00

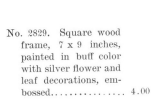

No. 2829. Square wood frame, 7 x 9 inches, painted in buff color with silver flower and leaf decorations, embossed.............. 4.00

Per Dozen

No. 829. Square shape silk plush frame, 5¼x7 inches, fancy pattern................... $1.75

No. 4837. Square shape embossed plush with oval opening 6 x 8½................... 2.00

No. 2832. Square shape silk plush frame octagon opening, 6½ x 8½ inches.............. 3.50

No. 6476. Square shape embossed plush (Flower pattern) frame, arch opening, 6½ x 8½ inches........................ 4.00

Per Dozen

No. 6698. Square shape embossed plush frame, oval opening, size 6½ x 8½ inches ... $4.00

No. 6240. Fancy shape silk plush frame with embossed flower on one side, beaded nickel arch opening, 7 x 8½ inches.............. 4.00

Per Dozen

No. 2834. Large square silk plush frame embossed fancy pattern, octagon opening, size of frame 8 x 9½ inches........... $4.00

No. 6256. Square shape silk plush frame with embossed oval ornament, rope imitation, beaded gilt metal opening, size of frame 8½ x 10½ inches.... .... 8.50

No. 7031. Fancy shape silk plush frame embossed pattern with beaded oval metal gilt opening, size of frame 9 x 10½ inches.. 9.00

No. 2802. Fancy shape combination of white enameled wood and silk plush frame with silver trimmings, arch opening, 8x10 inches, very handsome.................. 9.00

Per Dozen

No. 2808. Fancy shape combination white enameled wood and silk plush frame with silver trimmings, oval opening, size 8½ x 12 inches............. $9.00

NICKEL FRAMES, CABINET SIZE.

Per Dozen

No. 105. Swinging on stand...... $1.75

No. 101. Same style as before on a larger stand......................... .... 2.00

SILVER METAL FRAMES FOR CABINET PICTURES.

(All with Metal Backs.)

Per Dozen

No. 62. Fancy pattern $1.75
No. 1153. Fancy lace pattern.............. 2.00

No. 834. Fancy pattern.................... 2.00
No. 1158. Pansy ornamental pattern........ 2.00

No. 962. Fan shape filigree work.......... 2.00
No. 866. Fancy pattern, heavy style........ 3.75
No. 1013. Fancy pattern, heavy frame..... 4.00
No. 1154. Fancy ornamental pattern, heavy frame................................. 4.00
No. 1155. Oak-leaf engraved pattern....... 6.50

Per Dozen

No. 1156. Engraved ornamental pattern, over edged large shape................. $6.50

No. 1157. Fancy ornamental Cupid pattern.   6.50

No. 1154/1. Fancy ornamental pattern, double frame for two pictures.......... 9.00

No. 1013/1. Fancy pattern double frame for two pictures........................... 9.00

MIRRORS.
NICKEL MIRRORS.

No. 710/7. Round zinc pocket mirror, 3¼ inches in diameter..................... **Per Dozen**
$.35

No. 3. Round nickel rimmed pocket mirror, with handle 3¼ inches in diameter....... .37

No. 6. Same style as before, 5¼ inches in diameter.............................. .75

No. 900. Nickel frame square mirror on stand 2¼ x 4½ inches.... .40

No. 503½. Swinging stand square nickel frame mirror, size of mirror 3¼ x 5 ins.. .75

No. 205. Nickel rim swinging round stand mirror, 5 inches in diameter........ 2.00

No. 305. Nickel rim diamond shape stand mirror, size of mirror, 5 x 5 inches........... **Per Dozen** $2.00

No. 535½. Bevel edge swinging mirror on nickel stand, size of mirror 5 x 7 inches... 4.00

No. 547. Same style as before on heavy nickel stand, size of mirror 7 x 9 inches... 8.50

PLUSH HAND MIRRORS.

No. 204. Silk plush rim, paper cover back, size of mirror 3½ x 5½ inches........... .80

No. 223. Same style as before, bevel edge, large glass 4½ x 6½ inches............... 2.00

No. 10. Oval, plush rim mirror bevel edge large, glass 4¼ x 6¼ inches............ 2.00

No. 1½. Victor bevel plate mirror with folding nickel handle, size 3¾ x 5½ inches 2.00

Per Dozen

No. 11X. Same style as before, size 4¼ x 6½ inches............... $3.50

No. 21X. Same style as before, size 6 x 7½ inches................................. 6.00

No. 31X. Same style as before, size 7 x 8½ inches.............................. 8.00

SILVER METAL FRAME MIRRORS.
(This year's styles only.)

Per Dozen

No. 315. Fancy ornamental flower pattern with bevel edge glass, size of frame 6 x 7½ inches................................ $4.00

No. 1158. Fancy ornamental pattern, heavy frame 6 x 7½ inches, bevel edge mirror.... 4.00

No. 1153. Filigree pattern, bevel edge mirror 6 x 7½ inches....................... 4.00

No. 16. Flower pattern, 8 inches high, size of bevel edge glass 5 x 7 inches........... 4.50

No. 2. Gondola pattern, same size as before.................................. 4.50

Per Dozen

No. 54. Boy mirror 9 inches high, size of bevel edge mirror 5 x 5 inches........... $4.50

No. 14. Tallant, 3 figures, size of bevel glass 5 x 9 inches high; frame 10 inches high... 8.50

No. 5. Cherub pattern, bevel edge glass 7 x 9 inches frame 10 inches high.............. 8.00

No. 243. Filigree pattern, diamond shape, 12 inches high, size of bevel edge glass 6 x 6 inches........................... 9.00

MOON MIRRORS.

White Silver Metal Frames with Nickel Rim on the two smaller sizes and bevel edge rim on the two larger sizes.

Per Dozen
No. 5. 5 inches.......... ... $2.00
 " 7. 7 inches........... 4.00

No. 9. 9 inches........................... 8.00
 " 12. 12 inches....................... 15.00
 " 346. Round shape mirror on fancy white metal stand, scalloped edge (bevel) size of glass 9 inches...................... 9.00
No. 347. Same style as before, 14 inches high, size of glass 12 inches............ 21.00

ARAB PATTERN MIRRORS.

White Silver Metal Frames with Scalloped Bevel Plate Mirrors.

Per Dozen
No. 6. 14 inches high, size of glass 7 x 9 inches.................................. $8.00
No. 7. 15 inches high, size of glass 8 x 10 inches................................. 12.00
No. 8. 17 inches high, size of glass 8 x 10 inches................................. 13.50
No. 9. 20 inches high, size of glass 12 x 14 inches................. .... 24.00

METAL TOILET SETS.

SILVER METAL.

Per dozen
No. 2218½. Fancy tray with bevel edge mirror, fancy brush and comb to match.....$18.00

No. 1832. Plain finished tray with embossed sunflower ornaments, bevel edge mirror, fine brush and comb to match.......... 22.50

No. 2217. Oval shaped fancy embossed tray with bevel edge mirror, fine brush and comb to match...................... .. 27.00

No. 2154. Heavy silvered metal square shape tray with ornamental border, bevel edge mirror, fine brush and comb to match, beaded pattern................. 30.00

No. 2134. Square shape heavy silver metal tray with heavy open work border, bevel edge mirror, fine brush and comb, backs of mirror and brush in oxydized silver with silver flower........................... 33.00

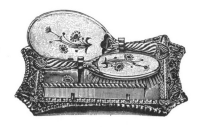

No. 2146. Fancy shape embossed silver tray with gold border and silvered bottom, bevel edge mirror with gold handle, fine brush and comb to match, backs of mirror and brush decorated celluloid........ 40.00

Per Dozen
No. 1560. Square shape silver tray with rose and daisy embossed border of open work bevel edge large mirror with brush and comb to match, backs of mirror and brush silvered rose and daisy decorated........ $40.00

No. 2147. Oval shape heavy silver embossed tray with sunflower and rose pattern open work border, bevel edge mirror, fine brush and comb, backs of mirror and brush engraved in silver............... 42.00

No. 2130. Square shape tray with silver border with gold ornaments and decorated celluloid bottom, large bevel edge mirror, silver handle with fine brush and comb to match, backs of mirror and brush decorated celluloid........................... 42.00

ODOR BOTTLES.

METAL COVERED.

Per Dozen
No. 9 3/4 oz. size. Square bottles with silver filigree covering... $2.00
No. 19 3/8 oz. size. Same as before with satin bow.............. 3.50

No. 10 8/12 oz. size. Same as before with satin bow, cut glass stopper........... 6.50

Per Dozen

No. 128. Tri-cornered shape, otherwise same as before.. $6.50

No. 141. Long neck, broad bottom shape filigree silvered metal covering, satin bow, cut glass stopper...................... 9.00

No. 104/1. Broad flat bottom with extra long neck, cut glass stopper and satin bow.................................... 9.00

SILVER METAL CANDY BASKETS.

Per Dozen

No. 96. Filigree work basket, octagon shape with fancy handle...................... $2.00

No. 680, 686 ane 689. Square, oval and oblong, assorted with silver white borders and silver tinted handle 8.50

No. 18. Fancy shape dull silver basket with small embossed star pattern with fancy twisted handle......................... 9.00

No. 24. Silvered high square shape basket with dented sides and silver ornaments and silvered border (white).............. 18.00

No. 6. Silver broad high shape, round fancy baskets with silver handle.............. 18.00

No. 109. Fancy shape, dented sides, silver white border with silver fancy handle... 18.0₀

WHITE METAL CRACKER JARS.

Per Dozen

No. 304. Round high fancy shape glass jar, covered with filigree white metal silver...$13.50

WHITE SILVER METAL FAIRY LAMPS.

Per Dozen

No. 5. Round shape, comes in assorted colors, White, Opal, Ruby and blue, the color of base and globe match, 7 inches high. $9.00

No. 2. Fancy shape lamp, pink base, shade to match, 9½ inches high................ 18.00

Per Dozen

No. 3. Fancy square shape, Celeste blue base with fancy shape to match, 8 inches high $18.00

No. 800. Round fancy shape, assorted colors, 9 inches high......................... 18.00

METAL PIN TRAYS.

METAL PIN TRAYS.

Assorted with motto or landcape decoration.

Per Dozen

No. 108. Oblong shape heavy silver tray with embossed decoration and motto......$1.25

Per Dozen

No. 54. Heavy white silver metal fan shape tray with figure of woman.............. $2.00

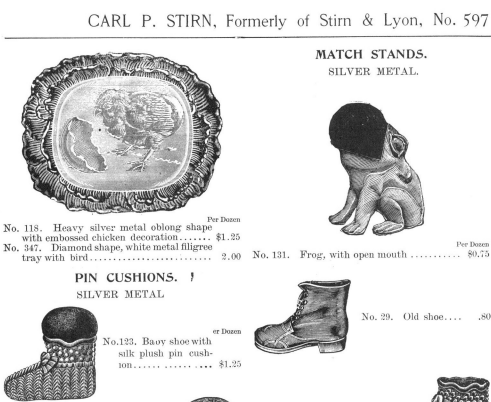

No. 118. Heavy silver metal oblong shape
with embossed chicken decoration....... $1.25
No. 347. Diamond shape, white metal filigree
tray with bird........................ 2.00

PIN CUSHIONS.
SILVER METAL

No.123. Baby shoe with
silk plush pin cush-
ion..... .... $1.25

No. 127½. Basket, silk plush
cushion.................. 1.50

No. 29½. Old Shoe pat-
tern plush pin cush-
ion................ 1.50

No. 111½. Lady's Slipper.................... 1.50

No. 68. Man's buttoned shoe with satin bow, 2.00

No. 104. Large Lady's slipper with large silk
plush cushion and satin bow........... 3.50

MATCH STANDS.
SILVER METAL.

No. 131. Frog, with open mouth $0.75

No. 29. Old shoe.... .80

No. 123½. Baby shoe, .80

No. 127. Basket............ .80

METAL MATCH HOLDERS.

No. 558/9. Metal sleigh $ .75

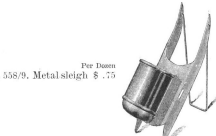

No. 762 Silver metal with oval decorations. .80

No. 944. Holder with oak leaf and rope decorations............................... .80

No. 941. White silver metal oak leaf with
acorn.................................$0.80

No. 943. White silver metal, oval shape
with Columbus' ship and American flag
decorations........... .... 2.00

No. 945. Fancy shape with butterfly decorations.................................. 2.00

METAL SMOKER SETS.

No. 836. Square shape with gold rim........ $8.50

No. 2639. Round shape, silver and gold finish. 8.50

No. 1044. Round shape, silver and gold smoking set on polished old oak wood base
with metal feet........................ $9.00

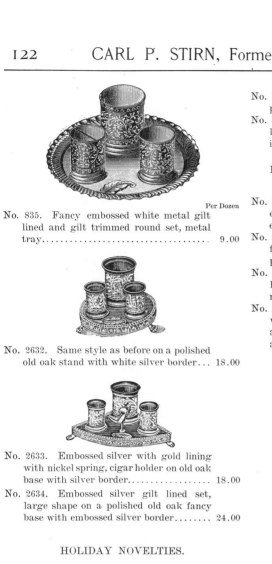

No. 835. Fancy embossed white metal gilt lined and gilt trimmed round set, metal tray...................................... 9.00

No. 2632. Same style as before on a polished old oak stand with white silver border... 18.00

No. 2633. Embossed silver with gold lining with nickel spring, cigar holder on old oak base with silver border.................. 18.00

No. 2634. Embossed silver gilt lined set, large shape on a polished old oak fancy base with embossed silver border........ 24.00

HOLIDAY NOVELTIES.

(Decorated China Plaques, Hand painted Flowers and Landscape Decorations)

Per Dozen
No. 5. 5 inch. in diameter...$3.25
" 6. 5 " " " ... 6.50

Per Dozen
No. 8. 8 inch. in diameter. $9.00
" 10. 10 " " " . 16.50

Per Dozen
No. 12. 12 inch. in diameter.............. $24.00

PAPER WEIGHTS (NEW.)

No. 830. Fancy glass paper weights, round snow ball with motto "Merry Christmas" in colors........................ 1.85

No. 831. Round snow ball on frosted sleigh with "Merry Christmas" motto hand painted................................ 3.00

Per Dozen
No. 832. Same style as before with hand painted landscape decorations...........$3.00

No. 835. Large snow ball with hand painted landscape and "Merry Christmas" motto in colors............................... 4.00

IMITATION OF LEATHER COVERED NOVELTIES.

Per Dozen
No. 324. Imitation alligator leatherette covered with everlasting calendars, paper and envelope stand........................... $2.00

No. 1077. Imitation lizard skin covered Portfolio with everlasting calendar and note paper and envelopes.................... 4.00

No. 728. Fancy white leather Portfolio with hand painted flower and bird designs with note paper and envelopes.............. 4.00

No. 725. Portfolio in fancy ribbed leather with hand painted rose and gilt fan decoration with two glass ink stands and paper and envelopes......................... 12.00

ARTIFICIAL FLOWERS.

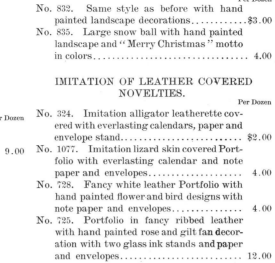

Per Dozen
No. 630/25. Artificial flowers in fine gilt squares and round wicker baskets. 9 inches high, ½ dozen assorted in a box.... $2.00

No. 630/50. Assorted gilt and colored straw braided wicker and fancy baskets with and without handles, with fine artificial flowers, 12 inches high, ⅓ dozen in a box 4.00

No. 630/100, Artificial flowers similar to the foregoing with finer artificial flowers. 18 inches high, ¼ dozen assorted in a box... 8.00

No. 630/125. Artificial flowers, fine large flowers in gilt wicker baskets. 15 inches high, ⅙ dozen in a box.................. 9.00

SHELL BOXES.

Per Dozen
No. 1977. Shell boxes, square shape, full shell top. 3x3¾ inches one dozen in a box.... $0.38

No. A. Shell boxes, assorted square and diamond shapes full shell top. Size 4x6 inches, one dozen in a box............. .75

No. B/25. Shell bureaus, assorted styles with shelves and with imitation book case. 4 inches wide, 6 inches high; one dozen in a box................................... 1.75

No. B/50. Shell Bureaus similar to B/25. 6 inches wide, 8 inches high. ½ dozen in a box................................... $3.75

Per Dozen
No. C. Shell boxes assorted with full shell cover and satin pin cushion on top, wicker woven sides, assorted square shapes. 5x7 inches, one dozen in a box.............. $2.00

No. D. Oval, round and diamond shape pin cushion boxes, full shell covered top with satin pin cushion, wicker woven sides, assorted fancy square, round and diamond shapes. One dozen in a box............ 1.75

No. E. Shell baskets, assorted shapes with single or double covers and handles. 3x6 inches, one dozen in a box.............. 1.75

No. F. Shell boxes, large square shapes, full shell covers, silk pin cushion, fancy insides, wicker woven sides. 7x9½ inches, half dozen in a box.................... 3.75

SHELL PURSES.

Per Dozen
No. 635/10. Shell purses with two shell sides, metal clasp and red inside cloth partitions; one dozen in a box...................... $0.75

No. 635/15. Same as before with silver chain .80

No. 635/25. Shell purses, square shape with metal rim and clasp and red inside cloth partitions, one dozen in a box.......... 1.75

GILT WIRE EASELS.

PICTURE EASELS, FINE GILT SOLID BRASS, TWISTED WIRE.

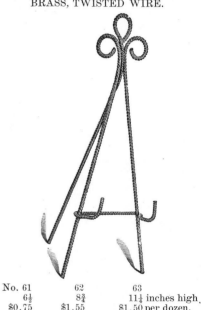

No. 61	62	63
6½	8¾	11¼ inches high.
$0.75	$1.55	$1.50 per dozen.

No. 272. Same style as before with silver sun flower ornament on top. 12½ inches high; per dozen..................$2.00

PLACQUE OR CARD EASELS.

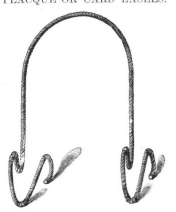

No. 103	104	106
3¼	3½	4¾ inches high
$.70	.75	1.75 per dozen

No. 460. Same style as before with gilt strawberry and leaf decoration; per dozen................................... $2.00

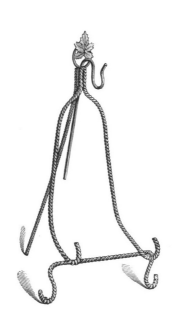

Per Dozen

No. 129. Cup and Saucer Easel for medium and large sizes........................ $2.00

No. 256. Same style as before with silver lily ornaments........ .... 2.00

No. 107. Album Easel, 8 inches high, 5½ inches wide.................... 2.00

No. 507. Same style as before with front ornaments (maple leaves), 10 inches high, 6 inches wide.......................... 4.00

No. 135. Cup and Saucer Easel, regular size, per dozen........................ 1.25

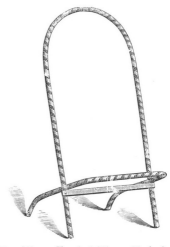

No. 384. Album Easel folding, 15 inches high, 7¾ inches wide, engraved solid brass, fine gilt, per dozen $6.00

STEREOSCOPES.

Per Dozen

No. 30. Stereoscope; imitation cherry wood hood and frame, and wood screw handle. $1.75

No. 31. Imitation rose wood hood, black walnut frame and black walnut screw handle....................... .... 2.00

No. 33. Cherry wood hood and frame, folding handle............................... 2.50

No. 38. Walnut hood with brass nails, walnut frame, patent folding handle........ 3.50

No. 37. Cherry wood hood with brass nails, cherry wood frame, patent folding handle................ .... 3.75

No. 45. Polished rose wood hood with brass nails, black walnut frame, patent folding handle, extra large and strong lenses.... 7.00

No. 46. Polished tulip wood hood with black walnut frame and patent folding handle, extra large and strong lenses.......... 8.00

STEREOSCOPIC VIEWS.

No.		Per 100
1.	New York city and vicinity, assorted...	$1.80
2.	Lake George and Niagara..............	1.80
3.	California and Union Pacific R. R......	1.80
4.	European Views.....................	1.80
5.	Comic Views.........................	1.80

Special Cases of Assorted Toys.

PACKED READY FOR SHIPPING.

The Best and Most Complete Assortments of Toys for the Price.

No. A—10.	Assortment................................$10.00 per case
No. B—15.	" .... 15.00 " "
No. C—25.	" .... 25.00 " "

Upon application I will send illustrated sheets of each of the above assortments which will also contain the specifications of the contents of each case.

Import Order Department.

On JANUARY 15th, my IMPORT SAMPLES will be ready for Inspection.

My specialties in this department are:

DOLLS, TOYS,
HARMONICAS, MARBLES,
TOY TEA SETS,
BOHEMIAN GLASSWARE,
ALBUMS and
EUROPEAN NOVELTIES.

☀ C. P. Stirn's Patent ☀
Photographic Concealed Vest Cameras
FOR TIME AND INSTANTANEOUS PICTURES.

Over 20,000 now in use all over the World.

Awarded Two Silver and Four Bronze Medals.

SEND FOR ILLUSTRATED CATALOGUE OF PHOTOGRAPHIC CAMERAS, OUTFITS AND MATERIALS WITH DISCOUNTS.

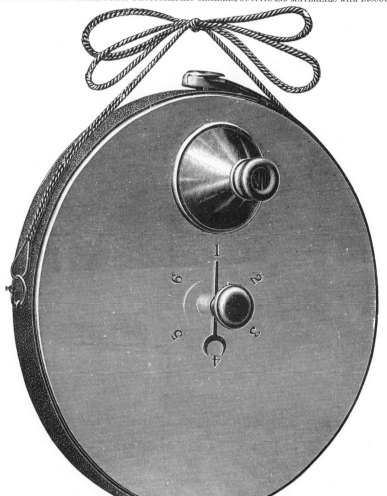

Photograph made with C. P. Stirn's Patent Concealed Vest Camera.

Photograph made with C. P. Stirn's Patent Concealed Vest Camera.

C. P. Stirn's Patent Concealed Vest Camera in position for time exposure.

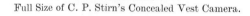

Full Size of C. P. Stirn's Concealed Vest Camera.

C. P. Stirn's Portable Dark Room Bag for changing Photograph Plates in the open air.

Enlargement made from picture taken with C. P. Stirn's Concealed Vest Camera.

Enlargement made from picture taken with C. P. Stirn's Concealed Vest Camera.

Price List of C. P. STIRN'S
Patent Photographic Concealed Vest Cameras
AND PHOTOGRAPHIC SPECIALTIES FOR THE SAME.

	Each
Stirn's Concealed Vest Camera, No. 1, with 6 plates	$10.00
" Star Tripod for Vest Camera	.60
" "Star" Enlarging Apparatus No. 1, complete	10.00
" Portable Dark Room Bag, No. 1	3.50
" Complete Outfit for Camera No. 1	3.50

	Per Dozen
Extra Quality Eclipse Dry Plates, No. 1	$1.20

	Each
Ruby Lantern, "Our Beauty," fine japanned	$0.75
C. P. Stirn's Finder for Vest Cameras	1.50
Developing Trays, japanned, No. 1, 6 x 6 inches	.25
Printing Frames for Concealed Vest Camera No. 1	.50
Folding Negative Racks, holding 18 plates	.40
Pure Rubber Caps or Lens Protectors for Vest Cameras	.05
Steel Die for cutting round Vest Camera Pictures, No. 1	1.65

	Per Bottle
C. P. S. Special Developing Solutions, No. 1, 3 oz. bottle	$0.20
" " " No. 2, 3 oz. "	.15
" " Toning No. 1, 3 oz. "	.20
" " " No. 2, 3 oz. "	.20

	Per Box
" " Hyposulphite of Soda, box of 6 oz.	$0.05

	Each
Graduates, 2 oz.	$0.20